Great Books
Written in Prison

# Great Books Written in Prison

Essays on Classic Works from
Plato to Martin Luther King, Jr.

*Edited by* J. WARD REGAN

McFarland & Company, Inc., Publishers
*Jefferson, North Carolina*

LIBRARY OF CONGRESS CATALOGUING-IN-PUBLICATION DATA

Great books written in prison : essays on classic works from Plato to Martin Luther King, Jr. / edited by J. Ward Regan.
    p.    cm.
    Includes bibliographical references and index.

    **ISBN 978-0-7864-7803-3 (softcover : acid free paper)** ∞
    ISBN 978-1-4766-1970-5 (ebook)

    1. Prisoners' writings—History and criticism.
    2. Prisoners in literature.   I. Regan, J. Ward, 1967–  editor.

    PN494.G74 2015
    809'.8920692—dc23                                    2015002327

BRITISH LIBRARY CATALOGUING DATA ARE AVAILABLE

© 2015 J. Ward Regan. All rights reserved

*No part of this book may be reproduced or transmitted in any form or by any means, electronic or mechanical, including photocopying or recording, or by any information storage and retrieval system, without permission in writing from the publisher.*

Cover image © Thinkstock

Printed in the United States of America

*McFarland & Company, Inc., Publishers*
  *Box 611, Jefferson, North Carolina 28640*
   *www.mcfarlandpub.com*

To all of the prisoners of conscience and
victims of political violence throughout the world.

# Acknowledgments

I would like to thank the book's contributing authors for their hard work and support in putting this book together. Thanks also to my research assistant Sarah Dunn and Lawrence Krauser for his editing work. I would also like to acknowledge the support of the Liberal Studies program at New York University through every stage of this project.—J.W.R.

# Table of Contents

| | |
|---|---:|
| *Acknowledgments* | vi |
| *Preface* | |
|     J. WARD REGAN | 1 |
| *Introduction* | |
|     J. WARD REGAN | 5 |
| Socrates' Trial and Death by Execution | |
|     FARZAD MAHOOTIAN | 17 |
| Boethius's *Consolation of Philosophy*: Why Do the Innocent Suffer? | |
|     HEIDI WHITE | 34 |
| Poetic Justice: The Civilization of the Heart in Malory's *Morte Darthur* | |
|     STEPHANIE KICELUK | 46 |
| A Prisoner of Circumstance: Cervantes, *Don Quixote* and Literary Self-Authorship in the Early Modern Period | |
|     SEAN EVE | 62 |
| Thomas Paine and *The Age of Reason* | |
|     J. WARD REGAN | 78 |
| Thoreau's Rhetoric of Resistance | |
|     PETER DIAMOND | 93 |
| Epistle from Prison: Oscar Wilde's *De Profundis [Epistola in Carcere et Vinculis]* | |
|     JOSEPH J. PORTANOVA | 107 |
| Bertrand Russell, World War I and Analytic Philosophy | |
|     PHIL WASHBURN | 123 |

His Majesty's Hotels: Gandhi's *Satyagraha in South Africa*
    MARTIN F. REICHERT    138

Jawaharlal Nehru's *Discovery of India*: The Writing of History, Fighting for Freedom in Ahmandnager Jail
    TILOTTAMA THAROOR    153

Drifter's Escape: Adolf Hitler and the Writing of *Mein Kampf*
    ROLF WOLFSWINKEL    167

Antonio Gramsci's *The Prison Notebooks*: A Humanist Reconstruction of Marxism
    BRENDAN HOGAN    180

Jean Genet: *Our Lady of the Flowers* in Prison
    AFRODESIA E. MCCANNON    192

In the Shadows of Prison: Sayyid Qutb's Visions of a Perfect World
    PETER C. VALENTI    204

Martin Luther King, Jr., "Letter from a Birmingham Jail" and Non-Violent Social Transformation
    JOYCE APSEL    230

*About the Contributors*    247

*Index*    249

# Preface

## J. Ward Regan

*Great Books Written in Prison* is a survey of culturally and historically important books written by prominent outspoken political or artistic figures while incarcerated or in exile. Gandhi shares this distinction with Martin Luther King, Jr., as do Hitler and Cervantes. The essays were written by faculty at New York University, and each looks at a different book and provides a short biography of the text's author and a description of the conditions surrounding the book's writing as well as a critical examination of the work and its impact. The essays reflect the diverse academic expertise of the authors and balance the different elements accordingly.

Throughout human history societies have erected ever more complex systems, both mental and physical, to help give meaning to their lives. The creation of these systems of order could be seen as an attempt to retool ourselves to create a fixed philosophical or moral perspective on life. The establishment of social hierarchy, the creation of laws and the subsequent emergence of institutions to keep the status quo has been an ongoing process throughout human history. The penal and criminal justice systems that developed can be seen as facilitating scapegoating for social problems. These systems allow for the definition, identification, and neutralization of those deemed a threat to the proper functioning of whatever the social order is at the time. This often leads to the conflation of the ideas and enforcement of legal and moral standards.

To understand how varied the categories "legal" and "moral" can be, look at history: the specifics have changed, but not the intent. The carceral system has been used not only to punish crime but also for moral compliance in the case of enforcing social "norms" on sex, relationships, and intoxicating substances. There is also the ongoing problem of the enforcing authority and its agents violating the laws and structures they are charged with administering.

## Contents of the Book

The chronological arrangement of the essays helps shed light on historical and contemporary discussions about the appropriate amount of force and violence and who it is used against. For the most part, history does not look kindly on the *incarcerators* in this book. The more the authors are respected for their actions and courage, the more one sees the opposite in the political powers who punished them. This should put citizens on alert now about their own government's actions and rationales.

Post–9/11 society has seen the global emergence of a new "security state" as governments (and private corporations) spend untold resources on monitoring, policing, and combating people or groups, both foreign and domestic, that are classified as threats. The criteria for being considered a threat are as vague, opaque, and flexible in favor of those in power as they have ever been.

## Law, Order and Violence

What really is the job of the police and the military apparatus? To serve and protect the citizenry from harm or to serve and protect the authority and individuals who run the institutions of power, law, and violence? Protecting the social and political status quo is not necessarily the same as protecting individuals and their lives and rights. We have learned that governments can unfortunately be the greatest purveyors of unjust and indiscriminate violence. Many of the writers covered here represent powerful examples of this phenomenon.

The authors in this book collided with the ruling power or government of their time, leading to all sorts of personal and historical ramifications. Most were already well-known figures, so the likely intent of their incarceration or exile was to remove them from public view and influence. In the process some were also targeted for physical torture and execution. These actions can be effective in the short term but sometimes blow back significantly. One of the most famous failed executions in that sense was a small state-run affair against a small-time agitator in a far-off province of a powerful empire—the crucifixion of Jesus of Nazareth.

In surveying the breadth and diversity of the authors and the books contained in this volume, we are confronted by one of the central issues in history: power. Power seeks avenues and opportunities for its expression and exercise. Institutions behave in ways that tend toward self-preservation. Once political authority began to be dispersed among institutions, there was something significant to protect. The establishment of these institutions usually leads to the creation and discovery of threats to their political authority, which must be contained or eliminated if possible. The ruling entities of the world, along with their organizing principles, show the desire that circumstances stay generally static. Unfortunately for them, conditions and ideas do not remain fixed. History is a kinetic event, and the authors here have contributed much to its dynamism.

## *How This Book Came Together*

This project started in 2006, when I realized several of the books I taught in my classes had similar origins. The authors of the Great Books (and the books themselves) were often seen as a threat in one way or another during their own lives, and it was not until the rest of society caught up with their ideas that they were properly recognized as trailblazers and not troublemakers. After some early research and writing, I soon realized I could not sufficiently cover the number of texts necessary for a whole book on my own, so the project sat on a shelf. It was several years later, while listening to a colleague give a talk on an author included this book, that I had the answer as to who could write all the different chapters necessary, and I did not have to go far to find them.

As the editor of this collection, I was lucky to work with such a talented group of faculty who are experts in their fields and teach in the Liberal Studies Program at New York University. The program has a Great Books–centered curriculum that emphasizes undergraduate pedagogy, critical thinking, and communication skills. We have all taught some of these texts in our classes at one time or another and spend a great deal of time discussing how to best teach these types of books. As teachers we cannot but enjoy the opportunity to engage our students in the big questions about individual and social rights and resposibilies that the Great Books always elicit.

# Introduction

## J. Ward Regan

The purpose of this introduction is to give a larger social, historical, and political context to the works and authors in this collection. This book is not about "prison literature"; that is a different category of writing. To understand the works here, some background and a few points of clarification may help. The books discussed are arranged in chronological order to place them easily in time and space, and to give a clearer view of the relationship between each work and its historical context. Many similar themes and questions emerge from the texts: justice, love, power, social obligation, and morality, to name a few of the more common and prominent. This creates a philosophical dialogue between the different authors, and between the authors and the reader—a discussion that spans the millennia. The conditions under which most of these works were written also sets them apart from other Great Books, and ties them together as a very distinct category of writing. The majority of the authors here were well aware of history and knew the risks they might be running with their words and actions—but they continued to write nonetheless. Each essay contains biographical and historical information and an analysis of the chosen text, as well as an examination of the authors' and the books' legacies.

## *What Are Great Books?*

What makes a book a Great Book? And in regard to the authors here, what gets you sent to prison? In this collection, the answers are often related. The first point to clarify is that a work is not "great" simply because it is popular or because we (personally) like it. "Great" in the literary and historical context means a text with unusual artistic or literary merit, daring political or philosophical insight, or cultural significance and historical impact—and often has more than one of these qualities.

The collection of Great Books continues to grow, becoming an ongoing record of the development of human culture. Part of what makes many of the works in this collection "great" is that they were written while the author was incarcerated or on the run, or both. Some of the writers did not survive the experience, and so their work arrived as an echo of their life and ideas. In other cases, the authors did survive and continued on to varying degrees of success, renown, or infamy. They were not all necessarily "good" people, in the simple understanding of the word; the status of their work is a reflection of its historical effect or extraordinary qualities. The works here are only a sampling of a large body of Great Books; they have been included partly because of their already acknowledged status and their special relationship to each other.

## *A Brief History of Prison*

Throughout time, there have been many different systems of imprisonment and punishment; consequently it needs to be clarified what is meant historically by "prison." For much of the past, as *The Oxford History of the Prison* points out, the use of prisons and imprisonment was much less frequent; prison as an organized system of incarceration was a relatively loosely-run affair in most places. That does not mean that there were no laws or criminal punishments. But prior to the modern era, physical punishment (branding, scarring, whipping, etc.) and execution—as well as slavery and exile—were much more common punishments, and were not associated with long-term detention. Prison as we think of it has only recently come into being. This change coincides with the rise of what Michel Foucault calls the "carceral system" of social surveillance and control. At the same time, governments were creating permanent military infrastructures as part of their national purpose and identity.

Over almost all of the past two and a half centuries, starting in the West—specifically the Anglo-American areas, and then spreading all over the world—a new mode of criminal punishment and judicial institutions was established, and has been steadily evolving. This is what we know as the "penal system"—typified by domestic incarceration with varying degrees of security; and loss of freedom of movement in proportion to the perceived severity of the crime committed. "The debate on whether to build or not to build prisons, and then simultaneously on how to reform them once they've been built, has been going on since the Quakers tried to redesign a wing of the first correctional institution in America, the Walnut Street Jail in Philadelphia in 1790" (Bencivenga). This carceral system helps shape the political and ideological mechanisms in a society that are necessary to keep the system functioning. The prison system has continued to grow even though the rates of interpersonal violence have been on a steady decline for centuries. "The findings again coincided with the long-term decline [in interpersonal violence] anticipated by Gurr, showing a drop from about fifty per 100,000 population in the fifteenth century to about one per 100,000 in the nineteenth century" (Eisner). At the same time, death from organized state violence has risen dramatically; eighty million people died in World War II alone.

The developmental trajectory of the prison and penal systems, like Western civilization and technology in general, has been one of specialization. Until the early modern period, prisons and jails were essentially large buildings, a world where men, women, families, lunatics, criminals, and debtors all lived in a semi-monitored state (think of La Force Prison as depicted by Charles Dickens in *A Tale of Two Cities*). Today, prisons have developed all the way into the "supermax" institutions in the United States. The supermax or "control unit" prison is where inmates can be in solitary confinement for twenty-three hours of the day, with one hour for exercise and extremely limited contact with the outside world. The United States currently houses 80,000 prisoners in these conditions (Kurshan). The power of the state, and its unquestioned position of ascendency, is nowhere more evident than in the supermax, perhaps even more than in the power to execute. In these prisons, there is absolute control of daily life functions, and total observation: a solitary confinement that never leaves you alone, forever. The modern prison system—from outcome-based strategies to the physical spaces of penal intuitional architecture—has also evolved in tandem with modern industrial global capitalism, into a system that requires compliance and uses institutionally established means of dominance.

From the early modern era onward, only the highly regimented, regulated, almost industrialized carceral system was able to handle the increasing number of people drawn into that system: its existence seemed to necessitate its utilization. This coincides with the physical manifestations of the judicial process and punishment being increasingly removed from public view, and from direct public participation. The spectacles of trial and punishment, including government-sanctioned executions, were now going on *inside* the new prison, police, and court infrastructure. The task of physically enforcing order and law and the flow of money moved under the purview of a rising private entity that has come to be known as the "state." This "state," in all of its historical-cultural manifestations, accrued to itself the power to enforce compliance with its needs as a ruling class.

Ideas can be dangerous, especially ideas and authors that question or challenge the ruling power structure. Historically, the amount of time, resources, and violence that authorities devote to quashing unwelcome ideas, and eliminating the messenger, have varied. But the ruling institutions and the people who populate them have never been reluctant to wield the authority they control in order to protect themselves.

## *Who Were These Authors?*

Several authors discussed in this book come from European countries, while a number of other authors come from the Anglo-American or English Colonial world, which includes the United States, United Kingdom, India, and Egypt. At least some colonial resistance was the result of claims to the rule of law by the colonial government, which ran a system that did not treat people equally. There is a direct relationship between political events and alignments in a given country and the coercive force applied by the state—as well as the resistance by the population to that force. The unfolding of this large-scale dynamic interplay between the governed and the governing is what makes history.

The authors in this book come not from the ranks of the criminal class—except perhaps Jean Genet, whose best-known novel, *Our Lady of the Flowers*, was written during one of his stints in jail. Some were specifically targeted for what they said or did, usually something political. As for the prisoners of war, such as Cervantes, they were seen as part of a specifically defined enemy group, and thereby automatically categorized as a threat. In many instances the authors here were singled out for what could reasonably be described as extrajudicial treatment.

The death of the Ancient Greek philosopher Socrates is one of the most famous state executions in history, and certainly the first recorded in such philosophical depth.

Eight hundred years later the philosopher Boethius sought to console himself, while a political prisoner, by turning to his classical philosophical education and his Christian faith. Both thinkers were victims of a government they had served faithfully, but later found disfavor with.

Thomas Paine, a famous author during the American Revolution, was under a death sentence from the British government and imprisoned in France by the revolutionaries when he wrote *The Age of Reason*. He was well acquainted with the aggressive actions of the state to persecute political activity.

Even though it is a story of unjust state persecution, Oscar Wilde's experience—his imprisonment and writing of *De Profundis*—was different from that of many of the authors in this book. His crime was not political; it was social. Conversely, Sir Thomas Malory was held in the Tower of London—where he wrote *Le Morte Darthur* during the last two years of his life—because of the political alignments he chose in the War of the Roses. And Antonio Gramsci's imprisonment and writing of *The Prison Notebooks* is a story of political repression backfiring. He was sent to jail by the Fascist government of Italy in the hopes that it would shut him up—it didn't.

These authors were sent to prison for all sorts of reasons: supporting war, not supporting war, violence against the state and nonviolence against the state, campaigning for equal legal status, etc. To put it simply, the powers that be wanted them out of the way.

Martin Luther King, Jr.'s, "Letter from a Birmingham Jail" written while he was in prison for parading without a permit during the U.S. Civil Rights Movement, became a rallying cry in the fight against injustice, and for human dignity and rights everywhere.

Sayyid Qutb is probably the least known of the authors in this volume, but two of his works written while he was in an Egyptian prison, *In the Shade of the Qur'an* and *Milestones*, have become immensely influential for twentieth-century Islamist movements, with significant historical implications.

*Discovery of India*, possibly Jawaharlal Nehru's most important work, was written while he was being held in prison by the British, in India. Along with many others, Nehru spent a great deal of time in prisons as punishment for his fight for India's independence. Gandhi, who during one of his many jail stays in India while fighting for the nation's independence, wrote *Satyagraha in South Africa*. In it, he recounts his time fighting for political equality in British South Africa. Also taking on the English government was the famous English philosopher Bertrand Russell, who was sent to jail for his antiwar activism during World War I. While in prison he wrote his influential *Introduction to Mathematical Philosophy*.

Tragically or thankfully (take your pick), considering the punitive treatment they received for their activities during their lives, history has vindicated almost all of the figures in this book. Ironically, the person treated best while in prison—and even let out early—has been judged one of history's great villains: Adolf Hitler. He was imprisoned in 1923 for attempting to overthrow the German government. The other authors were kept in conditions that ranged from austere but safe, to horrendous—where they were subject to torture and execution. Historically speaking, no country, people, or system can claim to be innocent of the abuse of its power to imprison or execute for political gain. This makes Henry David Thoreau's famous quote, "Under a government which imprisons any unjustly, the true place for a just man is also a prison," all the more imposing. Thoreau's essay *Resistance to Civil Government* is one of the most famous and influential pieces written on how a citizen should respond to the immoral or unjust laws and actions of their own government.

There are untold hundreds of millions outside the annals of history who have suffered at the hands of oppressive governments. Most were silenced through fear, incarceration, or death. What makes the subjects of this book different is that the attempts failed. Some got out of prison and went on to continue to be politically active and write more, while others were executed—but all of them live on in their words and the historical memory.

The authors here were directly confronted by the "carceral network," as Foucault describes it, of their respective governments. In many instances the legal process was designed to make the charges against them stick: trials were rigged and verdicts predetermined. Significantly, most of these authors were not targeted by specific individuals, but by a system designed and created to enforce general inequality, rooted in political power. From the personal level all the way up to the state, as far back as settled human history goes, people seem to have accepted organized collective violence as a means of maintaining order. The rituals and symbols surrounding collectively sanctioned violence are important in creating the experience of justice (as culturally understood by the participants). The public displays of seeking out and punishing actions and actors perceived as socially dangerous (prosecuting someone for witchcraft, for example) may be more important for people than capturing and punishing the guilty (many innocents have been executed over the millennia). There were always at least a few people in the societies of these writers, starting with Socrates, who were happy to see them put out of action; even dictators don't do it all on their own. Large segments of the U.S. population were not concerned that people like Martin Luther King, Jr., got sent to jail. Even though most societies claim to eschew the use of collective coercive force, it is a historical reality. Unfortunately, the rituals surrounding law and justice can be used toward unjust ends.

## *Institutionalized Violence as a Means of Control*

The next question that arises is: Why is physical and mental violence so consistently used by society to control criminal, political, and moral behavior—violence that is collectively sanctioned and institutionalized? (It's the unsanctioned violence that gets punished.) The institutionalization of violence legitimizes and authorizes its appointed purveyors. This apparatus can then be deployed against individuals or groups considered dangerous by whoever holds the hegemonic reins.

The habitus of punishment, specifically physical punishment, is cross-cultural and deeply embedded in human history. The use of coercive violence for social and political control is one of the few constants in human political systems. The modern nation state has refined and enhanced the carceral system into one of its most prominent features. It has been pointed out by historian Charles Tilly that the pursuit of the ability to successfully wage war is a driving force behind the creation of an internal protection system, which in turn provides the institutional means to enforce compliance with the needs of the new war state: taxation, forced military enlistment, and a stable apparatus to make the system work.

There are at least two types of collective coercion and violence that can be considered overtly oppressive. First, going after specific individuals or groups of people with certain characteristics (race, religion, politics, etc.) that are used to justify curtailing their rights and protections. There is also a more general level of control that preemptively limits the social and political freedoms of the whole population. As Ervin Staub has pointed out, these different actions can have varying amounts of acceptance, depending on the social and historical context. Both types are in evidence in the treatment of the authors in this book. In recent history, groups have often come to power with popular support, only to exhibit dictatorial and repressive tendencies later as a result of some "crisis," or as they attempt to hold on to power. In other instances, the existing apparatus of church and state are used as tools of oppression. The actions of these institutions are always "legal," and yet it seems that on some level the population is aware of the repressive reality—but has few options for changing it.

Over time, generalized mechanisms of control can develop that are also more or less supported, at least tacitly, by large enough segments of the population to keep them going. These sorts of mechanisms are often called "tradition," and their mere existence is used as the argument for their continued existence. The conglomeration of these traditions is referred to as "society." The European aristocratic system of the fifteenth to twentieth centuries depended on both popular support and violence to maintain itself. In England at the time of Thomas Paine's birth (1737), people were routinely executed for minor offenses such as theft; yet many rallied to support the monocracy. This system of "justice" was carried out on and by a largely willing or cowed populace, both up and—surprisingly—down the social scale, many of whom could easily, in the right (or wrong) circumstances, find themselves in the dock or on the hangman's scaffold instead of in the generally exuberant crowd. Aristocratic and theocratic societies seem especially inclined to develop harsh legal systems and punishments in their efforts to motivate compliance and maintain power. This is just as true for the actions of the seventeenth-century Puritans as it is today with the Taliban, as well as among the former and current monarchies of the world.

There are gradients of violence and coercion in any legal system, varying from monetary fines to the death penalty. Currently there are significant differences between nations in the level of physical violence visited on prisoners, and the lengths of incarceration. This variety of systems and orders of violence helps explain why some in prison are able to write, and others cannot. The production (and survival)—or lack thereof—of a prisoner's text may have nothing to do with the individual character of the incarcerated person. Historically, social rank has played some role in determining the severity of charges brought, and the types of punishment received. (This sort of tiered treatment creates privileged classes and subservient ones. Given this reality, how else but by forms of coercion, mental and physical, could the majority of a population be made second-class citizens—and in some cases even property?) The first requirement for a Great Book Written in Prison is that its author not be killed directly upon arrest and detention.

## *The Morality of Violence*

Captors, victors, slave owners, warriors, and jailors can never understand why subjugated people don't see how the world is and why resistance is futile. Many of the authors in this book found themselves in prison precisely because they challenged the unquestionable authority, actions, and morality of those in charge. They did so often enough, loudly enough, and successfully enough to have been targeted by the political establishment for silencing.

For the ruling elite, morality resides in submission to their orders and the satisfaction of their needs. Many an occupying army has justified its violence as necessary to maintaining safety and order. The question is, safety and order for whom? Certainly not the occupied population. It is always the ideas and actions that serve the ruling class which become codified as just, obvious, and moral.

## *Government Power, or the Creation of the State*

The last part of the picture that must be filled in is that, in order to carry out the necessary actions of institutional collective violence, governments and what Lenin called "special bodies of armed men" are created. Charles Tilly has likened state formation in Europe to the development of organized crime. The military, police, and carceral infrastructure could not function without people up and down the chain of command following orders and working toward stated and unstated ideological and institutional goals. It is through the functioning of these "special bodies of armed men" that a society's metanarrative of violence, suppression of thought, and incarceration emerges. Its ideas and institutions become tools wielded against dissent by the ascendant classes to achieve political and economic goals. Tilly wrote:

> Back to Machiavelli and Hobbes, nevertheless, political observers have recognized that, whatever else they do, governments organize and, wherever possible, monopolize violence. It matters little whether we take violence in a narrow sense, such as damage to persons and objects, or in a broad sense, such as violation of people's desires and interests; by either criterion, governments stand out from other organizations by their tendency to monopolize the concentrated means of violence.

The increasing stability of the historical social order was accompanied by institutionalized forms of coercion, namely war and slavery. The further removed violence became from interpersonal motives, the more it became the job of certain specialized workers in the society—the coercive branches of government; the "special bodies of armed men." In many ways, ever since its inception, human civilization has been pushed and pulled by religion and war. Two of the earliest institutional professions were priest and soldier. For the authors in this collection, the prison experience was a concrete manifestation of the power of the state—physically, ideologically, economically, and culturally.

## *Institutionalizing and Sanitizing Collective Violence*

Stable managerial societies, based initially on the oversight of agricultural practice, slowly created and institutionalized social and economic hierarchies. Much later, in the nineteenth and twentieth centuries, these structures were further strengthened by the development and diffusion of industrial society. Keeping the technologically advanced systems running required the work of highly skilled manual and intellectual workers, and a great deal of political and economic compliance.

The social and cultural rituals surrounding politics, religion, money, and law create an aura of legitimacy, and therefore authority; this gives the guise of order and permanence to the exercise of state power. Cultures and societies have distinguished themselves from one another by the different expressions their religious and political rituals took. In the twentieth century's longest political struggle, the Cold War, national identity, as well as political and military alignments, was established through economic theory, and concepts of ownership of the means of production in industrial society. The definitions, forms, and practices of crime and punishment reinforce different types of social bonds and obligations. A primary characteristic of post-agrarian society is the use of institutionalized violence to grease the gears of political and economic systems.

Coercive violence is certainly not the sole purview of institutions such as church and state. Organized crime and street gangs, as well as unpredictable mob violence, are real and dangerous. Corrupt political machines in the nineteenth and twentieth centuries were the de facto governments of some U.S. cities; they used coordinated violence similar to terrorism, and sometimes paramilitary organizations, to achieve their economic and political ends. The collusion of state institutions or individuals with other self-interested groups, and the willingness of social systems to sanction violence, make such actions more likely throughout the society. The use of violence by those in authority might encourage "outlaw" groups to believe that the path to legitimacy lies in violence (Staub). Violence in the name of the ruling class's idea of law enforcement invites and instructs violent responses.

It can be difficult to perceive the unanimity of the various forms of sanctioned violence for social control, since every culture is different; and in the modern period, governments may seem to at first have been civilized in their beliefs and actions. But it is simply the changing rationales for persecution and violence obscure a certain consistency of ideas and valuations across the centuries. It should also be noted how much money, in the form of collected taxes from the world's people, is currently spent by leaders on organized systems of "security" and war that are turned against the paying citizenry. In 2012 the world's governments spent a total of $1.75 trillion on military budgets; this does not include domestic military, intelligence, and police expenditures (Pollard).

One of the important characteristics of many writers featured in this book is that they directly stood up to their own government and social institutions for not acknowledging and protecting the humanity of each individual. If legal systems are to protect us, they should be able to protect us from themselves, as well as from interpersonal violence. And yet history shows that populations in fact need to be shielded from the violent actions of the very institutions created to control and maintain order. In effect, we must still find a way to protect ourselves from ourselves—possibly the oldest social problem there is. The question may be, not how or why do we have social systems, but why do we persist in flouting all the rules we set for ourselves, allowing the continued existence of violent and dehumanizing government and social practices? This problem, in one form or another, lies at the center of each of the books discussed in this collection.

## Works Cited

Bencivenga, Jim. "*PRISONS*; *The American Prison: From the Beginning... A Pictorial History*. Executive director/editor-in-chief, Anthony P. Travisono. American Correctional Association." Review. *The Christian Science Monitor*, 14 Mar. 1984. Web. 28 July 2014.

Eisner, Manuel. "Long-Term Historical Trends in Violent Crime." *Crime and Justice* 30.30 (2003): 87. Print.

Kurshan, Nancy. Introduction. *Out of Control: A 15-year Battle against Control Unit Prisons*. San Francisco: Freedom Archives, 2013. 1. Print.

Morris, Norval, and David J. Rothman. *The Oxford History of the Prison: The Practice of Punishment in Western Society*. New York: Oxford University Press, 1998. Print.

Pollard, Niklas. "World Military Spending Dips in 2012, First Fall since 1998." *Reuters*. Thomson Reuters, 14 Apr. 2013. Web. 28 July 2014.

Staub, Ervin. *The Roots of Evil: The Origins of Genocide and Other Group Violence*. Cambridge: Cambridge University Press, 1989. Print.

Tilly, Charles. "War Making and State Making as Organized Crime." *Bringing the State Back In* by Peter B. Evans. Cambridge: Cambridge University Press, 1985. 169–86. Print.

# Socrates' Trial and Death by Execution

### Farzad Mahootian

## Summary

The Socratic dialogues which examine Socrates' trial and execution are unlike the other writings collected in this volume in that they were not written by the imprisoned person. The dialogues are included because they address issues such as political persecution, criminal justice, and execution, and they had a profound influence on future philosophers. Written by Plato, Socrates' closest student, they are a reflection of issues surrounding the charges against Socrates, his defense, and the final questions he wished to bequeath to posterity. Throughout all these discussions, Socrates knew he was facing prison and execution. The *Apology*, *Phaedo*, *Phaedrus*, and *Epistle VII* deal with virtue—both personal and civic—and with the soul and immortality. Since Socrates considered it his mission to incite people to confront their own ideas and prejudices, it seems fitting that he is portrayed at the end of his life continuing with this process as if it is his only real concern. The dialogues are concerned not with death, but with the pursuit of the philosophical life.—J.W.R.

## Introduction

Socrates never wrote anything for posterity. Neither did Moses, Jesus or Mohammad; but unlike them, Socrates did not claim to be a messenger of God. In this and other interesting ways, Socrates resembled Buddha: neither claimed to be prophets, and both were devoted to advancing the collective good by exposing human ignorance. What differentiates Socrates so strongly from these great figures is that *he denied being a teacher*. On the one hand we have the tradition of great teachers, on the other we have Socrates' explicit *disavowal* of the very possibility of teaching (Plato, *Meno; Epistle VII*). If we take him at his word, the "teachings of Socrates" would be an oxymoron, and yet he is rightly considered to be one of the world's greatest teachers, the very exemplar of an ideal form of education: the so-called "Socratic method." It seems that the simple act of introducing Socrates introduces paradox but it becomes clear that Socrates himself provoked paradox intentionally and, as I hope to show, succeeds in purposefully deploying paradox for the sake of deeper self-understanding. A measure of his success lies in how easily he confounds anyone who encounters him, challenging them to retrace their steps, to examine how they became so quickly confused about their own opinions of right and wrong, love and desire, and a host of other basic issues.

## *Who Was Socrates?*

So how did Socrates teach if he never wrote? Most of what we know about him comes to us through Plato's famous Socratic dialogues, each of which (with the exception of the *Apology*) is named, significantly, after a conversation partner. What Socrates taught about teaching is captured in several of the dialogues concerned with two co-arising questions: what is virtue and can it be taught (Plato, *Meno* 70a)? The second question is deceptively simple when couched in binary affirmation-denial mode, as if such a complex and fluid reality as the human mind could be grasped by answering a question that has the same grammatical form as "What is chess and can you teach it to me?" It's no wonder that whenever Socrates encounters the question of whether virtue can be taught, he arrives at the same answer—albeit via different paths, depending upon the personalities of his dialogue partners. The answer is "no," but one ought not be content with a one-word answer to deep questions; if Socrates taught anything, it would be to keep the significant questions open. Understanding what—and how—he did and did not teach requires an examination of Socrates' ideas of knowledge, the soul and virtue. The story of his trial and death illuminates these points with unique clarity.

Socrates frequented the agora, the open market of Athens, immersed in the intense daily exchange of goods, services, information, opinion and the news of the day. Plato's dialogues show Socrates challenging the famous orators, demagogues and teachers of his time—the so-called "Sophists," and thinkers of ancient Greece, for the moral edification and intellectual arousal of the youth of Athens. Plato recreates Socrates' open-ended exploration and discovery of the underlying presuppositions, contradictions and unfounded beliefs of his interlocuters. Indeed, "open-ended arousal" is a more fitting description than the actual charges brought against him, namely, the corruption of youth, the creation of new gods, while disparaging traditional ones. The charges were brought by two Athenian citizens who represented the anonymous power elite that was threatened by Socrates' open criticism of Athenian politics. A war hero and a survivor of two political coups, Socrates was about seventy years old when he faced these charges in court. He was found guilty and executed by the state.

Most of Plato's dialogues feature Socrates in dialogue with two or more figures but they were never intended as transcripts of actual conversations. They were meant to recreate in the reader's mind a sense of intellectual curiosity and surprise, perplexity and frustration, etc., that could have arisen in actual conversation with Socrates. They are artful recreations whose purpose (it is obvious from their complexity) goes far beyond the intellectual entertainment and artistry contained in them. Plato's dialogues are literary masterpieces that interweave logic, psychology, politics, ethics, mathematics, mysticism, mythology and physics—as these were understood and integrated in the mind of the great Plato at the dawn of the western academy. (The very term, "academy," is one that we use in deference to the name of the school Plato founded.) Plato owed all of this and more to Socrates. While he may not have invented philosophy, it is certain that Socrates did invent the word *philosophy*, which means the love *(philo)* of wisdom *(sophia)* (Plato, *Phaedrus* 278). This word fits Socrates perfectly for it distinguishes him sharply from the Sophists (who, as their title indicates, claim to be "the wise") and, more importantly, it characterizes his powerful yearning for what he knew he lacked—his life and death were shaped by his love.

His last days were consistent with the rest of his life: he spent his time in dialogue with friends, inquiring into the nature of the human soul, its immortality and its proper care—even in his last hours he still inquired about how one might live the good life. Socrates would not have it any other way. This constancy in the face of death invites the reader to find new depth in what could otherwise be construed as mere ideas, transforming these from subjective personal convictions into objective ideals. In the remainder of this essay, we explore Socrates' paradoxical defense against these charges in court and in prison.

## *Socrates' Defense: The* Apology

The word *apology* derives from the Greek *logos*, an account, explanation, story (and several other meanings, including "meaning" itself), and *apo*, which means of, off, or from. In English, apology has had two major usages: speaking in defense of something to justify it, or to express regret about having done something. Beginning in about the 18th century, the latter meaning began to dominate, so that since the 20th century most people are familiar exclusively with apology as synonymous with saying "I'm sorry." In both cases one admits to an action, but in the former case one justifies it, in the latter case one accepts some level of blame, or guilt. In certain circumstances the two meanings are blended: somehow *both* meanings resonate. One needs only to consider an argument with an intimate to recall how a slight difference of emphasis and tone is sometimes sufficient to make one sense of apology slip into the other. Whether the difference of tone occurs in the mind of the listener or the speaker, or unevenly distributed in both, is not easily determined. There are many reasons for the reluctance of politicians to apologize for their misdeeds, but at least one of these lies in their cautious avoidance of the slippery line between the two senses. Regardless of how easily the two senses of apology may be confused, we can recognize the difference and, at least with those close to us, we can usually distinguish an authentic apology and a real explanation from their false counterparts.

Two accounts of the trial of Socrates, written about ten years after the event survive to this day: one is Plato's famous account, the other is by Xenophon; both are titled the *Apology*. The two are quite different, though they agree on the charges, sequence of events, the raucous atmosphere of the court—perhaps 500 jurors who also acted as judges—and, of course, the verdict. The two are radically different in tone. Neither is a transcript of the proceedings, nor an "objective" account, if such a thing can even be said to exist in such cases. Xenophon, a lesser student of Socrates, presents the lesser and more superficial account lacking all the subtlety, wit and defiance characteristic of the personality that attracted such charges to begin with. Classicist Paul Friedlander explains that it is a defense that anyone might give against trumped up charges: one which seeks to demonstrate that Socrates is like any other Athenian, that his religious expression and dialectical argumentation are (for many) practically indistinguishable from published authors and well-known Sophists of his day (Friedlander, *Plato* 159).

Bearing the two senses of apology in mind, we may note that Xenophon's portrayal of Socrates' defense tends to be an apology in the familiar contemporary sense of a sober explanation of a regrettable misunderstanding. Xenophon's Socrates acknowledges the charges as stated and proceeds to explain that, like many Athenians he discusses novel ideas that are readily available in the marketplace; and again, like most Athenians, he celebrates all of the city's traditional religious festivals. By contrast, in his *Apology,* Plato masterfully recreates the tone of Socrates' confrontation of unjust charges before an unjust court; this is a portrayal of a man who is anything but common. Plato pays tribute here to a man who was "among the living what Homer says Teiresias was among the dead—'He alone has comprehension; the rest are flitting shades'" (Plato, *Meno* 100). In Plato's portrayal, Socrates *defense* is anything but that—on the contrary, it is presented as his highest statement of self-justification: it is a countersuit. In his short time before the court Socrates takes his opportunity to challenge the leaders of the city in the same way he challenges each and every one of his dialogue partners. Plato's Socrates doesn't so much explain his innocence as demonstrate his moral superiority by putting his accusers, and all of the jurors, on trial. We may now set aside Xenophon's *Apology* and concentrate on Plato's work.

A key tradition in ancient western rhetoric, one that lasted for several centuries, grew around Plato's account of Socrates' defense. Within that tradition of commentary there is a strand that maintains Socrates said nothing in his defense. The "Silence of Socrates" trope occurs often enough that it must be addressed (Friedlander, *Plato* 158). How did such a strange notion arise? One source is Plato himself: in *Gorgias* and *Protagoras* his interlocutors point out that, were Socrates to appear in a court of law he would be so out of place that he would just stand there dizzy and tongue-tied. Socrates simply agrees with their surmises. The *literal* silence of Socrates is highly unlikely—the Platonic Socrates is at least as ironic as the historical figure was. What is signified by the image of a silent Socrates? Is it a simple refusal to recognize the court's authority?

The more closely one examines the Socratic defense the more paradoxical it seems. Socrates excuses himself at the start, noting that he is not accustomed to making speeches, then proceeds to make speeches of profound rhetorical artistry which have become examples of Greek rhetoric that have been studied and practiced ever since. And yet the most striking aspect of his speeches is their paradoxical and monumental failure to persuade the jury. Whereas proper use of rhetoric aims only at persuasion and has no necessary connection with the truth, Socrates sets out to differentiate rhetoric from truth. Some scholars claim that his speeches do not even try to persuade, that Socrates directs his rhetoric against *rhetoric*. He does this by action rather than by argument, by his ironic abuse of rhetoric itself (Allen 35). Perhaps the "silence" of Socrates refers to the self-consuming nature (Fish 1–20) of his speeches.

But what did Socrates "say"? Perhaps the more precise way of putting it is this, what did Plato understand of Socrates' day in court, and what aspect of this event does he want to leave to distant posterity? Plato knows the limitations of language well enough: much more than mere language is required to understand the depth of Socrates' meaning. What can be gleaned from his verbal and nonverbal communication in court? Socrates challenged all assembled to reject the baseless charges against him, not by answering the charges directly, but by demonstrating that his accusers, Meletos and Anytos, are unable to state their case without self-contradiction. He does this by his customary method of question and answer. This is the only point during his defense that he addresses the charges—or more accurately, his accusers—directly, and spends little time doing so. He says he regrets having only a few hours and not several days, for rather than making speeches he would prefer the modality of inquiry and dialogue to address the court—implying that he would like to engage each of the 500 jurors one-on-one, as he did with Meletos and Anytos. This, of course, does not happen. Nevertheless, Socrates gives the court a live demonstration of the techniques he uses to uncover ignorance. In even the most sympathetic reading, he appears to intellectually overpower the admittedly incompetent and malicious Anytos and Meletos by highlighting their inability to articulate their bogus charges. This exchange does not present the pair unfairly, but neither does it cast Socrates in the best light in the eyes of the jurors, who interrupt Socrate's interrogation several times with their outcries and objections. Rather than winning him friends, this courtroom tactic confirmed the jurors impression of Socrates as a trickster.

Nowhere in his speech does Socrates claim to possess the truth. He is not a Sophist (from the Greek, *Sophia,* meaning wisdom), a dogmatist, or a prophet. Not only is he innocent of the charges brought against him, he claims that he is incapable of claiming any knowledge except for this: he knows that he does not know. This juxtaposition of opposites is characteristic of Socratic philosophy: we have already seen this in his use of rhetoric to open the mind rather than to persuade his listeners of a pre-decided formula. This philosophical pursuit of open-ended self-discovery is the precondition that makes the good life possible. Socrates takes the stance of man on a mission instead of capitulating to the unreal game of the court to mount an equally unreal defense.

## *Putting Athens on Trial*

The focus of this essay is philosophical; space does not allow for treatment of the historical and political factors influencing the outcome of the trial. Many excellent sources for that kind of scholarship exist (Brickhouse and Smith; Waterfield). Nevertheless, an indication of Socrates' standing among his Athenian peers is made clear by a reference about midway through his defense. He notes that his divine sign, "the voice which comes to me and always forbids me to do something ... is what stands in the way of my being a politician," for

> if I had engaged in politics, I should have perished long ago and done no good either to you or to myself. And don't be offended at my telling you the truth: ... he who will really fight for the right, if he would live even for a little while, must have a private station and not a public one [Plato, *Apology* 31e–32a].

This is not idle philosophical talk and Socrates makes it much more personal by recalling for the judges his role in a specific military tribunal, "the trial of the generals who had not taken up the bodies of the slain after the battle of Arginusae."

> [Y]ou proposed to try them all together, which was illegal, as you all thought afterwards; but at the time I was the only one of the Prytanes who was opposed to the illegality, and I gave my vote against you; ... I made up my mind that I would run the risk, having law and justice with me, rather than take part in your injustice because I feared imprisonment and death [*Apology* 32b–c].

Socrates' attitude toward death, expressed so starkly here, is highlighted a number of times during the trial, usually in political and moral contexts. However, he expressed his ultimate and truly transcendental idea of death in the context of the seminal experience of his philosophical life: his encounter with the oracle at Delphi. In court, Socrates recounted the story how a fellow Athenian, well-known to the court, once asked the oracle "whether there was anyone wiser than I was, and the Pythian prophetess answered that there was no man wiser" (*Apology* 21a). Upon hearing this, one would rightly expect most Athenians to start planning a party in celebration of what the voice of the god Apollo had announced through the oracle. But Socrates is no ordinary person: his first reaction is not unquestioning acceptance but profound perplexity. Socrates does not think himself as wise, so he is skeptical. He treats this statement just as he would any other: he sets out to disprove the oracle by finding someone wiser than himself. In this pursuit he found that people who were expert in one area often thought themselves expert in others; Socrates helps them to see things differently. After much searching and finding no one that is wise (and none the wiser himself), Socrates says he came to believe that the oracle must have meant that he is wiser in just this one thing: he knows that he is not wise. Whereas others think themselves wise when they are not, Socrates knows that he does not know. This turn of events defined Socrates' mission in life. Plato skillfully employs this story to shape his response to charges of impiety in the form of the ultimate expression of Socratic wisdom on the matter of death:

> I might justly be arraigned in court for denying the existence of the gods, if I disobeyed the oracle because I was afraid of death: then I should be fancying that I was

wise when I was not wise. For this fear of death is indeed the pretence of wisdom, and not real wisdom.... Is there not here conceit of knowledge, which is a disgraceful sort of ignorance [*Apology* 29a]?

Here Socrates takes control and reverses trial, transforming it from a defense of himself to a concern for the well-being of his accusers and judges. He claims, as he has in several other dialogues, that a good man cannot be harmed by an evil one, that the attempt to do harm actually harms the perpetrator, not the victim of violence. Socrates treats the assembled company as he would any individual dialogue partner. The final sense of his defense becomes Socratic: he uses this occasion, with his own life at stake, to give them the opportunity to examine and perhaps come to know themselves better.

The "silence of Socrates" tradition expresses a definitive understanding that he did *not* defend himself, but instead gave the assembled company an opportunity to learn something that no one could teach them, something that is *in principle not teachable*: self-knowledge. The quintessential Socratic moment of this philosophic lesson is that *self-knowledge can be learned but not taught*. It cannot be learned by constructing logical proofs but only in response to provocations designed to arouse awareness and desire, a yearning for the life of philosophy. Socrates practiced this mode of education, offering himself as an example of living a philosophical life and dying a Socratic death. Upon receiving the death sentence, he admonished the jurors one last time:

> The difficulty, my friends, is not in avoiding death, but in avoiding unrighteousness; for that runs faster than death. I am old and move slowly, and the slower runner has overtaken me, and my accusers are keen and quick, and the faster runner, who is unrighteousness, has overtaken them [*Apology* 39a].
> ...
> Me you have killed because you wanted to escape the accuser, and not to give an account of your lives ... if you think that by killing men you can avoid the accuser censuring your lives, you are mistaken; that is not a way of escape which is either possible or honorable; the easiest and noblest way is not to be crushing others, but to be improving yourselves [*Apology* 39c–d].

## *Socrates in Prison: Practicing Philosophy and Planting Paradoxes*

Plato's *Phaedo* is a re-creation of Socrates' final dialogue with his friends, his last day in prison, his last hours before drinking the deadly draught of hemlock. What does he choose to talk about? He does not engage in a critique of the state, but focuses on the individual: at issue are questions about the nature of the soul and its immortality. He quips that no one can accuse him of discussing abstract matters of no immediate consequence this time! In the lengthy discussions that ensue, various ideas of the soul are considered. But as always, this discussion is simultaneously about the nature of philosophy. To engage in philosophy, says Socrates, is to "practice death and dying." This intriguing definition of philosophy is suggestive of multiple lines of interpretation. Some scholars have made a compelling case for reading death as the separation, not merely of soul from body, but more generally of *logos* from deed (Burger). This parallels in some ways the divergence between the *words* Socrates says in his defense and what he *does* in delivering them to the judges. The key divergence in *Phaedo* is the separation of the invisible soul from the visible body—a separation that we commonly fear and think we understand. If we follow traditional religious views about the soul's immortality it becomes imperative to understand its fate after its separation from the body. This could mean quite a number of things, many of which are depicted in the iconography of most, if not all, ancient religions about how the shape of one's life might shape one's afterlife. Socrates urges his friends to care for the soul both when it is with and when it is without the body. To practice death is to practice the separation and union of opposites. This becomes the complicated and lengthy task of the *Phaedo*.

Socrates takes advantage of the separation between between word and deed to couch many ironies, including his last words (according to Plato):

> The chill had now reached the region about the groin, and uncovering his face, which had been covered, he said—and these were his last words—"Crito, we owe a cock to Aesculapius. Pay it and do not neglect it" [*Phaedo* 118a].

Why would these be his last words? Why the groin? Why the cock? Why Aesculapius? Scholars have offered literally dozens of interpretations to answer these questions (Brickhouse, Smith 265–73; Burger 206–17). To those I venture to add one more: Aesculapius is the god of healing, so invoking his name is a puzzling juxtaposition: poison-as-cure. This begins to make sense when one considers Plato's Myth of the Cave, according to which the world we are conditioned to believe as real is only partially real. The world of the senses is a world of images, visible glimpses of an "invisible," i.e., intelligible reality. To emerge from the cave to the light of the real world is to awaken from a false knowledge and to be cured of a soul disease. A harbinger of new beginnings, the cock crows at dawn, at the threshold of the new day, turning consciousness away from the darkness toward the light. The belled caps of medieval European fools are modeled on the cock's comb for their function was to rouse the commoner from his slumbers, to trick one into seeing what is hidden behind a self-imposed veil of ignorance. The fool, like Socrates, lived to expose foolish ignorance by tricking people into seeing their own foolishness. Fools bestow opportunities to break free of illusion, to reflect upon and awaken to the reality of oneself (Willeford). The reference to the groin is also in keeping with the cock and the fool: the medieval fool is a bawdy character, and again like Socrates, modeled after the Greek god Pan, erotic fecundator of field and stream. Socrates' resemblance to Pan is noted in the work of Plato and other ancient authors. A quick comparison of busts of Socrates with representations of Pan on Pantikapaion coins from 4th century BCE bears this similarity out. There are key differences, however. Whereas the fool arouses passions to make fun, of and with, his audience, Socrates does the same in order to help his friends to detach from and rise above their passions. The fool arouses consciousness and his work is done: laughter signifies breakthrough and success. For Socrates, philosophy follows the fun, and hard work begins when the laughter is done. Where Pan's fecundity generates semi-divine natural creatures, that of Socrates generates semi-divine creatures of the mind.

Plato has provided several clues to unravel the riddle of Socrates' last words; it is up to the reader to pick these up and put them together to understand what can be found only indirectly in the words. Plato's readers must be alert to more than one mode of reading, for he often relies on the mute language of myth, metaphor and symbol to express his deepest reflections on the primordial source of philosophy.

Let us examine Plato's explicit statements about his own writing to better understand his systematic deployment of non-literal language. In *Phaedrus*, he equates the written word to an abandoned child to whose defense the parent cannot come. By contrast, he describes the living word, spoken in dialogue between student and mentor, as a seed: *logos spermatikos*. In a previous section we saw Socrates' refusal to be called a teacher in connection with the experience that self-knowledge can only be learned, not taught. Here we find a second reason for deflating the power of instruction through "great books." Socrates disavows the capacity of any and all forms of writing to contain wisdom. At best, books function as a potential trigger for remembering what one already knows. Planting words with ink on paper, will come to naught, but when

> one employs the dialectic method and plants and sows in a fitting soul intelligent words which are able to help themselves and him who planted them, which are not fruitless, but yield seed from which there spring up in other minds other words capable of continuing the process for ever [*Phaedrus* 276e].

Plato reinforces this in a rare autobiographical note about writing on wisdom:

> There does not exist, nor will there ever exist, any treatise of mine dealing therewith. For it does not at all admit of verbal expression like other studies, but, as a result of continued application to the subject itself and communion therewith, it is brought

to birth in the soul on a sudden, as light that is kindled by a leaping spark, and thereafter it nourishes itself [*Letter VII* 341c-e].

The central paradox should not escape notice: he who has written hundreds of thousands of words of philosophy writes that no written philosophy should be taken seriously:

> In one word, then, our conclusion must be that whenever one sees a man's written compositions—whether they be the laws of a legislator or anything else in any other form ... —these are not his most serious works [*Letter VII* 344c].

Plato dissuades readers from taking any written text seriously, but this must apply to his own writing: indeed the statement is self-referential. For a lover of paradox this is a delightful confection, but what is the lover of wisdom to do with it? What is the appropriate sense in which to take Plato's dialogues? Non-seriously, of course ... in other words: non-literally. The skillful play of irony, metaphor and myth puts the onus of examination and reflection on the reader, but also projects far more than a monomorphic literalist reading could ever provide.

## *The Role of Myth in Socratic Discourse*

In the strange mixture of seriousness and play that characterizes any myth, Plato finds the appropriate medium for conveying his most serious topic: the death of his mentor and friend, Socrates. But there is subtlety here that should not escape notice: Plato presents a myth of cosmic proportions about the fate of the soul after death *explicitly as a myth*. What is not verbally explicit is enacted in the arc of the dialogue: the Socratic *mythos* of the *Phaedo* provides a broader context for the logical analysis that precedes and follows it.

In general, Plato's dialogues demonstrate rather than discuss the relationship between myth and logic. Interjections of mythic references, and occasionally fully fleshed-out stories like the one found in the *Phaedo*, set the stage for conceptual analysis and dialogue. Plato's deliberate placement of these references indicates the transitional nature of this form of discourse: the myth goes where logic cannot go and it does so with full self-disclosure *as myth*. It can thus serve either as a culmination or a starting point of analysis (Friedlander, *An Introduction*). A musical analogy for the role that myth plays in Plato's dialogue, while imperfect, will nonetheless invite interpretations that are helpful to the discussion that follows. Improvisational interludes in a live musical performance work within certain constraints defined by the overall theme, but there are no actual *rules* that govern free exploration beyond the score. Just as the improvisational interlude seeks to capture the original aesthetic sense or intent of the musical piece, so too the myths take Socrates, his interlocutors and the reader on a journey back to the origins of thought, to the original set of projects, notions, and concerns that cluster around the "big" questions.

What Plato learned from Socrates is that articulating the right questions is much more fruitful than any single answer, regardless of the correctness of the latter or the strangeness of the former. For questions chart the terrain of viable answers. Thus, even though mythos and logos often seem to stand opposed we find that sometimes the best *logos* is a *mythos*. This often occurs at the limits of analysis; Socrates was wise enough to make the transition to myth explicit, thereby disclosing his rational ignorance through undisguised mythical discourse. Unlike many experts who keep talking in the mode of experts long after they cross the analytic limit of their own concepts, Socrates stops, explicitly notes the presence of the threshold then crosses it in the idiom of self-avowed semblance that is Socratic myth.

This manner of Socratic discourse, its recognition of the limits of logic, embodies a key point which Plato's student and younger contemporary, Aristotle, makes explicit in treatises that establish the beginning of formal logic in western philosophy. Aristotle understood the power of logic: he established the foundational concepts, language and procedures of formal logic that survive to the present day. He also understood its limits: first premises of an argument *cannot be derived by formal logic*. The sources of first premises are as varied as their reliability: observation, tradition, hearsay, rules of thumb ... and other "accepted truths." None are immune to error. In short, Aristotle established formally what Socrates demonstrated in discourse: logic cannot produce truth where it doesn't exist to begin with. Computer programmers know this as the iconic "GIGO" principle: garbage in, garbage out. Logical process, whether carried out by computer or by human intelligence, cannot *add* truth, it can only extend and apply truths present at the outset. The truth of the output necessarily depends on the truth of the input. At key points in his dialogues Socrates will recur to traditional mythologies—suitably modified to match his moral vision. These recursions most often occur at the culmination of inconclusive arguments. Whenever Socrates (or Plato) finds himself at such crossroads, he does not pretend that logical analysis can produce what it cannot. He presents such topics within the super-saturated context of myth and highlights pertinent aspects. While its details do not persist throughout the dialogue, the myth functions as a background that guides vision.

In *Phaedo*, the occasion that calls for a myth of cosmic proportions is a conceptual difficulty that arises when Socrates and his friends apply the "theory of forms" to the soul. "Forms" signify the ideal patterns which condition the existence of all material things, but are not themselves part of the material world. For example, geometrical forms enable us to develop designs and make predictions about material objects even though any given geometrical form (say, a triangle) doesn't actually exist as a material thing among material things. And yet, this non-existent ideal form shapes our behavior toward material objects and enables us to literally shape material objects themselves. As such, these forms condition but are not conditioned by objects.

In granting these forms ontological status, i.e., considering them as real albeit non-existent, Socrates and Plato create an intriguing problem: what is the relationship between reality and existence, between form and thing? It is clear that the number 33 is eternal, as are the geometrical properties of a sphere, for time has no affect on them: number 33 never grows old, never wears down to becoming 32.998. The passage of millennia will not reduce the sphericity of the sphere, but of the thirty-three ball bearings in a machine, it is inevitable that some number of them eventually become less than spherical and begin to fail to perform properly. Several questions arise in the relationship between form and thing. Socrates invites us to imagine that any object, e.g., a ball bearing, "participates" in the form of the sphere, benefiting from the properties of sphericity (until it wears down or breaks). If opposite forms (hot/cold, great/small, etc.) can be present in the same object successively, or perhaps even simultaneously, do the opposite forms destroy one another? Does one retreat as its opposite one advances? If so, where do the forms "go" when they depart? Furthermore, it is clear to Socrates that the soul is like the forms (insofar as it is intelligible and invisible) but because it is not changeless, it cannot be a form. So, how does the soul participate in the world of forms *and* in the life of the body? Can it be immortal if it is not changeless? These lines of questioning highlight the inadequacy of the concept of form, soul and body as initially stated by Socrates. Further adjustment is required in order to have any hope of achieving clear understanding. A shift in perspective is needed.

## *Shifting Frames and Reconciling Opposites*

At this point we ought to take note of the structure of the *Phaedo* dialogue. It opens with Phaedo narrating from memory the story of Socrates' last day to his friend Echecrates—and an amazing memory it is, given the length and depth of topics covered. Nevertheless, memory is naturally faulty on occasion, and in a Platonic dialogue the question of *when* becomes interesting.

Once at the middle and again at the end of the dialogue, Phaedo becomes a character in his own story. The significance of shifting the narrative frame is complex and admits of several interpretations. After all, Plato could have written this dialogue like most of the others, wherein the conversation unfolds with different characters coming and going in the "realtime" of the conversation. The dialogue is already a narrative, but Plato frames it as a literal narration (by Phaedo) to bring attention to the fact that this is a *story* told about the death of Socrates, years after the fact. Given that objectivity is difficult under the best of circumstances, objectivity in the highly emotional setting of an execution is nearly unimaginable. Phaedo notes that Plato was absent on that day due to illness; here Plato is made to stand in for all readers. Plato is said (by Plato, speaking through Phaedo) to be absent, so the reader who does not listen to the *mythos* of the dialogue is struck immediately with a profound cognitive dissonance: Plato is present and absent at the same time. Is this another clue about immortality: something—no, someone—always present, even when absent?

Plato, the master of his craft, uses various recursive self-referential loops which at times may tax the imagination if not the patience of the reader. At the center point of the dialogue is this: how do things participate in forms, or stated differently—and this is Aristotle's way of asking the central ontological question—what is the relationship between things and properties? More generally still: how can we best conceive and talk about the relationships between immaterial forms on the one hand, and material objects, i.e., bodies, on the other? How can forms be both "separate from" and "together with" bodies? How can a property sometimes be present in, and other times absent from, things? This seemingly abstract question is of dire existential importance to Socrates and his friends in the hour before his execution. How can his soul exist with or without his body? In what does his soul's immortality consist? Plato's later dialogues indicate that he continues to wrestles with these questions, refining the concepts and the logic of his argument over the course of his 50-plus years of writing. But here, in the *Phaedo*, these questions bear an inextricably personal dimension. The questions are discussed at length, but not resolved, and the dialogue shifts the question: can Socrates' *logos* persist after the death of Socrates? At the end, when Crito asks him how he'd like to be buried, Socrates replies,

> However you please, if you can catch me and I do not get away from you." And he laughed gently, and looking towards us, said: "I cannot persuade Crito, my friends, that the Socrates who is now conversing and arranging the details of his argument is really I; he thinks I am the one whom he will presently see as a corpse [*Phaedo* 115c].

None could restrain their wailing and tears, despite Socrates' lengthy demonstration that he himself will not be buried, that he himself will abandon his corpse. If those closest to Socrates were unable to understand the proofs that Socrates presented for the immortality of the soul, where does this leave the reader? Amid the emotional outbursts, the wailing and the tears depicted at the end of the dialogue, we cannot help but ask why Socrates' *logos* failed to help his friends watch him die. There are obvious inadequacies in asking, let alone answering, some of these questions—so much is embedded in each. Nevertheless, we must acknowledge that no matter how adequately or inadequately the questions are asked, they express deep-seated human needs. Many of these, such as profound love and profound grief, for example, cannot *ever* be adequately expressed by words or captured in concepts. Human cultures have evolved a broad variety of expressive forms, such as music and ritual, to reach certain aspects of human nature more deeply and effectively than words alone could.

Recall the first myth that is referenced in the *Phaedo*, in the opening frame, indeed, on the first page. Echecrates asks about the unusually long time between Socrates' trial and his execution. Phaedo explains that the entire city of Athens was waiting on the return of Theseus' ship. The unstated reference is to Theseus' defeat of the Minotaur, which had been celebrated every year since the mythical dawn of Greek history. The ritual purity of Athens was requisite during this festival, so no executions were allowed until the ship—the very ship in which Theseus set sail on his quest—returned from Delos. Despite the well-known fact that every plank in the original ship had been replaced over time, every Athenian still thinks of this as the *same* ship, the very ship invested with all the glory of that special day. What is it that allows one to identify this as the same ship? What aspect of Theseus' ship survives? Certainly not its material ... perhaps its shape— the simplest sense of its "form," i.e., its *structure*. Yes, but this is certainly not what is celebrated. Rather more significant is its meaning, its *logos*. During the celebration, the ship and its *logos* are together and whole, just as Socrates is in life. But here, now, as he faces execution, the question of the separation of Socrates' *logos*, his meaning, from his material presence, becomes most poignant.

Separation of soul from body is parallel to separation of Socrates *logos* from Socrates' physical presence in the prison. Plato provides clues to reinforce the separation of Socrates from his existence, of his *logos* from his deeds. Conversely, one must also learn to see them together, for philosophy as practicing death—in the sense of "practice makes perfect— makes no literal sense unless one considers the *separability,* not merely the separation, of those opposites. Philosophy requires mastery over the art of separation *and* combination as required by necessities at hand: not dogmatic literalism. To do philosophy is also to practice *living* in order to live *well*, for, as Socrates said during his trial:

> to talk every day about virtue and the other things about which you hear me talking and examining myself and others is the greatest good to man ... the unexamined life is not worth living [*Apology* 38a].

## *Conclusion*

Near the center of the *Phaedo* difficult discussions generate even more difficult objections and alternatives to Socrates' ideas of the soul. Anxiety among those present rises rapidly. Even Socrates fell silent, meditating. Phaedo admits that he had a moment of doubt. Socrates asked him at this point whether he would cut his "beautiful hair" in mourning tomorrow, to which he replied yes. Thereupon Socrates advised him, "You will cut it off today, and I will cut mine, if our argument dies and we cannot bring it to life again" (*Phaedo* 89b). According to Socrates, we should mourn the day that we distrust philosophical discourse and abandon the *logos*: misology is a fate worse than death ... even the death of Socrates!

Somewhat later, Phaedo admits to a lapse of memory about a key juncture: someone—he can't remember who—noted an apparent contradiction between how opposites were addressed at the outset and what they were saying at that moment (103a). Socrates praises the man's courage, then, proceeds to intensify the discourse to clarify (a) a key distinction between two kinds of opposites: opposite things vs opposite properties; (b) questions about alternative ways of employing the method of hypothesis; and (c) how these final considerations prove the soul's immortality. In Phaedo's telling, all of this "heavy lifting" is done in rather short order and Socrates' most articulate critics, Simmias and Cebes, readily consent to Socrates' reasoning. With this behind him, Socrates concentrates on the implications of the soul's immortality: one must learn to care for its fate. Here the mythic dimensions of the dialogue blossom as Socrates unfolds his grand cosmic vision of the soul's afterlife. Lest they forget themselves in its epic beauty, Socrates tempers his tale with gentle irony to dissuade his fellows from the allied delusions of literalism, dogmatism and escapism.

> Now it would not be fitting for a man of sense to maintain that all this is just as I have described it, but that this or something like it is true concerning our souls and their abodes, since the soul is shown to be immortal, I think he may properly and worthily venture to believe; for the venture is well worth while; and he ought to repeat such things to himself as if they were magic charms, which is the reason why I have been lengthening out the story so long [*Phaedo* 114d].

To practice philosophy as the practice of dying means to learn how to separate the eternal from its apparent presence in the changing instances at hand. It means the opposite as well: to learn how to see how the time-bound and the eternal are co-present. Is the separation ontological, epistemological, or psychological? For Socrates, the purpose of philosophy is purely practical: to live the good life. Rhetorical, analytical, psychological, social, political, metaphysical and every other intellectual consideration that philosophy may bring to bear on this central question are strictly secondary. By attending to how the stories of Socrates' trial and death are told, what happened and what was said, the reader may glean a sense of who Socrates is, and what his life and death mean.

## Works Cited

Allen, Reginald E. "Irony and Rhetoric in Plato's *Apology.*" *Paideia-Special Plato Issue.* New York: State University of New York Press, 1976. 32–42. Print.
Brickhouse, Thomas C., and Nicholas D. Smith. *Routledge Philosophy Guide Book to Plato and the Trial of Socrates.* New York: Routledge. 2004. Print.
Burger, Ronna. *The Phaedo: A Platonic Labyrinth.* New Haven: Yale University Press, 1984. Print.
Fish, Stanley E. *Self-Consuming Artifacts: The Experience of Seventeenth-Century Literature.* Pittsburgh: Duquesne University Press, 1989. Print.
Friedlander, Paul. *Plato.* Princeton: Princeton University Press, 1964. Print.
_____. *Plato: An Introduction.* Princeton: Princeton University Press, 1964. Print.
Plato. *Plato in Twelve Volumes.* Cambridge: Harvard University Press, 1966. Perseus Digital Library. Web.
Waterfield, Robin. *Why Socrates Died: Dispelling the Myths.* New York: W. W. Norton, 2009. Print.
Willeford, William. *The Fool and His Scepter: A Study in Clowns and Jesters and Their Audience.* Evanston, IL: Northwestern University Press, 1969. Print.

# Boethius's *Consolation of Philosophy*: Why Do the Innocent Suffer?

## Heidi White

*Summary*

Anicius Boethius was a theologian of late antiquity who struggled to reconcile the apparent existence of evil with his belief in a just God. In his *Consolation of Philosophy*, written while in prison, Boethius asks why God would permit injustice to occur at all. His outlook derives from the Stoic tradition of pagan antiquity, which posits the existence of an overarching moral universe, and Boethius advances many ideas that would later become recurring themes of medieval thought. Following the classical model of a Platonic dialogue, he imagines a conversation between himself and Lady Philosophy, who serves as his guide. Boethius had been imprisoned after falling out of favor with the current ruler, the Ostrogothic king Theodoric, and was eventually executed, though the exact circumstances of his downfall are hard to determine. Boethius ultimately sought to remain happy in spite of the existence of injustice, and his determined effort led him to consider free will, personal integrity, and the nature of God.—J.W.R.

> Why is there any misery at all in the world? Not by chance surely. From some cause then. Is it from the intention of the Deity? But he is perfectly benevolent. Is it contrary to his intention? But he is almighty. Nothing can shake the solidity of his reasoning, so short, so clear, so decisive; except we assert, that these subjects exceed all human capacity.
> —Hume, *Dialogues Concerning Natural Religion*, Part X

## Introduction

The ancient philosopher Anicius Boethius knew there were many ways to land in prison, but what often seemed to him most vexing was that he saw himself as innocent—whereas the people who put him behind bars were guilty. He expected that ultimately he would be executed, and he had many long hours to contemplate this fate, probably about a year, before he was killed. But he was also highly learned, and so he tried to analyze his predicament philosophically. He eventually came to view his story as a particular instance of a far more general problem: If the world was created, as Boethius believed, by a god who is all-powerful, all-knowing, and good, then why do the innocent suffer and the wicked prosper? Why does there seem to be so little justice in the world? And why is there evil at all? Does God not care? Does God lack the power to turn wrong into right? How, indeed, can one be happy in the face of so much injustice, since even if the injustice strikes others, it is still terribly wrong? Boethius was working through questions and problems that have often beset thoughtful people in many parts of the world.

These questions are probably as old as thought itself, and they appear in many literary traditions, including those of the classical Greeks, the ancient Hebrews, and the early Christians—all of which were well known to Boethius. But one of the greatest attempts to seek out answers to such questions was Boethius's own *Consolation of Philosophy*, which he composed while a prisoner and which he left behind, before being put to death in AD 524.

Prison has had different effects on many different people, but on Boethius the effect was to make him ever more reflective, ever more meditative, and ever more philosophical. His story is especially evocative because it is true, and because it concerns a man who suffered great injustice and still found a way to offer his readers an education in the things that he experienced. Boethius tried to supply a deeply philosophical consolation—to the effect that though we may suffer injustice, we may still call ourselves happy.

## Boethius's Service to the Ostrogoths

Many details of Boethius's life are unclear. The oldest biographical account, other than remarks in his own writings, comes from Cassiodorus, who had known him and had also served in the Roman Senate before becoming a monk. Boethius is generally thought to have been born in or around Rome, sometime between 475 and 480, and to have died sometime between 524 and 526, after having been imprisoned at Pavia for about a year.

Boethius was a member of the ancient Roman aristocracy, and he lived at a time when his native Italy was ruled by Germanic conquerors, the Ostrogoths. The Ostrogoths had swept down upon the remains of the old Western Roman Empire, just as other Germanic tribes had done before them, and in Boethius's day it was a given that these conquerors could not be dislodged. Instead, many reflective people in Italy had come to believe that the true task of men and women of good will, whether Roman or Germanic, was to try to make the best of a bad situation. Boethius accepted this view, and as a highly educated Roman, he was called to state service by the Ostrogoths' preeminent leader, their powerful king Theodoric.

Theodoric was in fact quite conscious of tensions between his Gothic army and the Romans over whom he ruled, and he was also conscious of religious differences that tended to separate Romans from Goths. Most Romans in those days were orthodox Christians, who held that God the Father and God the Son were "the same in substance." Most Goths, on the other hand, were Arian Christians, who held that the Father and the Son were only "similar in substance." Expressed in ancient Greek, these two doctrines had only an "iota of difference between them,"[1] and yet the difference was deep enough to generate profound resentments and occasional violence. Boethius was orthodox and Theodoric was Arian, yet none of this made any difference when Boethius was asked to contribute to the common good of the community. At Theodoric's request, he accepted a series of important government appointments, and he ultimately rose to be master of the offices—the head of Theodoric's civil service.

He said later that in choosing this path he had taken seriously a dictum of the Greek philosopher Plato—that the penalty for good citizens who refuse to participate in government is to be ruled by people worse than themselves. In his *Consolation*, he specifically relates Plato's view that "commonwealths would be blessed if they should be ruled by philosophers or if their rulers should happen to have studied philosophy." And he says that for Plato "it was necessary for philosophers to take part in government to prevent the reins of government falling into the hands of wicked and unprincipled men to the ruin and destruction of the good" (Bk. I, iv, 10).[2]

When Boethius was still a scholar, he said, he had been happy, but he believed he had a duty to serve the state, for the sake of others (I, iv, 10).

## *Boethius's Arrest*

Theodoric had initially placed great confidence in Boethius. Over time, however, the Gothic king began to suspect him. Theodoric continually feared threats to his rule, and he was especially concerned about alleged plots from the powerful ruler of the Eastern Roman Empire, centered at Constantinople, the emperor Zeno. It seems likely that Theodoric's fears were also stoked by ambitious men at court, and so, eventually, he ordered Boethius's arrest.

Boethius explains in the *Consolation* that the immediate reason for his arrest was that he had tried to protect the Roman senate—which still existed and which functioned in those days as an advisory body to the king. He saw the senate as a target of unjustified attacks, though, in fact, many senators eventually deserted Boethius out of fear, or so Boethius says. Whatever the particulars, Boethius was finally brought down, and Theodoric seems to have become increasingly paranoid during this period, fearing intrigues from many different directions. (Not long after Boethius's death, Theodoric even executed the Pope.)

After his arrest, Boethius was held at Pavia, and during his confinement he put the *Consolation* together, constructing it as a combination and merging of several different lines of thought. The *Consolation* (composed in Latin) contains the seeds of much that would later become widespread in Christian theology, but it also has much in common with the Hebrew Bible, the Old Testament, and it contains many doctrines that had come down to Boethius from the older pagan tradition of ancient Stoicism.

## *Lady Philosophy and the Stoic Tradition*

As a Roman patrician, Boethius was well versed in Stoicism, which stressed reason, the conscientious performance of one's duty, and a serene acceptance of one's external fate. The Stoics believed that as long as one did right and maintained a positive attitude, one's life was a life worth living. To the wise, pain, defeat, opprobrium, and death should make no difference. The *Consolation* adduces arguments in favor of this outlook in books 1 and 2, and this much of the text might have been written almost as easily by a pagan philosopher as by a Christian one. All of these points would have been available to Boethius from his reading of earlier pagan classics.

Yet there is a strong Christian metaphysic in the *Consolation* too, as well as many echoes of the biblical personage Job, who shuns evil, yet suffers horrible calamities for no apparent reason. Just as Job sought to complain to God of the injustice of the world, so Boethius complains bitterly to a sort of internal philosophical advisor, whom he calls "Lady Philosophy." Lady Philosophy personifies philosophy itself, and Boethius says that, having followed her lead, he has now been betrayed: "This, then," he says to her, "is how you reward your followers." He protests in the same way that Job does, and the intention of both men is to pose the same question to Heaven: Why do the innocent suffer, while the wicked prosper?

As it happened, Boethius wrote out the whole of the *Consolation* as a conversation between himself and Lady Philosophy, who attempts to console him by explaining the transient nature of earthly fame, wealth, and honor, and by extolling the superiority of virtue, the intellect, and what she calls the "one true good." Lady Philosophy is of course a creation of Boethius's imagination, and his conversation with her is his invention—to express philosophical ideas. But she is vividly drawn in his text, and she appears in his cell quite suddenly, just as he is in the middle of lamenting his fate. Boethius depicts himself as speaking with the Muses of Poetry, who attend him in his sorrow, and they induce him to write poetry: "So sinks the mind in deep despair," Boethius writes in verse, "And sight grows dim; when storms of life / Inflate the weight of earthly care, / The mind forgets its inward light / And turns in trust to the dark without" (I, ii, 5).

Boethius portrays Lady Philosophy as tall and ethereal, and he says she wears a garment of imperishable fabric, "covered with the dust of long neglect." There are Greek letters on her garment, from the letter Pi to the letter Theta, and these letters represent the two basic kinds of sciences according to the ancient philosopher Aristotle—the practical and the theoretical.

Lady Philosophy explains that she has learned of Boethius's predicament, and so she has appeared to him to offer help in his hour of need. He suffers, she says, not because of enemies or external circumstances, but because of his own internal sickness, which is his inordinate attachment to material and earthly things. Referring to his study of philosophy during earlier periods of his life, she admonishes him, "I gave you arms to protect you and keep your strength unimpaired, but you threw them away. Surely you recognize me? And yet you do not speak. Is it shame or is it astonishment that keeps you silent?" She lays her hand on his breast and says, "It is nothing serious, only a touch of amnesia." He has forgotten who he is, she explains, and so she promises to "wipe a little of the blinding cloud of worldly concern" from his eyes (I, ii, 6).

As it turns out, Lady Philosophy refers often to God in her remarks, yet the *Consolation*, as a philosophical text, does not invoke any particular religion. There is no reference to Jesus or to Christianity per se—or to any other religion. Nevertheless, Boethius's god is much like the god of the biblical Job in that Boethius sees God not only as eternal and all-knowing, but also as the source of all that is good. And like Job, Boethius questions the universal order of the world; both men protest that they are victims of injustice, and they demand an explanation.

One of the points to which Boethius's conversation with Lady Philosophy will tend is the idea that as a mere mortal Boethius cannot understand God's ways, or, as he puts it later, "it is not allowed to man to comprehend in thought all the ways of divine work or expound them in speech" (IV, vi, 109). God's actions, it seems, are far beyond human understanding, and this of course is a common biblical theme.

Yet one of the most striking things about the *Consolation* is that, while defending the notion that God is actually just and fair, Boethius gives voice, for the sake of argument, to the opposing view: the thesis that God is *not* just and *not* fair. For example, in one of the many poetic sections of the book (which alternates between prose and verse), Boethius asks,

> Why else does slippery Fortune change
> So much, and punishment more fit
> For crime oppress the innocent?
> Corrupted men sit throned on high;
> By strange reversal wickedness
> Downtreads the necks of holy men [I, v, 16].

## *Fortune as Fickle*

Early in his conversation with Lady Philosophy, Boethius indicates that he had been favored by Fortune and that he had come to believe that he fully deserved Fortune's benefits. It was not until he suffered that he began to reflect on whether he had really deserved his seeming good fortune after all. Just as the biblical Job had sought to question and challenge God in the heavens, complaining of his fate, so Boethius, in his prison cell, poses similar challenges to Lady Philosophy. He seeks to understand why evil exists in the world, and he seeks to understand it in terms of reason and common sense, not blind faith.

Boethius is particularly distressed that the wicked so often seem to enjoy prosperity.

> I seem to see the wicked haunts of criminals overflowing with happiness and joy; I seem to see all the most desperate of men threatening new false denunciations; I seem to see good men lying prostrate with fear at the danger I am in while all abandoned villains are encouraged to attempt every crime in the expectation of impunity or even in the hope of reward for its accomplishment; and I seem to see the innocent deprived of peace and safety and even of all chance of self defense [I, iv, 14–15].

In addition, one of the things Boethius finds particularly galling is that he is falsely accused—because he has striven to do good:

I will just say that the final burden which adversity heaps on her victims, is that when some accusation is made against them, they are believed to have deserved all that they suffer. And so, stripped of every possession, thrust from my offices, and with my reputation in ruins, for doing a favor I have received a punishment [I, iv, 14].

In these same passages, Boethius tells Lady Philosophy that he considers himself one of the unhappiest of all men and wishes for death. Indeed, the first book of the *Consolation* opens with profound grief:

> I who once wrote songs with joyful zeal
> Am driven by grief to enter weeping mode...
> Old age came suddenly by suffering sped,
> And grief then bade her government begin:
> My hair untimely white upon my head,
> And I a worn out bone-bag hung with flesh.
> Death would be a blessing if it spared the glad
> But heeded invocations from the wretch.
> And now Death's ears are deaf to hopeless cries,
> His hands refuse to close poor weeping eyes.
> While with success false Fortune favoured me
> One hour of sadness could not have thrown me down.
> But now her trustless countenance has clouded,
> Small welcome to the days that lengthen life.
> Foolish the friends who called me happy then:
> For falling shows a man stood insecure [I, i, 1].

Lady Philosophy's replies to these laments with a series of arguments, posed in the form of questions and much like the sort of conversation that one sees in a Platonic dialogue. Lady Philosophy explains that she will seek to cure Boethius of his "sickness" by offering him a series of treatments—from gentle treatments to harsh ones. The gentle treatments, being arguments that are conceptually easier to grasp, are drawn from the Stoic tradition, but the harsh and stringent one will be more abstract and difficult, being philosophical reasonings about the nature of reality and goodness, which in later centuries would become core elements of Christian metaphysics.

One of Lady Philosophy's key contentions, drawn from the ancient Stoic tradition, is that we truly control only our own will—not the external world. Our conduct and our attitude are within our power, but all external things are ultimately beyond our power. If we then seek to found our happiness on things that we cannot control, we will ultimately be defeated—and unhappy.

According to Lady Philosophy, Fortune is fickle: "Inconsistency is my very essence," she says, as she puts words into the mouth of Fortune. "It is the game I never cease to play as I turn my wheel in its ever changing circle, filled with joy as I bring the top to the bottom and the bottom to the top" (II, ii,

25). She invokes the famous Wheel of Fortune, which carries the low up high, and brings the high down low, and she says that the apparent goods of the external world are merely transient. What happens to those who chase after material things, she says, is that they become slaves—out of fear of losing the very things they chase.

Moreover, there is no *truly* bad fortune, she insists. On the contrary, the loss of anything material or temporal should not be cause for sorrow, because the only things of real value are things within ourselves; they are our virtues, which can never be taken away. Lady Philosophy's views of good or bad fortune recall those of the ancient Stoic philosopher Epictetus, who said: "Never say of anything, 'I have lost it'; but, 'I have returned it.'"[3] Lady Philosophy warns against calculating one's happiness according to more suffering or less suffering; in fact, we all receive what *appears* to be good fortune and bad fortune (II, ii, 25). But in truth, "nothing is miserable except when you think it so, and vice versa, all luck is good luck to the man who bears it with equanimity" (II, iv, 31).

In Lady Philosophy's view, the deceptive nature of apparent good fortune even applies to the friends that fortune sends our way. "The friend that success brings you becomes your foe in time of misfortune. And there is no evil more able to do you injury than a friend turned foe" (III, v, 57).

## *Boethius's Emphasis on Moral Motivation*

A profound moralism underlies most of Boethius's remarks on these matters, and he is particularly concerned with moral motivation. He is often concerned with *why* we do what we do, and he asks why we should even care to do right. What reason can we have to be just, he asks, in a world that often seems so unjust?

Lady Philosophy's attempts to answer such questions often turn on the idea of happiness, though the notion of happiness that she invokes is sometimes elusive and abstract. In fact, Boethius was well acquainted with the question of why we should bother to do right, because it is the subject of a famous discussion in Plato's *Republic*, from which Boethius often drew. In book 2 of the *Republic*, the character Glaucon argues that people do right only for the sake of rewards and to avoid punishments, and he asserts further that no one would bother to do right rather than wrong were it not for these incentives. To buttress this view, he tells the story of a man who acquires a ring of invisibility that allows him to practice injustice without penalty, and he says that anyone with a similar ring would regard justice as a waste of time. In Glaucon's telling, just conduct is merely a means to something else, a means to all the external, transient things that Lady Philosophy sees as a trap for the weak-minded.

In contrast to Glaucon's view (but in keeping with the general outlook of Plato), Boethius seeks to promote disinterested morality—morality for its own sake rather than for a reward. In fact, something similar seems to be at stake in the story of the biblical Job as well, because at the beginning of the story Satan complains to God that Job is righteous only because he has been rewarded. "Touch in all he has," Satan says to God, "and he will curse you to your face." Much of the wager between Satan and God is about Job's true motivation—the question of *why* he does what he does.

Lady Philosophy asserts that happiness (or felicity, as it is sometimes translated) is based on integrity. In other words, our happiness depends on our virtues, and not on external goods. And apparent bad fortune is often good fortune, precisely because it helps us to discover our integrity and helps to free us from bondage to earthly things. In fact, she says, no one is ever truly secure in this kind of happiness until finally forsaken by Fortune.

All this comes in the form of the "gentle" treatments that Lady Philosophy had promised early on in the story—the treatments that had been based on the tenets of ancient Stoicism. But there are also the harsher, more stringent treatments that Lady Philosophy had promised, and these turn out to consist in abstract, metaphysical reasonings, and it is here that Boethius conveys doctrines that would have much influence in later Christian theology.

## *Boethius's Theology*

Specifically, through a series of questions and inferences, Lady Philosophy argues that there is actually no such thing as evil in the first place. Evil is not really something, she says but rather, only the *absence* of something, as darkness is the absence of light, or coldness is the absence of heat. Evil is just the absence of goodness, she maintains, and goodness is everywhere present in the world, because God has made only good things. With these propositions, Boethius then seeks to explain how an entirely good god could still make a world that contains what we *perceive* as evil.

On this view of things, evil is not part of creation at all but rather a gap or vacancy in creation, where God, for reasons that we cannot fathom, has chosen to leave a blank. This outlook is often called the privative theory of evil—evil being only a privation of goodness—and this theory had already been articulated at considerable length by Augustine.[4]

This philosophical treatment is stringent, because it requires the patient to follow a chain of abstract argumentation and then to draw further corollaries. For example, on this privative view of evil, human wickedness becomes a kind of nothingness, because wickedness is a form of evil and evil does not exist. As a result, then, the souls of the wicked tend toward nonexistence. The wicked extinguish themselves through their own transgressions, and thus they supply a kind of punishment for themselves. The good, by contrast, become ever more real through their own, conscientious actions.

In addition, Lady Philosophy asserts that humans are naturally good and that if they then become evil, they cease to be human at all, because they cease to conform to their own nature. Evil people are thus sub-human. This is part of Lady Philosophy's claim that evil does not really exist in itself, but is only a lack of goodness, or life, or health: "The result is that you cannot think of anyone as human whom you see transformed by wickedness" (IV, iii, 94).

Lady Philosophy says that nothing external can give true happiness; instead, she contends that happiness must come from within and that one's virtue is all that one truly has. She equates happiness with the good and asserts further that since God, the creator, is the supreme good, all people are actually seeking God when they seek happiness, though they do not always know it.

Lady Philosophy also insists that all these effects come about as a result of our free will, our free choices in life, and not from any force applied to us externally, by circumstance or by God. Our will is free, she says, and yet at the same time God knows all things eternally, even how each of us will choose when we choose freely. In other words, our will is free and yet God knows how we will choose anyway—and Lady Philosophy says there is no contradiction in this position.

In making these remarks, Boethius has in mind a doctrine also defended by Augustine—to the effect that God is outside of time. God is said to be eternal in the same way that the truth of the Pythagorean Theorem is eternal. It makes no sense to ask *when* the theorem is true, or to ask what would be the case *before* it was true or *after* it is true. The theorem simply *is* true, and it is eternally so. Questions of *when*, *before*, and *after* are out of place. In a similar way, Boethius conceives of God as being outside of time such that questions of when, before, and after are out of place. God's material universe unfolds in time, and if it should last forever, it would then be *perpetual*, meaning it would last for an infinite time. But God is not perpetual, according to Boethius; God is eternal, meaning outside of time altogether.

God knows eternally what our free choices will be, he says, and yet God does not determine these choices for us—any more than the spectators at a chariot race determine how a charioteer will choose to turn his horses, even though everyone knows that a good charioteer will turn his horses at the far end of the track.

All these positions are strongly Augustinian, and Boethius apparently sees Christian theology as being not merely an intellectual curiosity, but as a true support in times of trial. And though the idea that wickedness makes us nothing, whereas conscience makes us real, may seem like a profoundly obscure hypothesis, it nevertheless expresses a recurring theme in later moral philosophy—the idea that our sense of self is strongest when we act from principle rather than from purely selfish motives. To act from selfish motives and only selfish motives is to feel less like a person, more like a thing. (As Jean-Jacques Rousseau would remark more than twelve centuries later, "To be governed by appetite alone is slavery. But obedience to a law that one prescribes to oneself is freedom.")[5]

In Lady Philosophy's telling, there is a just and good god who is beyond our understanding. God is just, she says, but we cannot see God's overall plan for the world, especially when Fortune and Fate seem so disordered. And Lady Philosophy admits that this is indeed a mystery—for everything takes place simultaneously for God, and we, like Job, in our temporal world, cannot understand this.

Ultimately, she says, happiness is the pursuit of God through intellectual and spiritual means. This is the supreme good, and the only good worth pursuing. All earthly goods, by contrast, are false, and only our intellect and our virtues can lead us to the true good of the soul. Happiness, as Lady Philosophy interprets it, is certainly not the restoration of one's worldly fortune (including wealth, home, and livestock, as happens at the end of the Book of Job). Reward is not the purpose. Instead, the good man is happy despite his seeming misfortunes. Material misfortune is not significant, and divine retribution in the form of physical torment is not important either. The just man who suffers injustice, Boethius tells us in the end, is happy anyway.

Perhaps, as Lady Philosophy asserts, understanding the suffering of the innocent will always be a mystery. But for us the important question remains how we should live our lives.

## Notes

1. In Greek, "the same in substance" was written *homoousios*, whereas "similar in substance" was written *homoiousios*.
2. Plato's views appear in the *Republic* at 473b–d.
3. Epictetus continues, "Is your child dead? It is returned. Is your wife dead? She is returned. Is your estate taken away? Well, and is not that likewise returned? 'But he who took it away is a bad man.' What difference is it to you who the giver assigns to take it back? While

he gives it to you to possess, take care of it; but don't view it as your own, just as travelers view a hotel." *The Enchiridion*, written in AD 135.

4. The privative theory of evil is defended, for example, in book 7 of Augustine's *Confessions*.

5. Rousseau makes these remarks in book 1, chapter 8, of his *Social Contract*.

## Works Cited

Augustine, *Confessions*. Trans. E. J. Sheed. Indianapolis: Hackett, 2006. Print.

Boethius, Anicius. *The Consolation of Philosophy*. Trans. Victor Watts. New York: Penguin Classics, 1999. Print.

Epictetus. *The Enchiridion* in *All the Works of Epictetus, Which Are Now Extant; Consisting of His Discourses, Preserved by Arrian, in Four Books, the Enchiridion, and Fragments*. Trans. Elizabeth Carter. London: J and F Rivington, 1768. Print.

Hume, David. *Dialogues Concerning Natural Religion*. Cambridge, MA: Hackett, 1998. Print.

Plato. *The Republic*. Trans. Desmond Lee. New York: Penguin, 2007. Print.

Rousseau, Jean-Jacques. *The Social Contract*. Trans. Maurice Cranston. New York: Penguin Classics, 1968. Print.

# Poetic Justice: The Civilization of the Heart in Malory's *Morte Darthur*

STEPHANIE KICELUK

## *Summary*

Caught up in the political turmoil of fifteenth-century England, Sir Thomas Malory found himself at one time or another on both sides of the War of the Roses, and finally in prison awaiting death. He was a purported bandit, rapist, vandal, and traitor. Weighted against all these accusations is his work, *Le Morte Darthur*, better known as the legends of King Arthur. One of the most recognizable characters in world literature, Arthur is not only the subject of academic study but a staple of popular culture. The frequently asked question is: How could so infamous a man write so convincingly about such chivalrous characters? The answer is that Malory and his stories have often been misrepresented. Like other authors in this book, he was not sent to prison for criminal behavior; political affiliations and dynastic intrigue got him there. His response to the prison experience was to re-create a lost world of heroes and noble causes.—J.W.R.

## *The Identity Crisis*

> We few, we happy few, we band of brothers.
> —*King Henry V*, St. Crispin's Day, Shakespeare

For hundreds of years, until the end of the twentieth century, the identity of the author of a book whose stories pervade the English imagination with a power comparable to that of Greek myth lay in doubt. William Caxton, its first publisher, called it "thys noble and Ioyous book," and the Prologue to the 1485 edition stated that it was "written for our doctrine, and for to be aware that we fall not to vice nor sin, but to exercise and follow virtue." More recently, it has been celebrated as the "book that changed the language we speak" (Lustig 155), "our first great work of English prose" (Lustig 114) and "a sacred and central possession of all who speak the English tongue" (Lewis 104). History has borne out the truth of these judgments. Today, few English-speaking people are not aware of the adventures of chivalry, knighthood, and pageantry that fill its pages, even if these came by way of Disney when they were children. This book is *The Hoole Book of Kyng Arthur and of His Noble Knyghtes of The Rounde Table*, otherwise known as *Le Morte Darthur*, an enormous compendium of Arthurian legends from both French and English sources, which Caxton edited and divided into 21 books comprising 507 chapters in all.

In 1934, a rival version came to light. Walter Oakeshott, a librarian at Winchester College, happened to come across an old, forgotten safe on its premises. Opening it, he found a stash of ancient documents and a "fat book," the manuscript of the *Morte*—the only one in existence. He had made one of the most remarkable discoveries in the history of literature. In the opinion of its eventual editor, Eugene Vinaver, the Winchester manuscript—as it came to be called—was more "complete and authentic" than the Caxton version, a text that brought readers "nearer to what Malory wrote" (Lustig 60). In both the Caxton and Winchester texts, the author had identified himself as Sir Thomas Malory, "knight prisoner," the "servant of Jesu both day and night."

The name solved little. There were multiple Thomas Malorys—with bewildering variations on the spelling of the name—who populated fifteenth-century England. In 1894, however, G. L. Kittredge persuasively argued that the author of the *Morte* was Sir Thomas Malory of Newbold Revel, a brigand and lawbreaker, who had spent close to a decade in English jails. This claim opened a moral gulf between the book and the man that would plague Malory studies for decades. As C. S. Lewis put it, "The work has long passed for a mirror of honour and virtue; the author appears to be little better than a criminal" (Lewis, "The English Prose *Morte*" 7). An unprecedented excavation of materials about Malory began. Hoping to find more suitable candidates, some scholars put forward other Thomas Malorys who could have written the *Morte*, none of them criminals. For Lewis and others, this was a "desperate expedient," a misguided attempt to substitute a specious teller for the one who had actually told the tale. In fact, until P. J. C. Field's masterful 1993 biography, the identity of the *Morte*'s author was still hotly contested. Field's exhaustive search of all the pertinent fifteenth-century historical documents and court records left no doubt that the Malory of the *Morte* was, in fact, the Malory of Newbold Revel.

Ironically, the *Morte*'s early readers would have welcomed the idea that its author was a criminal. Roger Ascham, schoolmaster to Elizabeth I, pronounced that the "whole pleasure of [it] standeth in two speciall poyntes, in open mans slaughter, and bold bawdrye: In which booke those be counted the noblest Knightes, that do kill most men without any quarell, and commit fowlest adulteries by sutlest shiftes" (Shepherd xxviii–xxix). Nathaniel Baxter, tutor to Sir Philip Sydney, condemned the entire Arthurian cycle as a vile chronicle of "the horrible actes of those whoremasters, Launcelot du Lake, Tristram de Liones, Gareth of Orkney, Merlin, the Lady of the Lake ... [and] King Peleus, etc." (Shepherd, xxix). This early censure resurged at the start of the nineteenth century. Like Ascham and Sydney, some Victorian readers dismissed the *Morte* as a sordid saga of incest and adultery featuring barbaric episodes of slaughter and perfidy, including matricide, patricide, and mass infanticide. This view in itself was not objectionable, but its eventual effect on the book—the *Morte*'s "sterilization" as T.S. Eliot called it—was troublesome. Editors set out to sanitize the book for a wider public—especially as its stories continued to be a magnet for children—producing new, revisionist versions that glossed over the carnal nature of the love between Lancelot and Guenivere and suppressed all references to Mordred as the product of Arthur's incestuous union with his sister, Morgause—the "foundation of ... the whole book," as T. S. Eliot declared (Lustig 132). C. S. Lewis emphatically rejected such revisionism, refusing to tar either the book or the man: "I at any rate will never blacken the book to make it match the man. But," Lewis asked, "was the man so black" (Lewis, "The English Prose *Morte*" 9)?

## *The Heroics of Crime and the War of the Roses*

Despite scant biographical data, Field proved to be an especially able and sympathetic architect of Malory's life and times. "Writing the life of a medieval Englishman," he noted, "is notoriously like making bricks without straw" (Field 1). To date, the year of Malory's birth remains unknown, with scholars placing it somewhere between 1400 and 1418. The basic facts are these: that Malory wrote most or all of the *Morte* in prison, that it took him about two years to write, that he completed it sometime near March 1470—in the "ninth year of the reign of King Edward the Fourth"—and, that roughly a year later, on March 14, 1471, Malory died, probably still in prison. Records of births, marriages, and exchanges of property also show that Malory married Elizabeth Walsh in 1448, that they had at least one son, Robert—perhaps named after an esteemed uncle—and that both lived to see the birth of their grandson, Nicholas, near 1466.

There are clues to suggest that Malory's uncle was the famous Robert Malory, a professional crusader and a "great magnate of the kingdom" who was the Prior of the Hospital of St. John of Jerusalem in England from 1432 to 1440, an office affording him enormous wealth, power, and access to the king (Field 68). When the Sultan of Egypt threatened Rhodes, the Prior promptly gathered a company of armed men and sailed to the Levant to defend the Holy Land. Malory's proximity to his uncle may have led him to define the ideal of knighthood less in terms of the rarified spiritual perfection demanded by the Grail and more in terms of the pragmatic discipline of service that dominates the *Morte* to its very end, where, contrary to his French sources, Malory has Lancelot's kinsmen go off on a crusade rather than retiring to a cloister after his death. Field speculates that Malory's hopes for advancement were shattered when Prior Robert died in 1440, and that his consequent sense of dispossession—Malory's income was only half the average for Warwickshire knights—may have prompted him to turn to a life of brigandry (Lustig 84). A revealing detail is that the sum of 40 pounds—the annual "income that for a century and a half had been associated with knighthood"—figures as a constant in his thefts (Lustig 89).

The extent to which Malory's criminal record coincides with his actual offenses is uncertain, given that the solicitors of his enemies compiled it. At the very least, in documenting his transgressions, it reveals the general contours of lawlessness in Malory's day. The first charges against Malory are entered on October 10, 1443; he is accused of injuring, insulting, and imprisoning Thomas Smythe of Spratton, while stealing property worth 40 pounds. Nothing comes of these accusations, but many more will accrue. Over the next eight years, Malory allegedly indulges in sporadic sprees of lawlessness, stealing livestock, raising mobs, and creating havoc in his native region, reaching a spectacular apex in his criminal activities on January 4, 1450, when he and twenty-six other armed men attempt to ambush the Duke of Buckingham in the woods of Warwickshire with the intention of taking his life. A hot-tempered and vengeful man, Buckingham would surprisingly take nearly a year and a half to bring formal charges against his ambushers.

In the interval, Malory's lawlessness continued. On May 23, 1450, and again on August 6, he supposedly "rapes" Joan Smith, taking 40 pounds worth of her husband's goods; on May 31, he extorts money from two monks at Monks Kirby and then returns to extract more from another monk on August 31. There is a brief hiatus until June 4, 1451, at which point Malory resurfaces, stealing 7 cows, 2 calves, 335 sheep, and an expensive cart from Cosford, Warwickshire. On July 20, he enters Buckingham's deer park at Caludon and absconds with 6 does, managing to inflict 500 pounds' worth of damage in the process. At this point, the Duke of Buckingham's patience appears to have worn thin. An attempt on his life was one thing, but the theft of his does was another. On July 25, the Duke and his men corner Malory on his own estate and hand him over to the Sheriff of Coventry for safekeeping in his manor. The maneuver is to no avail. Within hours, under cover of night, Malory breaks out, swims the moat and, the next day, he ransacks Combe Abbey with a small party of accomplices. The haul is 46 pounds in cash and valuables worth 40. The following night he returns with a mob of a hundred or so men for more loot.

Local authorities are slow to press charges, and it is not until August 23, 1451, that Malory is formally indicted at Nuneaton, Warwickshire, in the presence of the Duke of Buckingham. "The court was presided over by four justices," Fields notes, "among whom, undeterred by any scruples that the first and gravest charge was an attempt to murder himself, was the Duke of Buckingham" (Field 101). On January 27, 1452, Malory appears before the King's Bench, pleads not guilty to all charges, is placed in the custody of the Sheriffs of London, and committed to Ludgate Prison. A strange odyssey now begins. Malory is ushered from prison to prison, from Ludgate to the Marshalsea to the Tower of London to Newgate and back again to Ludgate in a futile circle of writs, summons, and deferrals worthy of a Dickensian novel. For the next eight years or so, Malory awaits a jury that never appears and a trial that never materializes. Why?

Malory's prison career, to a large extent, was entangled in the labyrinthine politics of the War of the Roses (1455–87), the dynastic struggle for the throne of England ignited by the rival Houses of York and Lancaster, whose emblems were respectively a white rose and a red one. A dispute over inheritance rather than ideology—neither side was contesting rule by monarchy—the ancestral feud cut its bloody swathe across an England rapidly descending into chaos. As the historian Riddy points out, Malory was born into the "worst political crisis England had known since the Norman Conquest" (Lustig 160). To make matters worse, French victories in the Hundred Years War—some under the banner of Joan of Arc—had forced the English to surrender all but one of the territories they once held, a humiliation that was felt to be part of the "larger failure of Englishness" (Lustig 160). When Lancelot is exiled from Arthur's kingdom of Logres—the ancient name for England—and returns to his native France, he distributes some of these very territories among his knights (Riddy 888). The English revenged themselves on a girl; the Duke of Buckingham himself was rumored to have "threatened the chained Joan of Arc with his sword," with the young Malory possibly looking on in the midst of the crowd (Lustig 98).

It is heady stuff to realize that Malory tread the same earth as Joan of Arc, and that he breathed and moved in the very world of the characters who stride deathlessly through the pages of Shakespeare's "histories." Humphrey Stafford (Duke of Buckingham), Richard Neville (Earl of Warwick), York, Lancaster, Clarence, and Somerset—these names cannot fall on deaf ears, and Malory lived in the blaze of their rivalries. In the course of his life, he was courted by two of the most powerful men in England—Buckingham, supporter of the Lancastrian Henry VI, and Warwick, supporter of Richard, Duke of York, and of his son, Edward IV. In 1445, Buckingham had used his influence to win Malory a seat in Parliament, but within five years Malory had rather dramatically severed their tie with an alleged attempt on his life (Field 96), earning him the vengeance of the Duke's solicitors if not also his henchmen. In the political upheaval of Malory's day, allegiances would dissolve just as swiftly as they formed. By 1450, for whatever reasons, personal or political, Malory had shifted his loyalty to the Yorkist Richard Neville, Earl of Warwick, the Kingmaker, Shakespeare's infamous "setter up and plucker down of kings" (Shakespeare 3 *Henry VI* 2.3.37).

Not surprisingly, the very aptitude that landed Malory in jail was precisely that which each magnate valued: "his ability to cause trouble." Although his role in the struggle between Warwick and Buckingham was "quite out of proportion to the social status suggested by the surviving evidence of his property, income, and family connections," both magnates could not help but take notice of Malory's talent for enlisting "scores of armed men, raised at very short notice" (Field 128). This marked interest in Malory the knight carried over to Malory the prisoner. As much care as his Lancastrian enemies had taken to bring Malory to prison, even more was taken to keep him there. A jury was never assembled, his pardon was "dismissed under suspicious circumstances, and his goalers were threatened with extraordinary fines should he escape," fines that broke all records in medieval England (Field 128). Most tellingly, Malory was never afforded a trial. "Trials do not always bring the truth to light now," Field observes, "and did not in the fifteenth century, but the absence of one makes it harder to estimate the truth of the charges against Malory. The number of people involved, the variety of the allegations, and ... their timing suggests that they were not wholey [*sic*] invented; but their comprehensiveness makes it plain that someone looked for people with grievances against Malory and organised them into court" (Field 105). In sum, "the legal process against him [was] suspect from the beginning" (Field 106). This is not to say that Malory's lawless behavior had been fabricated out of whole cloth but rather that it was of a piece with his times: raids, riots, and ambushes were common occurrences, and the destruction of property or breaking into deer-parks was "a recognized form of magnate-baiting" (Field 100). As a Yorkist knight—and perhaps even as Warwick's agent—Malory may have been "expressing political dissent in a manner that was becoming all too common" (Field 96), treading the line between incitement to violence and civil disobedience.

There is still, however, Malory's "rape" of Joan Smith. Notably, it was not Joan herself but her husband who brought this charge against him. This fact in itself cannot necessarily be used in Malory's defense. At the time, no married woman could bring suit on her own behalf. English rape law in England had evolved "so as to serve less the needs of the woman concerned than a complex of other social interests" (Bate 801). The Statute of Rapes of 1382 "accords the husband, the father, or next of kin, the right to make the accusation even though the woman may have consented ... and questions of material damage and compensation receive rather more attention than does the fact of sexual assault" (Bate 801). There is no evidence of any previous relationship between Malory and Joan Smith, but that means little and does not rule out the possibility of Malory loving her, as C. S. Lewis delicately put it, "*par amours*" (Lewis, "The English Prose *Morte*" 10). Whatever the circumstances, there are many "medieval cases in which rape (as abduction, forced coition, or both) features ... as [an element] in accounts of crimes against property, and the charge against Malory could conceivably pertain more closely to the issue of property crime than to a felony against Joan as an individual" (Bate 802–03).

## *The "Knight Prisoner": Ordeals, Plots and Defections*

The Lancastrian years of Malory's imprisonment were harsh and difficult. Life in fifteenth-century English prisons, foul and disease-ridden, could generally be made less horrific with amenities and privileges, including going about free during the day. Such comforts, however, had to be bought and were costly. Confronted by these expenses and by the irony that the flow of his income was impeded by the very circumstances that drained it, Malory soon found himself bankrupt and unable to alleviate his misery. Scenes in which knights suffer imprisonment recur almost obsessively in the *Morte*, but perhaps Malory's anguish is most fully glimpsed when Sir Darras imprisons Tristram for killing three of his sons in a tournament:

> So Sir Tristram endured there great pain, for sickness had undertaken him, and that is the greatest pain a prisoner may have: for all the while a prisoner may have his health of body he may endure under the mercy of God and in hope of good deliverance. But when sickness toucheth a prisoner's body, then may a prisoner say all wealth is him bereft, and then hath he cause to wail and weep. Right so did Sir Tristram when sickness had undertaken him, for then he took such sorrow that he had almost slain himself [Malory 225].

Such passages suggest that Malory had at times felt himself close to death, if not through illness, then by his own hand or the executioner's. "I pray you," he beseeched his readers, "all gentlemen and gentle women that readeth this book of Arthur and his knights from the beginning to the ending, pray for me while I am alive, that God send me good deliverance, and when I am dead, I pray you all pray for my soul" (Malory 527).

When Yorkist forces triumphantly entered London in July 1460 and besieged the Tower of London, Malory was at last freed from his Lancastrian imprisonment, and when the Duke of York ascended the throne as Edward IV, Malory was issued another general pardon that wiped his slate clean. One would think that at this point Malory's prison career had drawn to its close, but events to come would prove otherwise. After his release, Malory took up his life as knight and retainer. In October 1462, he joined a military expedition led by Edward IV and Warwick against Lancastrian strongholds in Northumbria, and returning home in January 1463, he resumed his life as a husband and father, attending to family and property matters. And, then, there is a stunning development: On July 14, 1468, Malory's name appears on a list of enemies to the Throne who have been denied pardon by King Edward, a list including King Henry VI himself and his most notorious supporters. Almost immediately, Malory is imprisoned again—this time in a scenario worthy of Kafka's making—without any charges whatsoever entered against him. It is now, during this second period of imprisonment (1468–70), that he takes up the work of writing the *Morte*.

What behavior could possibly have landed Malory in prison again, this time during a Yorkist regime? The ever-twisting maze of the War of the Roses may again supply an answer. Near the time of Malory's imprisonment, the Earl of Warwick seems to have had a political change of heart, abandoning the Yorkist cause. Hoping to forge a grand alliance between France and England, Warwick had long harbored ambitions of King Edward marrying a French princess. In the end, however, Edward chose for himself and married Elizabeth Woodville, the widow of a Lancastrian knight. Rebuffed by the King, Warwick rebelliously cast his lot with yet a third aspirant to the throne—Edward's brother, George, Duke of Clarence. In the spring of 1470, Warwick and Clarence fled to France where, by July, they had formed a Lancastrian alliance with Margaret of Anjou, wife of Henry VI. Where, one might ask, has *he* been all this time—the king whose "bookish rule hath pull'd fair England down" (Shakespeare 2 *Henry VI* 1.1.260)?

Beginning in August 1453, the hapless Henry lapsed into a state of "vegetative insanity," recovering only in December 1454. When his son, Edward, was born that month, Henry was baffled, "claiming he must have been conceived by the Holy Spirit" (Norton, xxi). Many believed this "spirit" to be Henry's closest councilor, Edmund Beaufort, Duke of Somerset. Nevertheless, there was now an heir apparent to the crown, which caused considerable consternation within Yorkist ranks. On May 22, 1455, the first major battle of the War of the Roses, exploded onto the scene at St. Albans, and by December 1460, the Yorkists had stormed London and detained Henry. Although released a few months later, Henry was captured again in 1465 and imprisoned in the Tower of London. Here he remained for the next five years until he was executed on May 21, 1471, two months after Malory's death.

It is jolting to remember that Malory was composing the *Morte* during the last two years of Henry's life with both of them imprisoned in the same tower, and even more chilling to consider that little more than a decade later— as Shakespeare portrayed it—it would be where Gloucester imprisoned the young sons of King Edward, his brother, before having them savagely murdered. During the last years of his life, efforts to rescue Henry intensified and came to a head in the Cornelius Plot, a conspiracy to restore him to the throne orchestrated by his French wife, Margaret of Anjou, and her supporters. The plot was uncovered when "Edward's agents in Kent had arrested a Lancastrian courier called John Cornelius with letters from the Lancastrian exiles to sympathizers in England" (Field 139). Cornelius was promptly tortured—the first time torture had been authorized in England before the reign of Henry VIII— and gave up the names of several men. Among them was Malory's. Why had he defected?

Had Malory decided to remain loyal to Warwick, crossing over to the Lancastrian side with him? Did he have a crisis of conscience in which he had resolved to make reparation to Henry VI, the king who had knighted him? Did he see his defection from the Yorkist party as a return to the fold, as a reckoning with the Lancastrian sympathizers among his kinsmen? There is no documentation of any kind that can supply the answer. Instead, there is the *Morte*. This is not to say that the book can be read as a *roman à clef* with neat parallels lining up Arthur's court with either Henry VI's or Edward IV's, but rather that Malory found the vast narrative cycles of Arthurian legend, of fellowship and betrayal, loyalty and treason, to be a perfect mirror of his troubled times.

## *The Book: The Motif of Wholeness in the* Morte

How Malory gained access to his Arthurian material while in prison has long been in dispute. Composing the *Morte* was a monumental undertaking that required him to "extricate and clarify a coherent pattern from the cyclic tangle of his sources" (Tucker 62). The English texts, among them the stanzaic *Morte Arthur* and the *Awntyrs off Arthure* (Meale 873), would have been readily available to a person of his social rank, but access to his French sources, including the *Tristan* and the French "Vulgate" series—the romance cycle containing the *Merlin*, the *Lancelot*, the *Queste del Saint Graal*, and the *Mort Artu*—would have been out of his reach unless he had entry to the royal library or the collection of a noble (Meale 877). If so, this collection was most likely the one owned by King Edward's brother-in-law, Anthony Wydeville, the Earl of Rivers, Caxton's most influential patron. It is likely, then, that Malory spent most of his second imprisonment in privileged conditions; certainly, his burial in Greyfriars, which held the bodies of nobles, was a mark of great distinction. It was also a stroke of poetic justice for the man who had authored "the whole book of King Arthur, and of his noble knights of the Round Table, that when they were whole together there was ever a hundred and forty" (Malory 527).

The word "whole" resonates throughout the *Morte* from beginning to end. The freight of its meaning must have been immense for a "knight prisoner" laboring to forge an identity that could yoke together two seemingly irreconcilable roles, one as a noble member of the knighthood and the other as its disgraced outcast. In Summers' study of prison literature, she points out that "Malory's almost oxymoronic self-definition of prestige and abasement/humility ... possibly should be read as a social and yet also spiritual exaltation—as a man of rank, and yet as one who humbly and nobly suffers misfortune" (Summers 184). As Michel Foucault reminds us, identity is necessarily predicated on subjection: a self or 'subject' comes into being and continues to exist only on condition that it is subjected to some form of power. Physical imprisonment all the more exposes and intensifies the inherent vulnerability of the subject. The doubly contingent nature of the prisoner—and the heightened tension between the exaltation and abasement of the self that it sets in play—is beautifully embodied in the figure of Lancelot, the consummate "prisoner" of love. In the *Morte*, he is Malory's ideal subject.

The yearning for "wholeness" appears immediately in the opening of the *Morte*, defining the motive for the sexual union of Arthur's parents, Uther Pendragon and Igraine, and Arthur's conception. "I am sick for anger and for love of fair Igraine," Uther tells Merlin, "that I may not be whole" (Malory 4). Uther is unhinged by his desire for Igraine, the wife of another man, and cannot be made "whole" either in body or mind until Merlin devises a ruse to get him into Igraine's bed. Desire cannot be resisted in the *Morte* except on pain of illness, psychic disintegration, or death. We see this principle at work not only in Lancelot and Tristram, but even in Merlin, who, with all his foreknowledge and wizardry, cannot save himself from the ineluctable pull of desire when he meets Nenive, a damsel of the Lake: "he was besotted upon her, that he might not be from her." Before Merlin suffers himself to be buried alive 'under a great stone' for love of her, he prepares Arthur for his disappearance:

> "Ah," said the King, "since ye know of your evil adventure, purvey for it, and put it away by your crafts, that misadventure."
> "Nay," said Merlin, "it will not be" [Malory 58].

Merlin has overseen and directed the consolidation of Logres, and in his last act of unification, which will find its fulfillment in Lancelot, he links Arthur's kingdom to that of Lancelot's father, King Ban, while at the same time connecting the Round Table to the Holy Grail. Just before his living entombment, Merlin follows Nenive to the court of King Ban, where he meets Lancelot as a boy, revealing that Lancelot was first named Galahad by his parents and predicting that he will be "the most man of worship in the world" (Malory 59). Once Merlin is imprisoned in the earth, he can no longer serve as the unifying force within the kingdom, or the text. This role passes to Lancelot, who represents the advance from the practice of magic to the practice of chivalry as the force that will now hold Arthur's kingdom—and the narrative of the *Morte*—together. As P. E. Tucker argues, "to understand Malory's presentation of Lancelot is to grasp the unity of the book; its theme is loyalty" (Tucker 102), and loyalty is absolute in Lancelot. It is one of the great paradoxes of the *Morte* that Lancelot's faithfulness to Arthur lies in his "traitorous" love for the queen and that this love, moreover, works to sustain rather than to disrupt the cohesiveness of the Round Table. In fact, the sundering of Lancelot and Guenivere spells the sundering of the fellowship, and eventually of the kingdom (Riddy 887). Malory makes it eminently clear—as does Arthur— that the blame for this disintegration lies not in the adultery of the lovers but in the villainy of Agravain, whose hatred and envy of Lancelot drive him to "bringeth up the noise" of their affair. As Malory summarily states at the end of Book XIX: "and here I go unto the morte Arthur, and *that* caused Sir Agravain" (emphasis mine; Malory 467).

Along with his brothers—Gawain, Gaheris, Gareth and Mordred—Agravain is a member of the treacherous Orkney clan. To avenge the slaying of their father, Lot, Gaheris beheads their mother when she is in the arms of her lover, Sir Lamorak, and later, together with Gawain, murders him as well. Except for Gareth, who is loyal to Lancelot, each brother successively threatens the unity of the Round Table. When Lancelot is discovered lying with the Queen in her chamber, Agravain strikes the first blow by publicly accusing Lancelot and Guenivere of treason. It is this "publicity," this "noise"—not the adultery—that unnerves Arthur. As the doom gathers, Guenivere stands ready to be burned at the stake, and, in his frenzy to rescue her, Lancelot unwittingly kills Gareth and Gaheris, earning him Gawain's remorseless hatred. Realizing that war with Lancelot and his kinsmen is now inevitable, Arthur is disconsolate:

> And much more am I sorrier for my good knights' loss than for the loss of my fair queen; for queens I might have enough but such a fellowship of good knights shall never be together in no company.... And alas, that ever Sir Lancelot and I should be at debate! Ah, Agravain, Agravain ... Jesu forgive it thy soul, for thy evil will that thou hadst, and Sir Mordred thy brother [Malory 482].

The "smiting and cleaving" will now start in earnest. "What the knights do individually to others is in the end done to them collectively: the split heads return in the form of a divided state" (Lustig 18). Without Lancelot the "center cannot hold," and the way is opened for the forces of evil incarnate in the child Arthur sought to murder in a mass infanticide, his son, Mordred, who, in a horrific enactment of the death drive, will impale himself on his father's sword while thrusting his own into his father.

## *A Binding Power: "Enfellowship" and Lancelot's Saving Grace*

"Even as a child," T. J. Lustig writes, "the infliction of head wounds in *King Arthur* struck me as symptomatic" (Lustig 14). According to Lustig's count, Lancelot holds the record for cleavings, proof of his superior prowess. What more importantly distinguishes Lancelot from his fellow knights, however, is that he repents of any cleavings he has inflicted for the purpose of winning "worship" or honor and that he willingly endures a grueling penance for this "sin." In the last two books of the *Morte*, Lancelot undertakes a lacerating self-examination as he prepares to seek the Holy Grail. To his shame, he finds that he has been too eager to succeed in the eyes of the world, too caught up in its vainglory and "bobbaunce," and ready to take up any contest—right or wrong—simply because he knows he will win it:

> My sin and my wickedness have brought me unto great dishonour. For when I sought worldly adventures for worldly desires, I ever achieved them and had the better in every place, and never was I discomfited in no quarrel [Malory 331].

When he begs the holy hermit to "hear his life," Lancelot adds another layer of significance to his sinfulness, confessing that he has loved Guenivere "unmeasurably and out of measure long": "And all my great deeds of arms that I have done, for the most part was for the queen's sake, and for her sake would I do battle were it right or wrong; and never did I battle all only for God's sake, but for to win worship, and to cause me the better to be loved" (Malory 332). When Lancelot and Guenivere encounter each other for the last time, he tells her that but for her—"had not your love been"—he would have "forsaken the vanities of the world" to attain the Sangrail (Malory 520). If he had striven to succeed in the world's eyes, it was solely because he had striven to succeed in hers, each being, for him, one and the same.

The moral point at issue is not so much that Lancelot loves Guenivere, but that he loves her "out of measure." Judged by the spiritual perfection necessary to achieve the Sangrail, Lancelot's capacity for such a love is a failing, but within the earthly realm of chivalry, it is a saving grace, for it extends itself not only to Guenivere but also to Arthur and to his knights. Even as the war with Arthur intensifies, Lancelot cannot bring himself to engage in it. He forgoes a display of the very prowess that is his *raison d'être*. To the objections of his men, Lancelot has only this answer: "I have no heart to fight my lord Arthur," he insists, "for ever me seemeth I do not as I ought to do" (Malory 489). In a pivotal moment of the war, Arthur is thrown from his horse in the chaos of battle; undone by the sight, Lancelot dismounts, gathers Arthur up, and reseats him. Tears burst from Arthur's eyes as he thinks on "the great courtesy that [is] in Sir Lancelot more than in any other man" (Malory 488). Later in the war, when Gawain insists on single combat with him, Lancelot balks, offering to abase himself in any number of ways to persuade Gawain to relent. When Gawain lies seriously wounded, Lancelot spares him and leaves the field at the expense of his own honor, moving Arthur to exclaim: "Now alas ... that ever this unhappy war began! For ever Sir Lancelot forbeareth me in all places, and in like wise my kin; and that is seen well this day, what courtesy he showed my nephew Sir Gawain" (Malory 503). Lancelot's unfailing nobility of spirit encapsulates "the civilization of the heart" that, despite all the *Morte*'s violence, infuses its narrative with "a fineness and sensitivity, a voluntary rejection of all the uglier and more vulgar impulses. We can describe it only in words derived from its own age, words which will now perhaps be mocked, such as courtesy, gentleness, chivalry" (Lewis, "The English Prose *Morte*" 9). When Lancelot lies dead at the end of the *Morte*, Malory's grief at the passing of these qualities in his own day is reiterated in Hector's lament over Lancelot's body:

> Ah Lancelot ... thou were head of all Christian knights.... And thou were the courteoust knight that ever bore shield; and thou were the truest friend to thy lover that ever bestrode horse ... and thou were the kindest man that ever struck with sword ... and the sternest knight to thy mortal foe that ever put spear in the rest [Malory 526].

The *Morte*'s valorization of Lancelot culminates, however, in its penultimate chapter, which describes an episode not found in any of Malory's sources and entirely of his own making: Lancelot's healing of the Hungarian knight, Sir Urry. Severely injured in an encounter with Sir Alpheus, Urry has been carried on a litter for seven years throughout the lands of Christendom by his sister and mother in hopes of finding the knight who can restore him, until the group finally happens upon Arthur's court. Sir Alpheus's mother, a sorceress, has "wrought by her subtle crafts that Sir Urry should never be whole, but ever his [seven] wounds should one time fester and another time bleed, so that he should never be whole until the *best* knight of the world had searched his wounds" (emphasis mine; Malory 460). After trying to heal Urry himself, Arthur—in an astounding sequence—calls forth each and every one of his knights to do the same, summoning all one hundred and ten by name. When each in turn tries but fails to make Urry "whole," Arthur commands Lancelot to try. Lancelot resists, saying he is in no wise better than any other knight: "My most renowned lord," said Sir Lancelot, "I know well I dare not nor may not disobey you; but and I might or durst, wit you well I would not take upon me to touch the wounded knight in that intent that I should pass all other knights—Jesu defend me from that shame" (Malory 465). Only after Arthur persuades Lancelot that he would be making the attempt "for no presumption, but for to bear us fellowship" does Lancelot submit. Praying to the Holy Trinity of God, Lancelot kneels beside Urry, "searches" his wounds, "and forthwith the wounds fair healed, and seemed as they had been whole seven years.... And ever Sir Lancelot wept as he had been a child that had been beaten" (Malory 465–66).

The power Lancelot has exerted throughout the entire course of the *Morte* here, at last, becomes manifest—literally embodied—in Sir Urry. In the presence of all the Round Table, Lancelot's *imitatio Christi* is a miracle that reveals his essential power to keep and make things "whole." Lancelot weeps in abject gratitude, pierced by the realization that, despite his humiliating failure with the Grail, he has all the while been a good knight—in fact, the *best* knight—in the eyes of God. At the same time, the scene is a tragic one, for it underscores not only Arthur's recognition of Lancelot's power but also his failure to call upon it to forestall the "smiting and cleaving" that will leave his kingdom in ruins. Instead, at Gawain's crazed insistence, Arthur banishes Lancelot from Logres.

At the end of the *Morte,* Arthur, caught in the masochistic grip of his guilt, cannot bring himself to "recall" Lancelot and ask for his assistance. Before his battle with Mordred, Arthur has a terrifying dream: He is sitting atop a great wheel and under him there is "a hideous deep black water, and therein was all manner of serpents and worms and wild beasts, foul and horrible. And suddenly the King thought that the wheel turned upside down, and he fell among the serpents, and every beast took him by a limb" (Malory 510). Its imagery is primeval, recalling the watery depths of Leviathan as well as the monsters of old that seethe in the currents of the unconscious. It is Gehenna, the dismemberment of the body politic, the dissolution of the self, the death wish.

The ending sentence of the *Morte,* circling back on itself, also serves as the beginning or title of the book, reiterating the cohesiveness of the Round Table and the combinatory power of Eros or—"enfellowship"—that binds its knights together and binds all the territories held by them into one "whole" kingdom. One could say that Malory enacts this same "enfellowship" in the making of the *Morte,* gathering up the scattered, episodic tales of Arthurian legend and literally binding them together into one "whole" book. In sum, the *Morte* can be read, on a metonymic level, as Malory's repair of the kingdom through the composition of the book. It is, of course, the kingdom of England as well as that of Logres. Throughout the *Morte,* each serves as a surrogate for the other, except that the fate of the first still hung in the balance in Malory's lifetime. As it moves inexorably toward "the day of destiny" on Salisbury Plain, the *Morte* unfolds as nothing less than the primal struggle between Eros and Thanatos, the life force and the death force, as they course through the rise and fall of civilizations. As such, it is not only a mirror of chivalry, but also a mirror of the dissolution that ensues in the wake of its failure, a mirror Malory held up to England, if not to the world.

## Works Cited

Bate, Catherine. "Malory and Rape." *Le Morte Darthur, or, The Whole Book of King Arthur and of His Noble Knights of The Round Table: Authoritative Text, Sources and Backgrounds, Criticism.* Ed. Stephen H. A. Shepherd. New York: W. W. Norton, 2004. 797–814. Print.

Field, P. J. C. *The Life and Times of Sir Thomas Malory.* Cambridge: D. S. Brewer, 1993. Print.

Lewis, C. S. "The English Prose *Morte.*" *Essays on Malory.* By J.A.W. Bennett. London: Oxford University Press, 1963. 7–28. Print.

Lewis, C. S. *Studies in Medieval and Renaissance Literature.* London: Cambridge University Press, 1966. Print.

Lustig, T. J. *Knight Prisoner: Thomas Malory Then and Now.* Chicago: Sussex Academic Press, 2013. Print.

Malory, Sir Thomas. *Le Morte Darthur, The Winchester Manuscript.* Ed. Helen Cooper. New York: Oxford University Press, 2008. Print.

Meale, Carol. "Manuscripts, Readers, and Patrons in Fifteenth-Century England: Sir Thomas Malory and Arthurian Romance." *Le Morte Darthur, or, The Whole Book of King Arthur and of His Noble Knights of The Round Table: Authoritative Text, Sources and Backgrounds, Criticism.* Ed. Stephen H. A. Shepherd. New York: W. W. Norton, 2004. 865–82. Print.

Riddy, Felicity. "Divisions." *Le Morte Dathur, or, The Whole Book of King Arthur and of His Noble Knights of The Round Table: Authoritative Text, Sources and Backgrounds, Criticism.* Ed. Stephen H. A. Shepherd. New York: W. W. Norton, 2004. 882–94. Print.

Summers, Joanna. *Late-Medieval Prison Writing and the Politics of Autobiography.* New York: Oxford University Press, 2004. Print.

Tucker, P.E. "Chivalry in the *Morte.*" *Essays on Malory.* Ed. J.A.W. Bennett. London: Oxford University Press, 1963. 64–103. Print.

# A Prisoner of Circumstance: Cervantes, *Don Quixote* and Literary Self-Authorship in the Early Modern Period

SEAN EVE

## Summary

Unlike many of the authors in this book, Cervantes' prison experiences were not related to his political activity. Rather, they were a result of war and economics. By midlife he had led a hard existence as a soldier of fortune, spent a significant time in captivity (as a prisoner of war and a pawn in Spain's political infighting), and was professionally disappointed. His literary output—first poetry, then theater, and finally prose works such as *Don Quixote*—was produced over three periods of writing, separated by many years "on the road." The story Cervantes tells in *Don Quixote* is reflective of his life in both Algiers and Spain. Like Jean Genet, Cervantes incorporated his prison experiences directly into his work, weaving them into the lives of his characters—characters who, like the novel itself, live on several intersecting plains of reality and fantasy.—J.W.R.

## The Trouble with History

History is a war against time, its evolution representing the slow and steady collapse of physical and mental distances within imagination and life. The journey is so easy for us now that we forget the inventions that made such travel possible, taking as a given the ways language and form translate another's reality into our own. We forget that the individuals who developed these forms of relation did so at great cost to themselves, reconfiguring meaning and communication in societies that were at best ambivalent to the new horizons opening up. The experience of the colonial adventurer and the historian may be different, but both seek out, in a world suddenly too small for existing cosmologies, a reality large enough to contain what they have seen, to find within and without a situation that more closely accords with the mental landscapes they have made for themselves. Such is the challenge to the newly forming conditions of power that resistance must start as internal journey, a private set of investigations, shrouded in fantasy, in the camouflage of invention.

We don't think of Miguel de Cervantes (1547–1616) as a historian. Despite the abundance of lived experience in his plays and the narrator's insistence that *Don Quixote* is a historical account, the novel's stylistics mark it as fiction, designed to capture the mind, not the body. This distinction protects the author and us from the subversion it contains, insulating the book from the law. That said, the interpenetration of history and fiction is at the center of the novel and the historiographic concerns of his time, a period marked by exposure to new societies, the emergence of widespread literacy and the recognition of the book as a distinct agent within the political sphere. *Don Quixote* represents a successful integration of all these forces into a text which establishes the author, not his characters, as the hero of the enterprise, and establishes the book as a distinct place of inhabitation, as real in its circumstance and consequences as any other course of action within his society. As exemplified by its title character's decision to realize his fantasies, the imaginative in Cervantes proves not only a means for its author to escape the marginalization of his birth and the violence that characterized his years of imprisonment, both in Spain and Algiers, but also ushers in a new space of transformation for us as individuals and social participants. The book becomes a field of action where self-awareness and societal critique challenge conquest as one of the primary drivers of change within a rapidly expanding world.

## *The Invisible Man*

> Behind the Miseracordia Hospital, in the heart of the old Jewish quarter, is a house with a certain elegance and charm, its patio graced by a fig tree.... It is there, they say, that the most illustrious of the sons of Alcala, the author of Don Quixote, was born. But this stage set is unfortunately only an illusion. The house where Cervantes was actually born, unknown to historians for a long time, was defaced over the centuries by its successive owners. Identified in 1941 ... it nevertheless fell to the demolisher's pick, and in its place stands a reconstruction built in perfect conformity with the architectural norms of the sixteenth century but incompatible with the modest origins of the great writer [14].

This passage from Jean Canavaggio's biography speaks to the difficulties faced by anyone looking for Cervantes amid the remnants left to us. He achieved fame only after *Don Quixote* was published in 1605, at which point the author was already fifty seven. Making matters worse, Cervantes chose to share very little about his life in Spain, concentrating his autobiographical efforts on the years he spent as a soldier and captive in Algiers from 1575 to 1580. The Spaniard's renown since the publication of his great novel has led to generations of scholars combing through the debris of a life lived largely in the shadows, and as a result we have the outlines of Cervantes' literary, military, and private activities. It's important to recognize, however, that sources from the period were created in an environment where even minor deviations from political and religious orthodoxy could lead to imprisonment, exile, or death. Personal narratives were governed by hagiography, accounts of those individuals who had lived abroad in particular marked by exaggerations and propagandistic rhetoric designed to justify Spanish military and colonial aggression. Cervantes' life, as it has come down to us, is a story of empire and corruption, of a soldier's sacrifice and a veteran's disappointments, a story every bit as entwined with the fictions and realities of his time as that of "The Knight of the Woeful Countenance."

The first record of Miguel de Cervantes is his baptism at Santa Maria Mayor in Alcala de Henares on October 9th, 1547, a year that saw the first index of prohibited seditious books issued and conversos barred from ecclesiastical office. His death will come in the same year as the final expulsion of remaining conversos from Spain, under Phillip III in 1616. The synchroneities are striking given the possibilty of Cervantes' Jewish ancestry, a link scholars base on the prominence of religious converts in his writing, the author's difficulties capitalizing on his years as a war hero and captive, and parallels between *Don Quixote* and certain Jewish texts. As Michael McGaha remarks: "It will probably never be possible to prove that Cervantes was a *cristiano nuevo*, but the circumstantial evidence seems compelling" (173). The *Instrucción* written by Fernán Díaz de Toledo in the Fifteen Century includes the Cervantes family among those of *conversos* origin. McGaha also notes that Cervantes' ancestors were in the cloth trade and his father was a barber-surgeon, "occupations almost exclusively in the hands of Jews and *conversos*" (173). Whatever his family's origins, the economic hardships of Cervantes' upbringing placed him at his society's margins.

## *First the Pen, Then the Sword*

Poetry and the theatre provided an escape, at least temporarily, from the constraints of finance and family. By 1567, Miguel had begun to make a name for himself in literary circles in Madrid. A poem of his is included in decorations celebrating the birth of the Infanta Catalina. This, and four poems produced in 1568 and later published in the *Relacion* of the funeral of Elizabeth de Valois, the wife of Philip II, mark the first time we meet Cervantes as an author. His early work, with its idealization of the monarchy, captures an element of his politics that resurfaces throughout the Spaniard's life, a deep respect for the secular and religious traditions of the society, even as his later writings criticize the country's bureaucrats and citizens for failing to uphold the moral objectives he sees these traditions as embodying. Our author is no revolutionary. Instead, the image we get is of a man committed to upholding his good name whatever the cost, and someone who held his society to the same high moral standards he expected of himself.

It would be nice to be more definitive about his life, but Cervantes rarely offers more than oblique references to his past. The frequent problem for the author and for many of his characters is, the truth is simply too dangerous to reveal. In order to take a post under the future Cardinal Acquaviva In Rome, Cervantes needed a certificate of proof of blood. Thus, in December of 1569, Rodrigo de Cervantes "certified that Miguel was not a bastard and that there are no Moors, Jews, converts ... among his ancestors" (Canavaggio 49). As evidenced earlier, this was almost certainly a lie. But like the lies Miguel's mother would tell to protect her family from destitution and those she would offer to get funds to free Cervantes when he was being held for ransom in Algiers, like the lies Cervantes would tell while attempting to escape captivity, or that the author, narrator, title character, inn keepers, and even the village priest tell on more than one occasion in *Don Quixote*, such transparent lies were the very currency of Spain. As Leo Strauss reminds us:

> Persecution ... gives rise to a peculiar technique of writing ... in which the truth about all crucial things is presented exclusively between the lines.... It has all the advantages of public communication without having its greatest disadvantage—capital punishment for the author [25].

It is in just this communicative condition that Cervantes is raised, and just this institutional environment, vis-à-vis language, out of which his sense of humor, playfulness with form, and commitment to interiority will develop.

The biographer's loss is the artist's gain. For language is not a prison for Cervantes' but the means of his escape, or rather the condition of his deliverance into a literary world in which the circumstances of power are inverted, the implicit becoming miraculous. As Don Quixote responds when challenged to present the incomparable beauty, Dulcinea, "If I were to show her to you ... what merit would ye have in confessing a truth so manifest? The essential point is that without seeing her ye must believe, confess, affirm, swear, and defend it" (44). The reference here is to the Inquisition's legal demand that Spain's citizenry assert in writing and in public its acquiescence to the religious authorities. The reference here is also to the Madonna, and by extension all veiled embodiments of the truth. In this way the conflation of the religious and secular offers Cervantes the opportunity to use religious ethics to expose social injustice. Authority and its subversion work through identical mechanisms, theatrical self-awareness pointing not just to implicit meaning as an ideological cipher, but focusing attention on the interior experience shared by the speaker and listener, or in Cervantes' case the writer and his audience.

Donald McCrory in his study of Cervantes notes he "was keen to show that in literature truth was what an audience can be persuaded to believe" (202). And the connection with that reader, "did not miraculously appear out of the void," but was based on having "read the major texts, theoretical as well as secular," and keeping up with "literary fashion and tastes" (203). I would add to this literary awareness, the social and legal conditions of meaning in Cervantes' time. His Spain is essentially a theatrical world, one which not only spawned a vibrant stagecraft and a poetic tradition of intricate implicit citation, but which carried its theatrical nature into the streets, the marketplace, the home. Cervantes democratizes irony, acknowledging the extent to which the rules of public assertion were understood and circumvented throughout his society, the real relegated to silence, the internal and external in an unstable and often antithetical relation to one another. Language manages this relationship, the subtleties of its application not just the purview of poets, but indicative of a common reality.

The "real" in *Don Quixote* is manifest both in the places where his story takes place—streets, inns, and roadways rather than palaces, monasteries and courts—and in the conspiracy his text presumes with the reader, a conceit represented in everything from the book's fictional Moorish author, Cide Hamet Benegeli, to the supposed madness of its title character, Quixote. The work's power rests on his ability to make both the outside and the inside equally real. The Old Hidalgo's madness is not simply the heroic attempt of a man to escape the drudgery of real life through living what he imagines, it challenges his society through the historical and cultural conditions of reference he appropriates. As Quixote says when threatened with arrest by a group of officers "in the service of the King and of the Holy Brotherhood" (360):

> Come now, base, ill-born brood ... do you name it highway robbery to give freedom to those in bondage, to release captives, to succor the miserable, to raise up the fallen, to relieve the needy? ... Tell me what ignoramus signed a warrant off arrest against such a knight as I? Who was unaware that Knights-errant are independent of all jurisdictions, that their law is their sword, their charter their prowess, and their edict

their wills? ... What Knight-errant ever paid poll-tax, duty, queen's pin-money, kings dues, toll or ferry? What tailor ever took payment of him.... What warden ... ever made him pay his bill? [360–61].

In speaking outwardly about the contradictions between the moral foundations of the church and crown and the realities of the state, Quixote is inducing a crisis, held at bay elsewhere in the society through a strict separation of the interior and literary from the sphere of political action. Surrounded as he is by soldiers, only a mad man would say such things; thinking them is a different matter. This collision of the internal moral compass of the Counter-Reformation and its literary manifestations with the political and economic realities of Spain was something Cervantes and his contemporaries confronted on a daily basis. Hypocrisy wasn't just tolerated, but institutionalized.

From immanent philosophy to mannerist poetry, the internalization of such contradictions is everywhere in the society. In terms of literary precedent, however, it is the theatre where we see this conflict break through to the surface. Lope de Vega's comedies, or the historical dramas and tragedies of Shakespeare, who died within weeks of Cervantes, depend upon identifiable contradictions as the basis for their action. The implications of the language and many of the components of plot rely on what is concealed by or from the characters. The contradictions may be internal or situational, ideally both, and are sustained for as long as possible, often until the narrative's conclusion, which coincides with the revelation of what the audience has already recognized.

This performed dissonance becomes the foundation for Cervantes' mature work, the book rather than the stage, mind rather than character, the ultimate site of realized subversion. Madness, feigned as in *Hamlet*, real as in *Lear*, shows up in Cervantes' fiction as a way to convert the internal and the poetic from reflective behaviors to components of the action itself. Unsurprisingly, it is in his own theatrical writings, on which Cervantes spent several years in the 1580s, that the interior world and its externalization are initially explored. In the Prologue to his *Eight Interludes,* published in 1615, he claims, "I was the first to portray on stage the imaginings and secret thoughts of the soul by bringing allegorical figures into the theatre" (4). It is also in his plays that Cervantes' disaffection begins to surface. *The Bagnios of Algiers* and *The Commerce of Algiers* preview how Cervantes will use his lived experience and the traumas and disappointments of captivity as a catalyst for his work.

What begins as observed contradiction becomes theatrical performance, and evolves into playing out the possibilities of political and personal subversion in the language and physical circumstances of the novel. The relocation of his theatricalized and reconfigured autobiography to the "fictions" of *Don*

*Quixote,* provides the author with both a context in which his thoughts can be actualized and a physical document, the book, through which his ideals and literary actions can find a tangible agent. Chock full of comedy and costume, poetic masques and soliloquy, mock battles and metaphysical argument, his novelistic space is one of enacted dissimulation. Legal hazard turns to dramatic irony, lies to license. This protects the author from prosecution, even as the book, which bears the same name as its principle character, is able to head out into the world and correct injustice. The "madness" that protects the Old Hidalgo and enables him to escape the consequences of his actions also becomes in the book's focus on mind, on the fictional and imaginative remaking of his society, the means through which Cervantes can challenge his society's institutions and misplaced authoritarianism.

The power of reading to effect change and the linkages between Cervantes' novel and dramatic precedent are discussed in the book itself, when late in Part 1, the Canon and Priest speak about literary works that have had an adverse effect on the title character and his larger society. The Priest complains that "drama ... should be the mirror of human life, the model of manners, and the image of truth" but "those which are presented nowadays are mirrors of nonsense, models of folly, and images of lewdness" (377). He then goes on to outline such a play: "what greater absurdity can there be than putting before us an old man as a swashbuckler ... a page giving sage advice ... a princess who is a kitchen maid" (377). That this is precisely the book we have just been reading, points to the degree to which Cervantes is happy for the text to be recognized as a type of theatrics, not so much a story, as a staged experience. That we are privy to the shared thoughts of two men commenting on what we have just read, speaks to the role literary community serves in the text. This is a book about books, about reading, and the private discussions and secret thoughts that result from exposure to literary reality.

By the beginning of the 17th century books had become as important on the political stage as living individuals. Cervantes' transfer of theatrical form to written accounts mirrors changes in the way the Inquisition used public spectacle to exert political control. Dale Shuger, in his study of the Inquisition's strategies, points to how a decline in revenues and shift from a focus on "eradicating the Jewish and *conversos* population from Spain" to "disciplining the old Christian population for minor transgressions" (407), led to mid-sixteenth century changes in the style and frequency of public executions by burning. While the last *Auto-de-fe* held in the Capital wasn't until 1680, Shuger outlines a steady move during Cervantes' time away from actual performances to their replacement by *Relacions,* which recorded the story of the events in printed form (408–09). The shift is from a "theatre of terror" located in the

town square to one within the reader's mind, now as significant a territory of political conflict as the contested seas of the Mediterranean.

## To Hell and Back

If the mechanisms that underpin Cervantes' mature work rest on a series of societal and formal dislocations, his motivations for such a critical attitude towards his society can be found in his life. As young man, the Spaniard exhibits none of ambivalence that will define him later. In 1571 he is fighting in the Battle of Lepanto, the most famous naval victory in Spain's war with the Turks. Though earlier that day he had been confined below decks due to illness, Cervantes insists on being allowed to participate in the combat. Badly injured, he will permanently lose the use of his left hand. He continues in military service for a few years, until it becomes obvious physical limitations preclude his promotion. He is going home when his ship is captured by Barbary pirates. Held for ransom in Algiers from 1575 to 1580, his time in captivity is equally dramatic. Cervantes repeatedly attempts to escapes. He is tortured and threatened with death repeatedly. Starved, bound in chains, confined to the deepest of dungeons for months, he is sentenced to die only to be miraculously saved. When questioned with a sword hanging over his head or a knife at his throat, the Spaniard always refuses to give up his accomplices.

Ultimately, Cervantes will spend the next twenty years travelling the roads of Spain, as a requisitions officer for the Armada and a tax collector, poorly paid positions that carried considerable personal risk. This was hardly the future he had imagined when sacrificing his youth and health to empire.

Cervantes' disappointments need to be seen in light of the unique circumstances he experienced during his captivity in North Africa. As a result of some letters of recommendation by Don Juan of Austria found on his person when captured, Cervantes was assumed to be important. His new position made Cervantes eligible to lead, and placed him in a shared struggle for survival with some of the very architects of empire. How frustrating then to find on his return home that all he had done, seen, risked, was forgotten.

Passed over for government appointments, Cervantes was briefly excommunicated and then imprisoned in Castro del Rio, in connection with his commerical service to the Crown, finally ending up confined for seven months to the Royal Prison in Seville in 1597 and 1598. Described as "a true picture of hell on earth" by a contemporary, Cristobal de Chaves (Canavaggio 175), it's here that Cervantes is assumed to have begun *Don Quixote*, and here also that the youthful optimist seems finally to have given way to the world weary veteran. Cervantes had done everything his society asked of him and had nothing to show for it.

## *And So It Begins*

To characterize his dissolution as a sudden, startling epiphany, would ignore the complications of his youth, the strangeness of his experience living in Algiers, and the religious and literary models of action we see both in Cervantes' work and his life as described by others. To live in an era of profound change is to exist where things move at different speeds. This divergence of perspectives can become increasingly difficult to manage, particularly for those like Cervantes who had served in a number of institutional settings, and who found himself by accident at the vanguard of his society. As Voigt remarks, "Early modern representations and uses of captivity ... point to epistemological ... transformations that predate and prefigure those associated with what would come to be known as the Scientific Revolution" (1–2). But this "privileging of experiential authority" (Voigt 2) came up against a legal system that demanded witnesses to verify one's testimony, a communicative environment that presumed concealment over honesty, and the wide-spread corruption of Spain's officialdom. *Don Quixote* is in many ways an attempt to bring the divergent elements of Cervantes' experience into a single, coherent framework. Idealities, the quotidian, the alien, all have a place in the book, the patois of Algiers playing out in the literary modeling of a consciousness that recognizes in its own contradictions both the violence and the opportunities of cosmopolitanism.

There is a parallel here between the diversities the individual has to accommodate and the divergence of perspectives that are present, but often silenced, in the public sphere. Cervantes is not simply building a space in which he can bring together the conflicting aspects of his own experience, he gives voice to his society's. The political resonance of exile in this era make it hardly surprising that Cervantes' time in Algiers and his periods of incarceration are particularly generative. He writes steadily for serveral years after his captivity and then slows for two decades. Likewise his months in the Royal Prison in Seville trigger a return to writing, perhaps as Maria Garces suggests, as a way to cope with trauma. She describes his writing as "haunted by images of captivity" (2), even going as far as asking "whether Cervantes could have become the great creative writer that he was without had he not suffered the traumatic experience of his Algerian Captivity" (2). Jonathan Shay's concept of moral injury (*Achilles in Vietnam*) may have the answer, Cervantes' position as a veteran, a survivor of prison, and a religious idealist pitting the moral dictates of each of these worlds against the other, and pushing him into a crisis that could only be resolved through the broad variety of perspectives and structural positions the novel accommodates. Cervantes himself tells us early in the Prologue to *Don Quixote* that the book is "just what might be begotten in prison" (9). The book is both a response to his captors, an act of defiant self-assertion; and a roadmap for those living with the fear and internal moral conflicts the author has had to face. It is a guide to how, in the most restricted circumstances, one can still achieve a measure of freedom.

The novel's storyline re-enacts the author's escape attempts. Don Quixote and Sancho Panza, who acts as his assistant in these adventures, leave home for the excitement of the open road. Though Quixote is at risk of recapture a number of times in Part 1, it is only at its end that he is returned home. Panza, promised the governorship of an island, something Cervantes had hoped to attain for his services to the Crown, returns also, largely empty handed, but full of memories and stories. He doesn't regret the adventure; "it is a fine thing to be on the look out for what may happen, crossing mountains … putting up at inns, all free" (402). Sancho's is a sentiment with which any armchair traveller or would-be pilgrim can identify.

The second part of the novel is more complex in terms of freedom. The men decide to escape home again, encouraged by the fact that they have become famous as a result of the book written about them. Sancho gets his island, at least for a short while, but does so as a consequence of exile. Quixote finds himself at last in the palace of a duke and duchess, but he is trapped there temporarily, a victim of his own delusions. Again, the two men are dragged home, this time with Quixote in a cage. Despite the ability of the men to elude authorities, the short-term realization of their dreams, and the principle achievement of the book's title character, which is to bring to life what he has only previously experienced in his imagination through reading, escape themselves any number of times from authorities, the book ends ultimately with Quixote's escape through Quixote's death, a reminder in this fallen word that only through divine consolation can sacrifice and suffering achieved the promised reward denied in life.

What is telling here is the way Cervantes has transposed his own dramatic experiences onto the more familiar landscape of Spain and of domestic dissatisfaction. His youthful ambitions are clearly on display here, but as the adventures are undertaken by an old man, and one who finds in books inspiration for his journey, it is also the mature writer we see in front of us, the distinctions on which memoir is based collapsed through the reinventions of fiction. As well as shifts and conflations of place and time, *Don Quixote* exploits transformations in tone. Among the numerous incidents of entrapment in the book, the title character's experience after the Captive's Tale section of Part 1 is particularly revealing. The Captive's Tale itself is one of the more sustained instances of autobiographical reference in the novel. In *Don Quixote*, the title character is left hanging by his wrist from a noose, after being tricked by a pair of women at an inn. Though the scene begins as a harmless prank, Quixote ends up in "such agony that he believed either his wrist would be cut through or his arm torn off" (348). The reference here is in part to Cervantes' injury at Lepanto. It continues:

> He struggled and stretched himself as much as he could to gain a footing, like those undergoing the torture of the *strappado* ... who aggravate their own suffering by their violent efforts to stretch themselves, deceived by the hope ... that with a little more effort they will touch the ground [348].

The mention of pain and reference to the *strappado*, a torture often used by the Inquisition, gives this passage a stark, visceral realism. At the same time, it is only "like" the *strappado*, in that Quixote is tied by one hand not two and will be released relatively unhurt just a moment later. As charged as this image is, it pales in comparison to another hanging figure in Cervantes' past, a Christian gardener named Juan who helped Cervantes attempt from Algiers, and when caught Juan was "hung from his foot and tortured in the presence of the fugitives, until he died choking in his own blood" (Garces 47).

Through his plays and novels, Cervantes attempts to draw a more complex human picture of the relation between Spain and its outcasts, one that acknowledges the impact of the internalization of social violence on a wide range of individuals across the society. Rather than celebrate Christian authority, he focuses on *conversos*, rather than side with soldiers or priests, he favors madmen and criminals, such as Ginesillo de Parapilla, a self-declared author who has also written an autobiography in prison, and whom Quixote frees along with other galley slaves in Part 1 (151–59). Sensitive to the injustices on both sides, Cervantes work offers, as one theatre director put it, "an impassioned song of tolerance" (Garces 130).

At the center of his attempts to articulate his years as a captive is a story of love, thwarted love, between Moor and Christian, convert and soldier. He returns to this frequently. If we look at the role of the woman in this pairing, and how the character's position changes in this sequence of stories, we can chart the evolution of Cervantes' attitude towards his society's human cost. *The Commerce of Algiers,* written shortly after Cervantes' return to Spain, centers on a secret love between two Christian slaves, Silvia and Aurelio, who are tormented by the unwanted affections of their Moorish masters, Ysuf and Zahara. This Zahara, sometimes translated as Zara, will reappear in *The Bagnios of Algiers*, written a few years later, now recast as a Moorish woman who has secretly converted to Christianity in childhood and who helps a group of Spanish captives to escape. Though one of the young men, Lope, is in love with her, her desire to leave Algiers is driven more by a wish for religious freedom than romantic entanglement. "It is not good for Christian lips to be sullied by Moorish women," she protests, when Lope attempts to kiss her, "I am all yours, not for you, but for Christ" (86). By the time we get to the Captive's Tale portion of Don Quixote, Zahara has become Zoraida. The couple is firmly in love, though it is still unconsummated, and the story now comes to us after the couple's arrival in Spain, the events of their escape and the struggle against her father much the same as in earlier versions, but the joy of their arrival in the promised land tempered by the young man's concerns for his beloved's future. "The happiness I feel in seeing myself hers, and her mine, is disturbed and marred by not knowing whether I shall find any corner to shelter her in my own country" (334). The young man's concerns are focused both on his own status, as a returned captive who needs to find "anyone who knows me" (334) to vouch for him, and Zoraida's, as a Moorish convert in a world that no longer sees her chosen faith as legitimate.

Scholarship has identified Zoraida as loosely based on the daughter of Hajji Murad, a prominent figure in Algiers who saved Cervantes life. Cervantes' work is full of such young lovers, pulled apart not just by religious differences, but by class distinction, sexism, parental hubris. In the same section of *Quixote*, in the same inn, Clara and her suitor, Don Luis, who appears dressed as a muleteer, emphasizing their economic differences, are struggling to come together despite their fathers' shared disapproval. In an echo of the annunciation and other moments of visionary religious experience, we first meet Don Luis singing outside Clara's window. His voice is so beautiful that Clara's friend wakes her, the sound of his voice causing Clara to tremble all over. "Love resolute," he sings, "Knows not the word impossibility, / And though my suit / beset by endless obstacles I see, / Yet no despair / shall hold me bound to earth when heaven is there" (342). This verse, equating human love with divine providence, and spoken by lovers who are kept apart by social norms, repeats a set of parallels Cervantes will use throughout the pastoral elements of *Don Quixote*. The author's insistence on the transformative power of spiritual faith, and his recognition of its ability to lead us both to moral insight and socially transformative action, firmly place Cervantes within the tradition of Counter Reformation thinking, and its trajectory from Thomas Aquinas to Ignatius de Loyola.

Cervantes' own story, and that of Don Quixote, bear a striking resemblance to elements of Loyola's. The founder of the Society of Jesus was, like Cervantes, a soldier turned writer. Badly injured during a battle, Loyola entertained himself while recovering by reading courtly romances and imagining his ideal love. After a few weeks, he realized how little consolation these entertainments offered and decided to write a more serious work, his *Spiritual Exercises* (1548), one of the best know religious pamphlets of Cervantes' time. The text, with its daily readings, demand for self-examination, and promise of personal redemption through faith, anticipates aspects of Cervantes' own philosophy. Its commitment to immanence mirrors our author's focus on interior space, and the acknowledgement of presence of the divine within the world represents a challenge to act with justice in life. Clearly an influence, Loyola is in both the storyline and underlying premises of Cervantes' masterwork; the echoes of Loyola's life on Cervantes' prefigure the ways the novel's namesake reflects and refracts its author.

Fortunately for us, Cervantes is not Loyola, and neither is Quixote. Cervantes shares some of the objectives of counter-reformation thinkers, but his ideas go beyond the somber tones and overt religiosity of Loyola's attempts, to craft a pluralistic version that includes religious imagery, the pageant of theatre, the joys of poetry, and the seductions of narrative as mechanisms for self-redefinition. Cervantes' novel uses consciousness and the complex and varied ways it mediates experience through language, to transform everything around him, offering us a landscape which is familiar and realistic for the most part, but has been subsumed by imaginative transfiguration.

This is a literary move. The world is peopled by characters from daily life and from literature, sharing a reality. He introduces the writer's experience of writing and ours of reading into the novel, bringing together many layers and dimensions of immediate, remembered, and vicariously experienced reality in an equivalent immediacy that mirrors how they appear in our thoughts, particularly when we read and write. By drawing on different states of consciousness and the variety of meanings within the words he chooses, he mobilizes our affective relations to the world. Sadness gives way to laughter, seriousness to awareness of the little we can change beyond ourselves. Cervantes uses the mechanisms of transpersonal identification and the fluidities of language to invert his relations, and ours, to the given conditions he finds around him, those conditions remain as they are, but how they impact us becomes a function of our attitude towards them. Subjectivity, as mobilized by language, becomes the ultimate agent of transformation.

## *Free at Last*

Quixote, the character, represents a sustained exploration of the relation between language and self-construction. "'Who knows,'" he says in Book 1, "'whether in time to come, when the ... history of my famous deeds is made known, the sage who writes it ... may not do it after this fashion?'" (30). He narrates his own story, in an archaic, overly poetic language, to be sure, but for him this is the language that grants him self-authorship. He speaks of "Rubicund Apollo," "little birds of painted plumage," "the coming of the rosy Dawn" (30), the very ridiculousness of the language showing us a man who is no great writer finding ways to become exceptional by drawing on the old stories he is familiar with. Through this, Cervantes exposes us to the power of traditional ideas, the ways the past can inform and transform the present.

Later Quixote uses his prior reading to push past his own inertia. "Finding that in fact he could not move, he thought of having recourse to his usual remedy, which was to think of some passages in his books" (44). This is literary agency writ large; not only do we have Quixote thinking of himself in terms of written posterity, he employs past readings as a way forward. " I know who I am," the character says a few pages later, "and I know that I may not only be those I am named, but all the twelve Peers of France and even all the Nine Worthies" (46). The archaic formulations underlie his ideals show his limits. This distance, however, enables us to see the place of story, of reading, within our framework of conscious awareness, and to acknowledge the discrete limits of literary experience within our own rational counter-perspective. Going forward, Quixote will use his experiences as a reader and the moral compass he has obtained from them, to free prisoners, defend unjustly threatened lovers, and on his death bed, in the final moments of the novel come to understand reading itself as a means to spiritual fulfillment. What he changes is not only the present, but himself.

> My reason is now free ... rid of the dark shadows of ignorance that ... chivalry cast over it.... It only grieves me that this revelation came so late that it leaves me no time to make amends by reading other books that might be a light to my soul [826].

The joke here, is that Quixote is still reliant on the books he has read. He fails to see that he has already become a man whose life is worthy of admiration. He does not need to read about saints; he has become one, his sanctity that of literature not sermon, his ambitions realized by force of his imagination and by leveraging that imagination into actionable will. The character's failure to understand that he has already become a book, even when he embarks on this volume of the novel out of the discovery of that very fact, points to the ways we misunderstand reading, or shy away from its more radical possibilities. The book precedes the character and comes after him, just as his reading lead him to actions which transform his present and the social status quo. It doesn't matter that there is historical distance between us and them. What matters is that we understand the power of ourselves and of our consciousness at the moment, that we recognize the book as a vehicle for insight, reading the first step in a course of action that will help us correct the injustices of our world, if only, like Quixote, we allow it to do so.

It is through the multiple ways we experience the text that we can inhabit it, the combination of conditions of relation, granting us a present akin to lived, perceptual experience. The novel's prologue is both a playful commentary on prologues and an enactment of the writing of a prologue, action and reaction intertwined in ways that speak to ways we embody and transform conventions within our society in the same moment. This recognition also points to how can achieve dominion over them and thus self-authorship. For our experience of the various mock dedications, bogus authors, and breaks in narrative continuity and form, to build a space for the reader that is relational, but not deterministic, and through language, a range of experiences that in their combination, and in what remains implicit, enact consciousness.

If "[e]very specific situation is historical" (Bakhtin 33), then this is as true of every kind of discourse as it is for each individual perspective. It is only through proliferation and "the co-habitation of languages working side by side" (x), to borrow a phrase from Barthes, that these perspectives become interilluminative. "One Language can," Bakhtin reminds us, "see itself only in the light of another language" (12), a relation to language that the novel is uniquely positioned to take advantage of because, "of all the major genres only the novel is younger than writing and the book, it alone is organically receptive to new forms of mute perception, that is, to reading" (3). Language is the vehicle, but it is perception, and our awareness of the conditions of our reception that make the literary work habitable, offering "a living contact with unfinished, still evolving contemporary reality (the open-ended present)" (7).

In *The Voyage to Parnassus*, where Cervantes criticizes his literary contemporaries, the ship carrying him to the muses is literally made of language: "From keel to the round top, O Extraordinary / The ship with verse was wholly fabricated. Its country of origin is not a country at all, but poetry: The flags which trembled in the yielding air, / Of sundry rimes ... composed" (8–9). There is no place beyond language: it is the primordial material of creation. Moreover, it offers a place to view the world at a distance, thus master it, occupying it as will and fancy dictate. It offers an epistemological location that may come in already familiar ways, but we reassemble on our own terms, and thus re-signify, the act not simply one of abstract realization, but the replacement of one condition of lived reality by another. This is why Spain is necessary for the book's setting, and why its realism and discussion of topics of immediate relevance to his audience is so important. For the things being changed as we read *Don Quixote*, which the novel and its characters and author are teaching us to reconfigure, are the same things that are already all around us, the powers that are challenged are those that govern us.

Cervantes is like the ironically positioned Ricote, a Moorish convert whom Sancho Panzo meets in exile in Book II of Quixote and who tells us, "'now I know by experience the meaning of the saying 'sweet is the love of one's country'" (726). Alternatively, the reference is to nostalgia, memory, to a place we are subject to but cannot possess. Indeed, the passage that leads to this line speaks of the Barbary Coast, of those exiled from Spain, and the reception they receive in their new home. He says, "It is there they insult and ill-treat us most" (725). The exile is trapped between worlds, at home in none. If we understand Ricote as speaking of his present, however, and the choice of tense here emphasizes this, then the country of which he speaks is where he stands at that moment, a place outside of Spain, beyond Algiers, a place he is forced to by circumstance, but which as a no-man's-land, unclaimed and unclaimable, offers him the consolations of self-possession, the space within.

It is this Cervantes has given us, a home of our own, ourselves.

## Works Cited

Bakhtin, Mikhail. *The Dialogic Imagination*. Austin: University of Texas Press, 1981. Print.
Barthes, Roland. *The Pleasure of the Text*. New York: Hill and Wang, 1975. Print.
Canavaggio, Jean. *Cervantes*. New York: W. W. Norton, 1990. Print.
Cervantes, Miguel de. *The Bagnios of Algeirs" and The Great Sultana*. Philadelphia: University of Pennsylvania Press, 2010. Print.
_____. *Don Quixote*. New York: W. W. Norton, 1981. Print.
_____. *Eight Interludes*. Rutland, VT: Charles E. Tuttle, 1996. Print.
_____. *The Voyage to Parnassus: Numantia, Tragedy, The Commerce of Algiers*. London: Alex, Murray, and Son, 1870. Print.
Garces, Maria Antonia. *Cervantes in Algiers*. Nashville: Vanderbilt University Press, 2002. Print.
McCrory, Donald P. *No Ordinary Man*. Chester Springs, PA: Peter Owen, 2002. Print.
McGaha, Michael. "Is There a Hidden Jewish Meaning in Don Quixote?" *Cervantes, Bulletin of the Cervantes Society of America* 21.1 (2004):173–88. Print.
Shay, Jonathan. *Achilles in Vietnam: Combat Trauma and the Undoing of Character*. New York: Scribner, 1994. Print.
Shuger, Dale. "A Curious Relacion: Event and Account of the Auto de fe." *Bulletin of Hispanic Studies* 90.4 (2013): 403–23. Print.
Strauss, Leo. *Persecution and the Art of Writing*. Chicago: University of Chicago Press, 1988. Print.
Voigt, Lisa. *Writing Captivity in the Early Modern Atlantic*. Chapel Hill: University of North Carolina Press, 2009. Print.

# Thomas Paine and *The Age of Reason*

## J. Ward Regan

## Summary

Thomas Paine, hero of the American Revolution, was in an especially convoluted and dangerous situation. His status as a well-known and highly controversial political writer had kept him politically active since 1774. In 1792, Paine was living as an exile in France under a death sentence from England. Unfortunately, he then also became the target of factions in the French Revolutionary government during the Reign of Terror. His ten years in exile—including ten months in prison—were trying, and he narrowly escaped death, but he produced some of his most important work during this time. Among them is *The Age of Reason*, Paine's Deistic account of God and nature, and a direct assault on religious institutions around the world. The first draft was hurriedly completed while Paine was eluding the police, who had an order for his arrest from Robespierre. He then revised the work in Luxembourg Prison while awaiting execution—which he luckily avoided.—J.W.R.

## Introduction

One wonders what occupied Thomas Paine's mind as he languished in Luxembourg Prison in Paris during the summer of 1794, in the midst of the French Revolution. Perhaps he contemplated his impending death from illness or beheading. Maybe he wondered if his dire circumstances might have been avoided, or if *The Age of Reason* would be his last words to the world. It seems that Paine, always the optimist, distracted himself with ideas for rewriting it.

He almost certainly looked back on the American and French Revolutions and his part in them. There was a lot to survey; over the past eighteen years he had been a best-selling author, political philosopher, international revolutionary, soldier, spy, and inventor. Many of the political elites on both sides of the Atlantic would have been happy to see him go. John Adams described Paine as one of the world's great troublemakers, yet did not underestimate his importance: "I know not whether any man in the world has had more influence on its inhabitants or affairs for the last thirty years than Tom Paine.... Call it then the Age of Paine."[1]

Paine wrote *The Age of Reason* in exile and prison at the height of the Reign of Terror during the French Revolution. The book is a critique of institutionalized religion, as well as a call to reason and morality. *The Age of Reason* sets forth the main tenets of a theistic universe without institutionalized religion, and has been seen as a foundational text by free thinkers and radicals for over two centuries.

The first part was written feverishly while Paine was eluding arrest, and rewritten in prison as he awaited execution; he completed a second part after his release. *The Age of Reason* is not as well known to Americans as his political works *Common Sense* or *The American Crisis*, perhaps because it was more controversial. Even though it was demonized, many of Paine's ideas about religion were shared by other Founding Fathers. The book's detractors and Paine's critics unfairly characterized him as an atheist in an effort to discredit the book and his ideas.

## *Biography*

Thomas Paine was born on January 29, 1737, in Thetford, a small town in Norfolk, England. His mother was Anglican, his father a Quaker and skilled craftsman (he was a stay-maker for women's corsets). He received a common grammar school education until the age of thirteen. This taught him how to read, write, and do math, as well as providing some instruction in history and the Bible. In his youth he was apprenticed and tried twice, unsuccessfully, to join a pirate ship.

After two marriages and several careers—including shopkeeper, teacher, and excise officer—Paine decided to emigrate to the North American colonies. He had previously met Benjamin Franklin in London and they had become friends. When Paine decided to go to the colonies, Franklin wrote him a letter of introduction, which he carried with him on his long life-threatening ocean passage. Paine finally landed in Philadelphia in late 1774.

## *The American Revolution,* Common Sense *and* The American Crisis

In 1775, Paine's job as editor of the *Pennsylvania Magazine* in Philadelphia put him in the middle of an ongoing political crisis. He quickly became acquainted with both the politics and the major figures of the American Revolution. At the end of 1775 he turned his literary attention to the conflict with Britain and wrote *Common Sense*, in which he makes the case for American independence. The pamphlet made him an instant celebrity, sold hundreds of thousands of copies, and came at exactly the right time to nudge public opinion in favor of independence (Claeys, 12).

By the time Paine arrived, the relationship between the colonies and England had deteriorated significantly, but after the Declaration of Independence the conflict intensified. During the war, Paine fought in the Continental Army and was even at Valley Forge in the winter of 1777. *The American Crisis Papers* (1777–1783) drew from his experiences in battle and living with the hardships of war.

When the American Revolution ended in 1783, Paine turned to other endeavors, and began work on the design and manufacture of cast-iron bridges. Unable to find financial support in America, he went to Europe in 1787. He was in the middle of his bridge project in England when the French Revolution erupted. Once again a revolution would bring Paine to the forefront of a political transformation.

## *The French Revolution,* The Rights of Man *and Exile*

Paine wrote *The Rights of Man, Part I* in 1791 in response to *Reflections on the French Revolution*, written against the French Revolution by Englishman Edmund Burke a year earlier. Paine's book, in support of the French Revolution and its ideas, was astonishingly successful and made Paine one of the best-known authors of his day. It was one of almost six hundred books written during what is known as "The French Revolution Debate" in England in the early 1790s; most sold several hundred, maybe a few thousand. Burke had sold more than 30,000, but *The Rights of Man, Part I* sold hundreds of thousands of copies (Foner 219, Keane 307, Thompson 108). Paine differed from and surpassed his contemporaries in the depth and breadth of his audience. His books were read by the professional and middle classes, the working class, and even the "poor" (Stone 69–139).

He followed *Part I* less than a year later with *The Rights of Man, Part II*, which made a strong and sustained attack on the English monarchy and its related institutions. Paine additionally described a plan for social security and public education funded by income and property taxes. The criticisms in *The Rights of Man, Part II* were sharper than the government would permit, and Paine was charged with seditious libel. Knowing that a guilty verdict was preordained, Paine left for France and was tried and found guilty in absentia.

## *From International Hero to Political Prisoner*

When he arrived in the French city of Calais in 1792, Paine was warmly welcomed and promptly elected to the National Convention. He went to Paris and took his place in the Convention, and became deeply involved in the revolution. Paine was one of only two foreigners in the legislative body, the other being Anacharsis Cloots.

By 1792, the idea of a French Republic had been accepted—but it needed a constitution. Paine was appointed to the committee in 1793 to write one, but the committee never finished its work. This was also when Louis XVI was on trial. During the trial, Paine took to the floor of the National Convention and made a powerful argument to exile rather than execute the king. He was unsuccessful, and the king was guillotined.

As the revolution progressed, Paine increasingly became a vocal critic of the new French and American governments. During the Reign of Terror, he was seen as a political threat and targeted by Robespierre and the Jacobins. A note in Robespierre's handwriting stated, "Demand that Thomas Paine be decreed of accusation, for the interest of America, as well as of France" (Paine and Conway 87). It was around this time, in early 1793, that Paine published a first draft, now lost, of *The Age of Reason* under a different title.

From October to December 23, 1793, he worked on a new version of *The Age of Reason*, even as political events brought danger closer. The night he finished, he stayed in Paris; very early in the morning he was awakened by the police and arrested. (In the introduction to one version of *The Age of Reason*, Paine recalls the date as being December 28, though several historians date these events to December 23 and 24.) By delaying the police for a few hours, he was able to deliver the manuscript to his printer before being taken to Luxembourg Prison.

## Luxembourg Prison

At the beginning of his prison stay, Paine's health was good and the rules were lax. Over the next ten months, both these conditions would deteriorate. The Reign of Terror went through perhaps its most chaotic, violent, and dramatic stages while Paine was in prison. In a letter Paine wrote to Sam Adams in 1803 he recalled, "My friends were falling as fast as the guillotine could cut their heads off.... I every day expected the same fate." When he was first imprisoned, there was a great deal of activity by friends and allies to get him released, but the political situation of the revolution and an unhelpful American ambassador kept him in jail.

Initially Paine was able to buy the basic items he needed in jail. He wrote letters as well as edited new editions of *The Rights of Man* and *The Age of Reason*. The introduction for a 1795 London edition of *The Rights of Man* lists the "Luxembourg Prison May 19, 1794" as the location of its writing. The title page of the same edition describes Paine as a "Member of the French Convention; Late a Prisoner in the Luxembourg in Paris." The dedication in *The Age of Reason* to "The Citizens of the United States of America" was written about a month into his imprisonment.

Paine's prison stay came to a crisis point on July 24, 1794, when his name appeared on the list of prisoners to be executed the next day. But the morning of July 25 came and went without the guards collecting him. Four days later, in one of the most dramatic political turnarounds in history, the Jacobins were removed from power and Robespierre was executed in the "Thermidorian Reaction" of July 1794. This significantly altered the political landscape, putting Paine in a safer position. He was finally released in November 1794 with the help of the new American ambassador, James Monroe.

## After Luxembourg

Paine went to recuperate at Monroe's house in Paris. While there, he expanded then published a new edition of *The Age of Reason*. After his recovery he returned to the National Convention, and in 1797 he wrote *Agrarian Justice*, which included his most radical political critique and proposals. In this work, he expanded his social programs from *The Rights of Man*, describing more fully the attributes and rationale of his robust welfare state.

Paine left the National Convention in 1797. He continued writing and trying to get back to the United States. In 1802, Paine suggested the Louisiana Purchase to U.S. president Thomas Jefferson and the French government. That same year, Paine returned to the United States and took up residence at his farm in New Rochelle, New York, and in Greenwich Village in New York City.

His reputation had diminished because of controversy surrounding *The Age of Reason* and an earlier public conflict with George Washington over his imprisonment. In his last years, when he felt well enough, Paine continued his involvement in politics and writing, and he saw visitors right up to the time of his death. He died on June 8, 1809, and was buried on his farm. Soon afterward, in a misguided effort to honor him, his bones were exhumed and subsequently lost by William Cobbett, an English admirer.

## *Historical Context and Importance of* The Age of Reason

Throughout his life, Paine's ideas and writing spread to a wide audience, well beyond the usual reading public of other political and philosophical writers of the eighteenth century. Open political debate and activity had only recently become part of a new and growing public sphere. At this time, England and other parts of Western Europe had the basic elements necessary for modern politics; one major component was a growing reading public who bought newspapers and books, and talked about what they read. By the end of the eighteenth century the number of commercial presses had grown into the thousands. They produced printed material of every description. Simultaneously, mechanisms for the broad and relatively quick dissemination of these new commodities, and the ideas they contained, had fallen, or been forced, into place.

This was the beginning of a global era in trade, politics, and culture. The European countries had established colonies all over the world, the English and French being the fastest-growing in the eighteenth century. England, especially, had been unconsciously experimenting since the 1500s with new business, banking, and social models that had transformed a small nation into a global power. Increasingly, business and political activity expanded—from what had been a very small circle of economic and political players—outward and downward in the social order. Thomas Paine was a beneficiary of this relatively dynamic society, even though he was born near the bottom.

## *Summary and Analysis of* The Age of Reason

Paine maintained that *The Age of Reason* was aimed at all religions, though he most often references Christianity and the Christian Bible. The book also promotes Deism as the "natural religion" of God, based in reason and nature. He clearly and often trumpets the success of science in explaining many of the former "mysteries" of the universe. In this sense, *The Age of Reason* is as much pro-science as anti-religion.

Paine's general opinion is that the Bible is not history, but a product of the cultural process of mythmaking. *The Age of Reason* was seen as a threat by the political and religious ruling elite at the end of the eighteenth century. To most people and institutions the Bible was an actual history of the earth's creation, Egypt, and the Jews, as well as the biography of Jesus. *The Age of Reason* was considered so dangerous that its sale was banned, and publishers and booksellers in England were prosecuted for years after its initial publication. Ironically, the state prosecutor against *The Age of Reason* in one early case was the same attorney who had defended Paine in his treason trial, Thomas Erskine.

Paine's questioning of Biblical authority and his understanding of Natural Law are closely tied to his political ideas. He argues that God's benevolence—giving humans the bounty of the earth for support—should be emulated by humans through supporting and assisting others; man "can now provide for his own comfort, and learn from my munificence to all, to be kind to each other." Paine is straightforward in his assessment of the various aspects of different religious traditions and texts. He sees the Bible, and all "sacred texts," as suspect. He contends that they are all either immoral or unbelievable.

In questioning the main elements of organized religion, particularly those of the Abrahamic traditions, Paine establishes a clear division between himself and most of his contemporaries. In different parts of the book he highlights the historical connections between church and state. He describes how a system was created with each institution pointing to the other for justification and enforcement, much to their mutual benefit. Moreover, he believes that this relationship distorts the function of both. He then examines the means by which specific dogma and ritual have been created, transmitted, and justified: revelation as written in holy books; divine inspiration.

Paine also notes the influence of local non–Christian stories and beliefs about the supernatural that were incorporated into the Christian story. Paine made it clear that he believed the iconography, mythology, and ceremonial practices of Roman religion and society were the foundation upon which the Roman Catholic Church and Christianity in general were built. He writes, for example, that "the deification of heroes simply changed into the canonization of saints" (Paine).

## *Textual Analysis of* The Age of Reason

### Book I

"I believe in one God, and no more; and I hope for happiness beyond this life" (Paine). Paine starts *The Age of Reason* with this straightforward statement of personal belief, yet for the past two centuries he has been accused of being an atheist. During his life, he was constantly frustrated by critics who had not read *The Age of Reason*. In an 1803 letter to Samuel Adams, Paine accuses him of making statements about Paine's beliefs based on hearsay and without actually having seen the text. Paine's statement of belief is clearly Deistic. Throughout the book, Paine consistently refers to the existence, wisdom, and moral authority of God—not a common practice of atheists. Furthermore, he contrasts his description with the cruel and immoral picture of God painted by many stories in the Bible.

Paine then proceeds with a discussion of the nature and history of organized religion, looking at the stories' teachings and credibility. He moves easily back and forth between theological and scientific discussions, and writes that nature is the only act of God that can be equally examined and understood by everyone. For Paine, science is a democratic endeavor. In order to explain the scientific view of the universe, he gives a basic lesson in astronomy, describing the planets and their movements in the solar system; this was still relatively new information at the time.

Paine's intention is not to limit the possibilities of religion or worship, but expand them. He makes the bold assertion that "my own mind is my own church." Since the mind is a place of reason and imagination for the Deist, both of which are God-given, he is invoking here the highest authority possible for the Enlightenment. The statement might also betray some of the Quaker influence on Paine. Quakers believe that everyone has a personal connection to God, and that there should be no religious institutions standing between humans and the Creator.

Paine makes a daring accusation when he writes, "All national institutions of churches, whether Jewish, Christian, or Turkish [Islamic], appear to me no other than human inventions set up to terrify and enslave mankind, and monopolize power and profit." Here, Paine draws a strong connection between the political realm and the religious. He asserts that they play off each other's falsehoods in order to maintain their positions of wealth and power. Previously, in *Common Sense* and *The Rights of Man*, Paine referred to these institutions being intertwined; in *The Age of Reason* he delves deeper into the psychological and intellectual reality of a world where spiritual and moral truths are essentially dictated by those in power. He maintains that changes in one institution would bring changes in the other: "Soon after I had published the pamphlet *Common Sense*, in America, I saw the exceeding probability that a revolution in the system of government would be followed by a revolution in the system of religion."

The American and French Revolutions marked a major transformation in how people thought about politics and government. The western world had not seen many non-hereditary political institutions. During the Enlightenment there was growing doubt concerning the traditional ideas maintained by the Church about the physical and moral universe. Paine uses the persecution of Galileo by the Catholic Church as an example of the extremes to which religious institutions will go in order to maintain their power and suppress dissent.

In chapter two of *The Age of Reason*, Paine addresses the problems with religious institutions' claims about their knowledge of God's will. As part of his attempt to demystify religious claims to exceptionalism, he writes, "Every national church or religion has established itself by pretending some special mission from God, communicated to certain individuals." These divine revelations are claimed by major Biblical figures such as Abraham, Moses, and the Apostle Paul, and are important because they are used to justify the authority of the Bible and, consequently, the power of religious and political institutions. In addition, Paine does not accept the traditional attributions of authorship for the books of the Bible.

Paine is not averse to the idea of divine revelation. He might argue that if God wanted to communicate directly, He would; but the passing-on of stories about other people's revelations is a different matter. As Paine points out, "It is revelation to the first person only, and hearsay to every other, and, consequently, they are not obliged to believe it." Paine points out that this initial problem with Biblical accounts of divine revelation is compounded by the passing of time and the amount of copying involved. As an example of how easily content and meaning can be corrupted over time, in the Introduction to Book II of *The Age of Reason*, he uses the insertion of text he had not written into some editions of Book I, very recently published.

Paine then closely scrutinizes the Gospels. His first comment is that the story of Jesus' birth was consistent with other contemporary supernatural origin stories. He concedes that, at the time the Gospels were written, there were no scientific standards for proof, so any story might do—but then points out that by the eighteenth century there were scientific explanations for many supernatural claims made in the Bible.

Paine's examination and critique put the stories of the Bible in a historical and cultural context. From this perspective it is not surprising to Paine that stories attempting to persuade about matters divine have miraculous elements—but these are exactly what he attacks: the fantastical and supernatural. God, as the Deist sees Him, would not suspend or violate the laws of nature. Paine asserts that the Gospels' attribution of divine parentage and Jesus' rising from the dead would not be unexpected: "He was born when the heathen mythology had still some fashion and repute in the world, and that mythology had prepared the people for the belief of such a story."

He continues by giving more examples in which the Christian Bible borrowed from Classical and Jewish stories, such as "The statue of Mary succeeded the statue of Diana of Ephesus." These similarities call into question the accuracy and veracity of the stories. For Paine, such elements dilute and obscure the moral teaching of the Bible, and diminish the authority it *might* have. While the story of Jesus' life is suspect, his message corresponds closely with that of other moral philosophers, and their similarities make it possible to see Jesus' teachings in a different light. "He [Jesus] was a virtuous and an amiable man. The morality that he preached and practiced was of the most benevolent kind." For Paine, it is not the nature of Jesus' birth or miracles that give his words authority. The ideas themselves have value, not the stories surrounding them.

Paine, like many before him, saw geometry as an example of universal truths that, once discovered, can be communicated unchanged over time. He now invokes *Euclid's Elements of Geometry* "because it is a book of self-evident demonstration, entirely independent of its author" (Paine). The Gospels, unlike Euclid, do not stand up to scientific scrutiny. Paine maintains that geometry and science need no justification for their acceptance other than the reliability of their ideas. Like any good Enlightenment thinker, Paine believes ideas and assertions must be verifiable on their own merits, without supernatural authority.

Paine's promotion of the Enlightenment's scientific perspective is clear. In a separate section, he recounts his discovery of scientific ideas through the attendance of lectures, and by working with scientific instruments and a moving model of the solar system (an orrery). He sees the laws of nature, discovered by humans, as examples of God's wisdom and reason. In effect, Paine argues that things are only mysterious until explained by reason and science. God's works are knowable by examining how the laws of the universe work. Paine concludes that, "so far as relates to the supernatural part, [the Bible] has every mark of fraud and imposition stamped upon the face of it."

Building his argument, Paine reminds the reader of the Bible's canonization over time by man-made institutions—and of the events at the Council of Nicaea in AD 325. By showing that the Bible is a product of human invention—"They decided by vote which of the books out of the collection they had made, should be the word of God, and which should not"—he invalidates its claim to supernatural authority.

Even when writing about religion, Paine sees the political aspects of the Bible's stories. He questions the ruling class's constant claims of innate superiority when he wryly notes, "It is somewhat curious that the three persons whose names are the most universally recorded were of very obscure parentage. Moses was a foundling; Jesus Christ was born in a stable; and Mahomet [Muhammad] was a mule driver." He points out that their achievements are impressive, and that each faced persecution by contemporary religious and political institutions. He describes Jesus as a radical who challenged the Jewish religious establishment, which then used the Roman legal system to rid itself of the threat.

Jesus' persecution might have spoken to Paine personally; he was still under a death sentence in England. Paine had always rejected the death penalty, and was one of the few members of the French National Convention to speak against the execution of Louis XVI. He'd made two arguments: first, that Louis XVI, as Louis Capet—a French citizen—was also a victim of the monarchal system. Second, he argued that sparing the king would be an act of mercy signaling the rise of a new government in France that valued human life. This latter motive also lies behind the writing of *The Age of Reason*; in a letter to Thomas Jefferson, Paine wrote that he feared France and the French Revolution were veering toward atheism and tyranny.

As part of his overall discussion, Paine was willing to make assertions about the nature of God; they were not all new ideas, but they were clearly and succinctly expressed. One was "There is a Word of God; there is a revelation. The Word of God is the creation we behold." He describes God, both the concept and the thing, as "the first cause. The cause of all things." This is a thoroughly Deistic concept, one easily accepted by the eighteenth-century intellegencia.

An interesting but often overlooked aspect of *The Age of Reason* is Paine's articulation of an interconnected physical and metaphysical cosmology that is connected through his understanding of the laws of nature and Natural Law. As part of his discussion of the size of the universe, Paine asks the reader to imagine the size of the earth relative to a never-ending space: "A world of this extent [earth] may, at first thought, appear to us to be great ... it is infinitely less in proportion than the smallest grain of sand is to the size of the world.... It is difficult beyond description to conceive that space can have no end; but it is more difficult to conceive an end."

Paine puts forth several ideas about space and exobiology that sound contemporary in their ruminations. He speculates that the universe is widely populated: "Since then no part of our earth is left unoccupied, why is it to be supposed that the immensity of space is a naked void." While Paine is not as well known for scientific research, he worked and communicated with many scientists and theologians, such as the Reverend Joseph Priestley and inventor John Fitch. Paine's scientific literacy is evident when he explains scientific theories and his ideas about God, whom he refers to as the "Great Architect."

The last chapter of Book I is titled *Of the Means Employed in All Time, and Almost Universally, to Deceive the Peoples.* In this chapter Paine examines three supernatural aspects of religion, which he describes as "the three principal means that have been employed ... to impose upon mankind. Those three means are Mystery, Miracle, and Prophecy." Throughout the chapter Paine uses natural science to counter miraculous religious claims. With the example of the lighter-than-air balloon, invented in the eighteenth century, he illustrates how something can simply be not-understood, rather than not understandable. He writes that misunderstood natural phenomena can be mistaken for the supernatural, and that study of nature leads to knowledge of God.

## Book II

In the preface to Book II, Paine gives an account of his recent imprisonment and recounts the story of Robespierre seeking his arrest. He also explains that when writing Book I he did not have a Bible on hand, and had to rely on memory; but that when he started rewriting *The Age of Reason*, he had one. He writes that he was too forgiving in Book I, and that the Bible was even more objectionable than he'd remembered. Book II is a close reading of textual elements of the Bible. Examining the Old Testament, Paine asks simple questions about its history and the authenticity of the different books: "The first thing to be understood is, whether there is sufficient authority for believing the Bible to be the word of God, or whether there is not?"

Paine does not ascribe divine origin to the Old Testament, nor does he think the traditional attributions assigned to its books are correct. His criticism applies as much to the Pentateuch, credited to Moses, as it does to the books of the Prophets. There is also a short discussion of the history of the word "prophet." Paine writes that many of the stories in the Old Testament are morally repugnant. He recounts the brutal military conquests and supernatural feats in order to impugn the credibility of the whole book: "There are matters in that book, said to be done by the express command of God, that are ... shocking to humanity."

Rather than read the Gospels in the order they appear in the New Testament—Matthew, Mark, Luke, and John (vertical)—Paine examines them in a side-by-side reading (horizontal). By reading the texts this way, one can see that even where they seem to be retelling the same incident, the Resurrection for example, the narrative and "facts" are not consistent. "It is not then the existence or the non-existence, of the persons that I trouble myself about; it is the fable of Jesus Christ" (Paine). He returns to the historical moment of the accounts of Jesus' life to examine their accuracy, credibility, and authorship. He again points out that the stories should not be seen in the same way as the teachings. Paine provides a more detailed history of the Council of Nicaea and the work of later ecumenical councils that over the centuries decided Church doctrine and proclaimed it the word of God.

A significant problem for Paine with the New Testament was the lack of agreement about the facts of Jesus' life in the Gospels. Throughout *The Age of Reason* Paine contends that the supernatural elements of the Bible, and especially the stories about Jesus, only put the text in greater doubt. Paine again connects the Bible's stories to its pagan analogues. The question for Paine was, since the stories of Zeus and Hercules are held to be myths, why should what is essentially the same story, but with God and Jesus, have any more credibility?

Rather than try to summarize Paine's conclusion in Book II, it is more illustrative to quote from it. Each of the following excerpts gives us a concrete theme or action connected to the larger cosmology Paine proposes throughout the text:

> MORALITY: "The most detestable wickedness, the most horrid cruelties, and the greatest miseries, that have afflicted the human race, have had their origin in this thing called revelation, or revealed religion."
>
> POLITICS: "It has been the scheme of the Christian church, and of all the other invented systems of religion, to hold man in ignorance of the Creator, as it is of government to hold him in ignorance of his rights. The systems of the one are as false as those of the other, and are calculated for mutual support."
>
> SCIENCE: "All the knowledge man has of science and of machinery, by the aid of which his existence is rendered comfortable upon earth, and without which he would be scarcely distinguishable in appearance and condition from a common animal, comes from the great machine and structure of the universe."
>
> PROGRESS: "Certain as I am that when opinions are free, either in matters of government or religion, truth will finally and powerfully prevail."

## *Conclusion*

There are two major turning points in eighteenth-century Anglo-American and French politics. Both England and France experienced seismic disruptions at the end of the eighteenth century, in 1776 and 1789, respectively. These events perhaps mark the beginning of a new politically dynamic, volatile, and transitional world. A world perched on the edge of the modern industrial era. Paine played important roles in both revolutions, and in the larger political landscape of the era.

The impact of Paine's writing cannot be overstated; his ideas were both ahead of and firmly rooted in his own time. In Paine's later work, especially *Agrarian Justice*, he sought to assert Natural Law and Natural Rights not simply as abstract principles. He proposed specific plans—such as public education and social security—to move society toward a material manifestation of those political ideas.

Paine believed that democratic institutions and social justice could arise from changing the ideas and mechanisms that govern society. Like many of the social-contract theorists, Natural Law proponents, and philosophers, he believed that knowable, unchangeable laws govern the universe and human society. Since humans are all equally endowed with reason and rights, none can be denied the protections and privileges owed by nature and society. In this respect, Paine was part of what is called the "Cosmopolitan" movement of the late eighteenth century. Other thinkers, such as Hume and Kant, also saw themselves as citizens of the world, with basic rights that could not be abridged. In their mind, citizenship was not bestowed by a government but chosen by the individual. If they considered the world their country, perhaps reason was its national religion.

To understand the continued relevance of Thomas Paine and *The Age of Reason* or *The Rights of Man*, try a web search; he will be found referenced in a wide range of political and religious writings and discussions. One of the most interesting aspects of his popularity is that he is often invoked by the Liberal, Conservative, and Radical political establishments alike. *The Age of Reason* is especially pertinent in the twenty-first century, given the global political situation, and in view of how religion and religious worldviews have been used by all sides to condemn, justify, and exonerate war and terrorism. It is the persistent immediacy of the questions raised in *The Age of Reason* that makes it a constant classic.

## Note

1. Full quote: "I am willing you should call this the Age of Frivolity as you do, and would not object if you had named it the Age of Folly, Vice, Frenzy, Brutality, Daemons, Bonaparte, Tom Paine, or the Age of the Burning Brand from the Bottomless Pit, or anything but the Age of Reason. I know not whether any man in the world has had more influence on its inhabitants or affairs for the last thirty years than Tom Paine There can be no severer satyr on the age. For such a mongrel between pig and puppy, begotten by a wild boar on a bitch

wolf, never before in any age of the world was suffered by the poltroonery of mankind, to run through such a career of mischief. Call it then the Age of Paine." (John Adams to Benjamin Waterhouse, letter, October 29, 1805).

## Works Cited

Foner, Eric. *Tom Paine and Revolutionary America*. London: Oxford University Press, 1977. Print.

Keane, John. *Tom Paine: A Political Life*. Boston: Little, Brown, 1995. Print.

Paine, Thomas. *The Age of Reason*. Online Library of Liberty. N.p., n.d. Web. Accessed July 11, 2011.

_____. Letter to Samuel Adams, 1803.

Paine, Thomas, and Moncure Daniel Conway. *The Age of Reason: Being an Investigation of True and Fabulous Theology*. Mineola, NY: Dover, 2004. Print.

Stone, Lawrence. "Literacy and Education in England 1640–1900." *Past and Present* 42.1 (1969): 69–139. Print.

Thompson, E. P. *The Making of the English Working Class*. New York: Vintage, 1966. Print.

# Thoreau's Rhetoric of Resistance

PETER DIAMOND

## Summary

While Thoreau's *Resistance to Civil Government* was not written while he was actually in jail, the effect of the experience on his thinking and writing was significant—as would be the work's influence upon future political thinkers. A reevaluation of this essay reveals that the ideas of resistance and civil disobedience generally attributed to him are not accurate—or at least don't tell the whole story. The notion that Thoreau advocated only passive resistance to questionable actions of the government is further proven wrong by his essay in support of Captain John Brown's raid at Harpers Ferry. Thoreau argued that the existence of a government law did not automatically make something ethical or unethical, or rightfully compel citizens to accept it, as was the case with slavery. Slavery's presence in the Constitution did not validate its existence for Thoreau and others. In his writing, Thoreau shares with Gandhi and Nehru a certain attitude toward the prison experience: that it was a necessary part of the process of political struggle. Both Thoreau and Gandhi believed that political enlightenment, personal growth, and resistance to injustice all go hand-in-hand. *Resistance to Civil Government* is included in this collection because of its historically significant impact on social and political movements around the world.—J.W.R.

## Introduction

Henry David Thoreau's "Resistance to Civil Government" (1849) is among the most celebrated and influential accounts of principled action in modern American letters. The action—Thoreau's refusal to pay his poll tax, for which he was arrested and briefly jailed—embodied his principled refusal to recognize the authority of a government that did not just sanction, but supported, slavery. While he did not write "Resistance" *in* prison, his imprisonment became the centerpiece of his rhetorical efforts to raise the consciousness of those of his countrymen who were "well-disposed" to lead a just and moral life but were "daily made the agents of injustice" by a wicked and tyrannical society (65). Thoreau's essay has subsequently inspired a diverse range of figures and organizations to principled law breaking, including Mohandas Gandhi, Martin Luther King, Jr., British suffragist Constance Lytton, anarchist Emma Goldman, as well as the African National Congress in South Africa. They all were convinced of the need *to act* in defiance of unjust laws, though they differed widely over the nature and purpose of such resistance. Although Thoreau's essay is widely recognized as a defense of "civil disobedience" he did not think of principled action as necessarily nonviolent, nor did he call for organized, mass demonstrations in which participants willingly accept punishment as an affirmation of the state's sovereignty. Indeed, despite the posthumous publication of his essay under its familiar title, "Civil Disobedience," Thoreau never used that term in any of his published works.

Thoreau placed more faith in action than in words, which is why he used his incarceration as the touchstone of his principle of resistance. But actions do not always speak for themselves; at least not in the way we would hope. According to a well-known, though apocryphal, anecdote, Ralph Waldo Emerson visited Thoreau in jail. "'Henry, why are you here?'" Emerson is said to have asked his young friend. "'Waldo, why are you *not* here?'" came the reply (Jones 15). While the story is often repeated to dramatize their mutual disapproval, it also illustrates the difficulty Thoreau would face in convincing his fellow townsmen that "action from principle," even if it entailed breaking the laws of an unjust state and accepting the consequences, is an obligation that they all should recognize. As to the utility of a night spent in jail, Thoreau admonished those who, like Emerson, believed his action to be pointless and ineffective: "[T]hey do not know by how much truth is stronger than error, nor how much more eloquently and effectively he can combat injustice who has experienced a little in his own person" ("Resistance" 87, 88). Of course writing is also a form of action, one to which Thoreau dedicated immense time and attention. He took care to adopt rhetorical forms designed to frustrate passive readers and to compel them to engage in the struggle to discern the truth in all its complexity. He reveled in paradoxes and contradictions, rewrote popular slogans so that they acquired entirely new meanings—all in an effort to create a productive uncertainty in his audience. As he wrote in his *Journal*, "'Yes and No are lies—A true answer will not aim to establish anything, but rather to set all well afloat'" (qtd. in Golemba 7).

Not surprisingly, scholars have disputed the meaning of Thoreau's "Resistance." Some have treated it as a private expression of individual conscience, devoid of political intent (Arendt 59–60; Walzer 6, 13). Others have celebrated it as a work of political education mindful of our democratic commitments and the need for social reform (Cavell 83–88; Rosenblum 15–38). Still others insist that its fundamental moral values require that we go beyond the necessary limitations of democratic government (Jenco 355–81; Shulman 39–88; Mariotti 117–44). To understand Thoreau's intentions, we will need to examine the evolution of his commitment to resistance, which began with a solitary act of self-reform, and culminated in as a deliberately social act of public persuasion. In fact, Thoreau's resistance started well before, and extended well after, the night he spent in jail. It began in 1842, when he first refused to pay his poll tax (a fee levied on all males between the ages of twenty and seventy), continued with his arrest in July 1846, and ended with the publication of "Resistance" in May 1849.

## Thoreau's Opposition to Social Reform

At the time of his arrest Thoreau had lived for a year at Walden Pond in Concord, Massachusetts, where he built his own small house on land owned by Emerson. He had just turned twenty-nine, and was fully immersed in the radical project of self-reform that had seized his imagination while a student at Harvard. Inspired by Emerson's writing, Thoreau decided to withdraw from the dulling comfort of mass society, to cultivate his intellectual and moral faculties, and to find his vocation by turning to unmediated nature. It would take Thoreau the better part of a decade to commit himself to spending time in the woods, as he put it, "to live deliberately, to front only the essential facts of life, and see if I could not learn what it had to teach, and not, when I came to die, discover that I had not lived" (*Walden* 90).

After graduating from Harvard College in 1837, he tried teaching, but without much success. Yearning for some measure of independence, Thoreau accepted Emerson's offer of room and board for a year in exchange for help around the house and garden. The year stretched into two, as the burgeoning friendship between the two men deepened. Thoreau spent much of his time reading, walking the woods, and thinking during this period. Emerson had suggested that he keep a journal and encouraged the young man to write. Fourteen years Thoreau's senior, Emerson had taken a personal interest in the young man's welfare while he was still at Harvard, and Thoreau, for his part, looked to his elder for guidance. Emerson was then becoming widely known as a public intellectual whose rejection of the growing materialism and conformism of American life resonated deeply with those—young people especially—who doubted the value of what was commonly extolled as "progress." Emerson did not just seek to undermine the regnant values of a morally and culturally flaccid society, he also provided young people with a secular religion, a call to action whereby the very nature of society might be transformed.

Transcendentalism, as this perspective was called, had its origins in the writings of Immanuel Kant and G.W. F. Hegel, two German philosophers of the late eighteenth and early nineteenth centuries, who argued that there is a body of knowledge innate within humans and that this knowledge transcends the senses. They posited that this knowledge is the voice of God within us— what the Transcendentalists called conscience or the moral sense. It was central to their belief that all humans are born with this innate ability to distinguish between right and wrong. Unfortunately, as people grow older, they tend to listen to the world around them rather than to the voice within, and thus their moral sense becomes corrupted. It is consequently the duty of all good citizens to resist established conventions and expectations, and to avoid undertaking work that does not reflect a deep personal calling.

The Transcendentalists were nominally led by Emerson, whose first book, *Nature*, became a manifesto for a small, informal group of like-minded men and women who explored the ethical and political implications of the new movement in German thought. They were also engaged in radical attempts to alter the American political and economic system by establishing new alternatives to it. A number of the Transcendentalists attempted communal agrarian experiments, the most famous of which was Brook Farm, a commune established by the Unitarian minister, George Ripley, in 1840. The idea was to create a secure and noncompetitive environment through cooperative labor. Intellectuals would gain time for their creative efforts, and the whole would serve as a model by which class divisions between laborers and intellectuals might be overcome. Most of the Transcendentalists were invited to join, but neither Emerson nor Thoreau wanted any part of it. As Thoreau wrote in his journal, "As for these communities—I think I had rather keep a bachelor's hall in hell than go to board in heaven" (1:277).

Both men lectured on the subject of reform in 1844 before groups of radical reformers gathered at Boston's Amory Hall. Emerson took the opportunity to praise solitary examples of resistance to government, but he criticized those reformers who joined "associations," finding them to be "tediously good in some particular but negligent or narrow in the rest; and hypocrisy and vanity are often the disgusting result." Emerson also believed that the very act of association is self-defeating, for it forces persons to submerge their talents and compromise their best ideas and values. He argued that while reformers mistakenly believe by uniting they increase their strength, they are in fact diminished by the demands imposed by any collective enterprise. "What is it we heartily wish of each other?" Emerson asked. "Is it to be pleased and flattered? No, but to be convicted and exposed, to be shamed out of our nonsense of all kinds, and made men of, instead of ghosts and phantoms" (*Essays, Second Series* 154, 161). When Thoreau's turn came to address the Amory Hall reformers, he took Emerson's advice literally, brutally calling them "the impersonation of disorder and imperfection," and advising them that they would be better off reforming themselves than seeking to reform others. Instead of healing themselves, he complained, reformers preferred to "rely solely on logic and argument, or on eloquence and oratory for success," rather than on deeds ("Reform" 182, 184).

Thoreau also gave another of Emerson's arguments his own unique twist, explaining that associations would cause individuals to lose confidence in the value of their own best efforts, not by their disapproval, but by their approval. Both men regarded dissent as the proper expression of self-reform, and popular approval, even within a small association, its death. They believed that associations suffered from the same herd mentality as society at large, and were consequently an obstacle to human progress. "There is no objection to action in societies or communities when it is the individual using the society as his instrument, rather than the society using the individual," he explained.

> While one's inspiration is so high and pure as to be necessarily solitary and not to be made a subject of sympathy or congratulation, he may safely use any instrument in his way, whether wood or iron or masses of men. But when the vote of the society rises to a level with his own prayers, and its resolution in the least confirms his own, he may suspect himself, or he may suspect his companions [186–87].

Such was the case, for example, when Nathaniel P. Rogers, editor of New Hampshire's abolitionist journal, the *Herald of Freedom*, called for the dissolution of all anti-slavery societies because, like all organizations, they inevitably impede self-reform. When Rogers was fired, Thoreau published an essay in *The Dial*, the Transcendentalist journal, praising him for his "clean attachment to the right" ("Herald" 49–50).

Thoreau continued to oppose organized social reform in the following year, when the noted anti-slavery orator, Wendell Phillips, was invited to speak before the Concord Lyceum. When conservative members of the Lyceum committee resigned in protest, Thoreau defended Phillips's right to speak in a letter to the *Liberator*, William Lloyd Garrison's abolitionist newspaper. Referring implicitly to the conservatives, Thoreau pointed out that Phillips "at least is not responsible for slavery, nor for American Independence; for the hypocrisy and superstition of the church, nor the timidity and selfishness of the state; nor for the indifference and willing ignorance of any. He stands so distinctly, so firmly, and so effective, alone, and one honest man is so much more than a host" ("Wendell Phillips" 59–60). Thoreau's sarcasm recalls a complaint he voiced to his Amory Hall audience: that people learn little of value in associations, where conformity is the norm and opposition voices are silenced ("Reform" 185). And yet, for all his celebration of Phillips' potent solitariness, Thoreau must surely have known that lecturing on behalf of solitary self-reform was itself an eminently social, or "outward," practice that relied on the sort of argument and oratory he had dismissed in his Amory Hall lecture. Perhaps he had begun to realize that self-reform was less likely to occur in societies that attempt to silence dissenting voices.

## *The Context of Thoreau's Reform Writings*

While the young Thoreau urged his listeners to obey their individual callings, rather than adhere to the expectations or desires of their "neighbors and kind friends and patrons," as time passed he would find it increasingly difficult to disparage organized efforts at reform, especially the abolition movement, as the country became more embroiled over the problem of slavery. In 1836, upon gaining its independence from Mexico, Texas immediately sought to join the Union. As Len Gougeon points out, its admission as a slave state threatened to increase the influence of the South in national politics and, consequently, abolitionists throughout the North vociferously fought Texas' petition. Despite their opposition, Texas entered the Union in December of 1845. In May of the following year, Mexico, which had never accepted Texas' independence, declared war on the United States ("Thoreau and Reform" 200–01). For Thoreau, opposition to the war meant opposition to public opinion and a politics that tolerated slavery, militarism, and imperial expansion.

In addition to his published support of particular reformers, Thoreau's opposition to slavery initially took the form of passive resistance. By refusing to pay his poll tax, he was following the lead of abolitionists in Massachusetts who were attempting to demonstrate their opposition to a government that supported slavery. In 1840 Thoreau's friend, Bronson Alcott, was arrested for refusing to pay his poll tax, though he spent even less time in jail than Thoreau, for his tax was paid within a couple of hours by Samuel Hoar, Concord's leading citizen. In 1843 the English reformer and friend of Alcott, Charles Lane, was similarly arrested, and just as quickly rescued by Hoar. This may have been one reason why Thoreau was reportedly "'as mad as the devil'" upon being turned out of his cell the morning after his arrest (qtd. in Harding 204–05). A man who did nothing lightly, who welcomed the opportunity "to occupy an honorable and manly position" in society (to use the words he used to praise Rogers) ("Herald" 49), he resented having his incarceration appear to be merely symbolic, rather than a substantial act of conscience.

In the months following his arrest, Thoreau remained at Walden Pond, where he completed two drafts of his first book, *A Week on the Concord and Merrimack Rivers*, his meditation on America's founding. Like "Resistance to Civil Government," *A Week* bears witness to injustice, in this case by reminding Americans of the cruelty and injustice suffered by American Indians at the hands of their European forbears. In the book Thoreau also sought to awaken what he saw as an increasingly complacent contemporary society by furnishing Americans with stories of heroism that would inspire them to combat such current moral evils as slavery and imperialism. "In my short experience of human life," Thoreau wrote, "the *outward* obstacles, if there were any such, have not been living men, but the institutions of the dead ... for it is not to be forgotten, that while the law holds fast the thief and murderer, it lets itself go loose" (130). Thoreau may well have had in mind an incident that occurred shortly after his return to Walden, in 1851. A fugitive slave was discovered aboard a ship in Boston harbor, and promptly returned by the ship's owner, who feared reprisals by the slave's master. The event infuriated abolitionists, and led Emerson to complain that commercial interests were leading to the moral bankruptcy of society (Gougeon, *Virtue's Hero* 127–29).

Thoreau also continued to lecture before the Concord Lyceum while at Walden and thereafter. In January and February of 1848 he delivered two lectures on "The Rights and Duties of the Individual in Relation to Government." Alcott attended one of the lectures, and was pleased that Thoreau had mentioned Alcott's own brush with the law. He must have been surprised when, in May of the following year, Thoreau published his essay in Elizabeth Peabody's *Aesthetic Papers* under the title "Resistance to Civil Government," without mentioning his friend's arrest.

## *Thoreau's Rhetoric of Resistance*

Thoreau's revisions to his essay are significant, for they reflect his decision to signal his opposition to "non-resistance," the doctrine of William Lloyd Garrison's New England Non-Resistance Society. Non-resistance combined pacifism with anarchism insofar as it prohibited not only all violence, but also all cooperation with any state that relies on coercion to enforce its laws. From that standpoint, holding public office, paying taxes, or even voting, were considered immoral acts. Thoreau's new title implicitly demonstrated his rejection of Garrison's doctrine. And since Lane defended Alcott's tax refusal in the pages of the *Liberator* as an act of "non-resistance," it is probable that Thoreau no longer wished to have his disobedience associated with that of Alcott (Rosenwald 155). Indeed, by the time he published "Resistance," the country was at war with Mexico, and Thoreau now recognized that social reform could not depend on individual acts of self-reform alone, such as those he had undertaken at Walden Pond. Rather, Thoreau had come to believe that justice demanded active resistance to the government. Passive and private resistance—such as one's refusal to pay a poll tax—would not suffice. Rather, just resistance called for a public, and, if need be, violent, response to the state's shedding of innocent blood.

Thoreau wrote "Resistance" in response to a simple question: "How does it become a man to behave toward this American government today?" He answered that a man "cannot without disgrace be associated with it. I cannot for an instant recognize that political organization as *my* government which is the *slave's* government also" (67). While he reached the same conclusion as those who advocated non-resistance, Thoreau insisted at the outset that he did not wish to be associated with "those who call themselves no-government men." Instead, he would "speak practically and as a citizen," which meant giving a clear and sensible account of what one should expect from *any* government. For Thoreau, that meant adhering to the revolutionary principles associated with America's founding. "To be strictly just," he wrote, "[a government] must have the sanction and consent of the governed. It can have no pure right over my person and property but what I concede to it" (89). Thoreau's language harks back to the Declaration of Independence, though we should not assume that he was relying on the *mythos* of America's founding as an example of consent. As the author of *A Week*, Thoreau well knew that America's actual founding entailed the violent conquest of native peoples long before the revolution of 1776 or the compact of 1787. As Thoreau pointed out in "Resistance," adherence to that fraudulent *mythos* allowed Daniel Webster to say of slavery: "'Because it was a part of the original compact, let it stand.'" Webster may have deserved to be called "the Defender of the Constitution," but in Thoreau's opinion he was "unable to take a fact [such as slavery] out of its merely political relations, and behold it as it lies absolutely to be disposed of by the intellect." Webster was not able to recognize that the Constitution, as a pro-slavery document, was itself "the evil" because he was "not a leader but a follower. His leaders are the men of '87" (74, 87–88). For Thoreau, each individual must literally express the consent idealized in our founding documents for him or herself.

It must surely have struck his fellow townsmen as bizarre that Thoreau, who had refused to contribute to the support of a local clergyman, gave the Concord town clerk the following declaration in support of his refusal: "Know all men by these presents, that I, Henry Thoreau, do not wish to be regarded as a member of any incorporated society which I have not joined." But what others may have considered strange, Thoreau regarded as an example of "the free exercise of judgment or of moral sense" that was badly lacking among the great "mass of men" (79, 66). Thoreau refused to pay his church tax in 1840, two years before he stopped paying his poll tax. Both refusals were private, passive acts of resistance. Through his act of "public" resistance, Thoreau undertook the political education of his fellow citizens, thereby intending to create "corporation[s] of conscientious men" whose conduct would serve as a "counter friction" to the machinery of state power. Such associations, he believed, could make a tangible difference in society: a "minority is powerless while it conforms to the majority" but "irresistible when it clogs [the machine] by its whole weight" (65, 74, 76).

Thoreau's position has not gone unchallenged. Critics contend that it is implausible and even dangerous to imagine, as Thoreau famously put it, that "the only obligation which I have a right to assume, is to do at any time what I think right" (65). The inherent subjectivity of Thoreau's position, critics point out, would result in anarchy or worse, since it militates against promises to obey all laws and governmental institutions, as such, for their very existence is based on the public's recognition of their right to command. For his part, Thoreau believed all persons possess a faculty of judgment he referred to as a "moral sense" and a constitution "written in [their] heart" by God ("Slavery" 103). By calling for "action from principle," which he defined as "the perception and performance of right," he implied that everyone has a duty not only to do what is right, but also to ascertain the meaning of "right," through unfettered deliberation. Thoreau believed in the existence of a higher law that imposes strict ethical standards on everyone. He was aware of the potential for disagreement, but he was also confident (perhaps naively so) that "the faintest assured objection which one healthy man feels will at length prevail over mankind" (*Walden* 216).

Critics have also complained that Thoreau misconceived the extent to which we are interdependent beings, whose collective lives require that we solve our problems through the democratic political process. He regarded politics as an essentially sordid business, which a virtuous citizenry must learn to transcend. By contrast, Thoreau regarded John Brown, recently captured after his violent raid at Harpers Ferry, as "a man of rare common sense and directness of speech, as of action; a transcendentalist above all, a man of ideas and principles.... For once we are lifted out of the trivialness and dust of politics into the region of truth and manhood" ("A Plea" 115, 125). Lincoln opposed Brown's violent abolitionism because it failed to recognize that such lawlessness not only erodes the rule of law but also undermines the ability of politicians—citizens taking part in the democratic process—to *build* consensus. It is important to recognize that Thoreau brooked no opposition on this point. To those who feared that action from principle would produce violence, he replied, "But even suppose blood should flow. Is there not a sort of blood shed when the conscience is wounded? Through this wound a man's real manhood and immortality flow out, and he bleeds to an everlasting death. I see this blood flowing now" ("Resistance" 77).

It is not difficult to understand Thoreau's contempt for "what is called politics," as he put it. The growing equality of condition that for Alexis de Tocqueville marked the triumph of democracy in Jacksonian America, had allowed majorities to exercise a despotic and insidious control over the formation and expression of ideas. "The same equality," wrote Tocqueville, "which makes [a person] dependent of each separate citizen leaves him isolated and defenseless in the face of the majority. So in democracies public opinion has a strange power of which aristocratic nations can form no conception. It uses no persuasion to forward its beliefs, but by some mighty pressure of the mind of all upon the intelligence of each it imposes its ideas and makes them penetrate men's very souls" (435). It was in this context that Thoreau declared, "the mass of men serve the State thus, not as men mainly, but as machines, with their bodies. They are the standing army, and the militia, jailers, constables, *posse comitatus*, etc. In most cases there is no free exercise whatever of the judgment or of the moral sense" ("Resistance" 66). In these circumstances, given the climate of opinion in the country, being "political," that is, involving oneself in the affairs or institutions of government, entailed the implicit legitimization of slaveholding and imperial expansion. Moreover, for Thoreau it was no longer enough to be a law-abiding citizen, for one's presence in the majority only served to legitimize immoral laws and practices; one now had a duty to be a dissident.

The rise of equality during the first half of the nineteenth century also meant the decline of hierarchical and paternalistic groups and classes that had characterized American society in pre–Revolutionary days. People were increasingly faced with the task of creating identities for themselves and others in a marketplace dominated by public opinion. Then, as now, politicians soon learned that it was easy to produce and exchange false or misleading images and statements in such an environment (Pocock 538). Not surprisingly, Thoreau rejected "what is *called* politics" on grounds that politics had become a superficial and coarsening affair, whose essential falsity follows from the nature of what could be achieved politically ("Life Without Principle" 177). It was from this standpoint that he declared government to be "at best but an expedient; but most governments are usually, and all government are sometimes, inexpedient." As Tocqueville observed (650), this is especially so in time of war, which tends to destroy political liberty. "Witness the present Mexican war," offered Thoreau, "the work of comparatively a few individuals using the standing government as their tool; for, in the outset, the people would not have consented to this measure" ("Resistance" 63).

Thoreau's response to this state of affairs was to deny the efficacy of politics, as it was then understood. "Is a democracy, such as we know it, the last improvement possible in government? Is it not possible to take a step further towards recognizing the rights of man?" (89). For Thoreau, the problem with democracy "as we know it" inheres in the electoral principle of majority rule. Voting is a feeble expression of an individual's conscience, for one's capacity for vital action is submerged in the will of the majority. Although democracy invites individuals to "cast [their] whole vote, not a strip of paper merely, but [their] whole influence," in fact "the mass of men" are more interested in earning a living than they are with seemingly abstract and far-off concerns, "and are not prepared to do justice to the slave and to Mexico." Indeed, in such circumstances justice is not likely to be done by encouraging more people to vote. Even those "who are *in opinion* opposed to slavery and to the war" will be unlikely to commit themselves to acting on what is right when the majority is disposed to continue the status quo (76, 68, 69).

What is needed, Thoreau argued, is for the conscientious individual in the minority to give up what is called politics in favor of action from principle, which, in the face of injustice, requires the transgression of unjust laws. He did not argue that the individual is morally obliged to contribute to the public good, by "devot[ing] himself to the eradication of any, even the most enormous wrong; he may still properly have other concerns to engage him." Thoreau denied that conscientious individuals have a moral obligation to devote themselves wholly to public service; indeed, he was rarely more caustic than when musing about "Doing-good." "If I were to preach at all in this strain," he wrote in *Walden*, "I should say rather, Set about being good.... If I knew for a certainty that a man was coming to my house with the conscious intention of doing me good, I should run for my life." This does not imply that Thoreau was careless or oblivious of the common good; rather, he understood that nothing a person does is unconnected with the life of a society. For a person serves society, not by devoting himself to a cause, but by pursing his calling wherever it leads. What Thoreau said, ironically, of the Do-gooder—

"I would not stand between any man and his genius"—applies without irony to all (73–74).

Everyone *is* morally obliged, Thoreau argued, "at least, to wash his hands of [any wrong], and, if he gives it no thought longer, not to give it practically his support" ("Resistance" 71). And when the state fails to act justly, he argued that private individuals have a duty to try to reform the state: They must help to create the conditions in which individuals are able to engage in "essentially revolutionary" acts of self-reform, or in other words, in "action from principle." For Thoreau, all meaningful social reform starts and finishes with that. More specifically still, Thoreau recognized that active resistance—breaking the law—is the only means by which to effect such change. He was aware that most people fear the consequences of such action, believing that resistance will only make things worse. What they need to understand, said Thoreau, is that "it is the fault of the government itself that the remedy *is* worse than the evil. *It* makes it worse. [But] why is it not more apt to anticipate and provide for reform?" Besides, the state is nothing other than the coercive means by which the people execute their will. "*It* does not keep the country free. *It* does not settle the West. *It* does not educate. The character inherent in the American people has done all that has been accomplished; and it would have done somewhat more, if the government had not sometimes got in its way" (73, 64). In an unjust world, breaking the law may be the only means to get government out of the way, and to create the conditions for individuals to engage in self-cultivation.

## *Thoreau, Prison and Persuasion*

For Thoreau, self-reform entailed continuous intellectual effort to live a "life of principle," and thereby to embody the higher law. His life at Walden, including his continuing refusal to pay his poll tax, followed by his night in jail, were the beginnings of that ongoing project. By publishing "Resistance," Thoreau turned what began as an act of self-reform into one of social reform, as he realized that the time had come to do "my part to educate my fellow countrymen." He now fully realized that resistance isn't actualized until it becomes a public act. This meant convincing, first his fellow townsmen at Lyceum meetings, and then the public at large by publishing "Resistance," that they needed to withdraw their support, "both in person and property," from the government (84, 74). Moreover, it entailed a most unlikely course of action: persuading them that going to jail was not merely the right thing to do, but a politically effective response to the government's economic and military policies.

To those who believed a night's incarceration to be pointless and ineffective, Thoreau offered a dramatic account of his brief incarceration that inverted the prevailing images of prison and outside society. Whereas most prison narratives rely on the prisoner's suffering to enhance the authority of their moral and political claims—one thinks of Socrates and Jesus, Boethius and Thomas More—Thoreau's story depicts his prison experience in idealized terms, as a place of refuge from the brutalizing oppression of a state that must physically compel its citizens to obey by threats and by force because it cannot appeal to their intellectual or moral faculties. In this reversal, the relaxed geniality of the prison atmosphere, the whitewashed walls and simple furnishing of his cell are made to evoke his circumstances at Walden. Rather than being a site of confinement, the prison affords Thoreau an occasion for inward-looking self-reform and hence self-liberation from the soul-corrupting world without. "It was like travelling into a far country," he wrote, "such as I had never expected to behold, to lie there for one night." He was now free to see through the town's practices and institutions, and to glimpse how much the town's residents resembled the old burghers of pre-revolutionary Europe (82).

In *Walden* he likened himself to "chanticleer in the morning, standing on his roost, if only to wake my neighbors up" (84); in "Resistance" the image of Socrates' gadfly is more apt. Like Socrates, he sought to persuade and reproach his neighbors and fellow citizens for failing to live up to their own ideals. His voice could be strident, and his expectations unrealistic, but his message was underwritten with the authority of his own action. As he proclaimed in "Resistance," "it is not so important that many should be as good as you, as that there be some absolute goodness somewhere; for that will leaven the whole lump" (69). Thoreau was not claiming the mantle of "absolute goodness," but rather bearing witness to its existence in the higher law, and urging his listeners and readers to undertake the project of self-reform upon which he believed all genuine social reform rests.

Thoreau's doctrine and his example have spread far beyond its intended audience. Decades later Mahatma Gandhi and Martin Luther King, Jr., both claimed him as the inspiration for their practice of passive or nonviolent resistance, though Thoreau himself was quite willing to endorse violence in opposition to chattel slavery, as he did when he praised John Brown's failed raid on the federal armory at Harpers Ferry, Virginia. The dramatic and far-reaching changes brought about by the efforts of Gandhi and King, manifest as they are in the democratic political practices and institutions of their respective societies, are apt to draw our attention away from where Thoreau would have us place the emphasis. He would have us maintain a certain intellectual distance from "what is called politics" in modern democratic societies; the better to see through the empty talk and corrupting practices that we tend to take for granted. Instead, he would have us focus our energies on self-reform, on becoming self-reliant individuals who are willing and able to engage in the political action and resistance upon which social reform depends. Such action takes courage, and a determination to resist the comforting illusion that public opinion is the measure of all value.

## Works Cited

Arendt, Hannah. *Crises of the Republic*. San Diego: Harcourt Brace, 1972. Print.
Cavell, Stanley. *The Senses of Walden*. Chicago: University of Chicago Press, 1981. Print.
Gougeon, Len. *Virtue's Hero: Emerson, Antislavery, and Reform*. Athens: University of Georgia, 1990. Print.
\_\_\_\_\_. "Thoreau and Reform." *The Cambridge Companion to Henry David Thoreau*. Ed. Joel Myerson. Cambridge: Cambridge University Press, 1995. 194–214. Print
Harding, Walter. *The Days of Henry Thoreau*. Princeton: Princeton University Press, 1982. Print.
Jenco, Leigh Kathryn. "Thoreau's Critique of Democracy." *Review of Politics* 65.3 (2003): 355–81. *JSTOR*. Web. 3 Feb. 2014.
Johnson, Linck C. "Reforming the Reformers: Emerson, Thoreau, and the Sunday Lectures at Amory Hall, Boston." *ESQ* 37.4 (1991): 235–89. *JSTOR*. Web. 3 Feb. 2014.
Jones, Samuel Arthur. *Thoreau's Incarceration, As Told by His Jailer*. Berkeley Heights, NJ: Oriole Press, 1962. Print.
Mariotti, Shannon L. *Thoreau's Democratic Withdrawal*. Madison: University of Wisconsin Press, 2010. Print.
Pocock, J. G. A. *The Machiavellian Moment*. Princeton: Princeton University Press, 1975. Print.
Rosenblum, Nancy. "Thoreau's Democratic Individualism." *A Political Companion to Henry David Thoreau*. Ed. Jack Turner. Lexington: University Press of Kentucky, 2009. 15–38. Print.
Rosenwald, Lawrence. "The Theory, Practice, and Influence of Thoreau's Civil Disobedience." *Historical Guide to Henry David Thoreau*. Ed. William E. Cain. New York: Oxford University Press, 2000. 153–79. Print.
Shulman, George. *American Prophecy: Race and Redemption in American Political Culture*. Minneapolis: University of Minnesota Press, 2008. Print.
Thoreau, Henry David. "Herald of Freedom." *Reform* 49–58. Print.
\_\_\_\_\_. "Life Without Principle." *Reform* 155–79. Print.
\_\_\_\_\_. "A Plea for Captain John Brown." *Reform* 111–38. Print.
\_\_\_\_\_. "Reform and Reformers." *Reform* 181–98. Print.
\_\_\_\_\_. *Reform Papers*. Ed. Wendell Glick. *Writings of Henry D. Thoreau*. Princeton: Princeton University Press, 1973. Print.
\_\_\_\_\_. "Resistance to Civil Government." *Reform* 63–90. Print.
\_\_\_\_\_. "Slavery in Massachusetts." *Reform* 91–110. Print.
\_\_\_\_\_. *Walden*. Ed. J. Lyndon Shanley. *Writings of Henry D. Thoreau*. Princeton: Princeton University Press, 1971. Print.
\_\_\_\_\_. *A Week on the Concord and Merrimack Rivers*. Eds. Carl F. Hovde, William L. Howarth, and Elizabeth Hall Witherell. Princeton: Princeton University Press, 1980. Print.
\_\_\_\_\_. "Wendell Phillips Before Concord Lyceum." *Reform* 59–62. Print.
Walzer, Michael. *Obligations: Essays on Disobedience, War and Citizenship*. Cambridge: Harvard University Press, 1970. Print.

# Epistle from Prison: Oscar Wilde's *De Profundis* [*Epistola in Carcere et Vinculis*]

JOSEPH J. PORTANOVA

## Summary

The circumstances surrounding Oscar Wilde's imprisonment and the writing of *De Profundis* are perhaps the most singular of any in this volume. Ultimately, he was incarcerated as part of Victorian England's policing of sexual behavior. It would seem, however, that this was a situation he might have avoided had he not first pursued a lawsuit of his own—against the man who then became the accuser in his criminal case. Regardless of the possible hubris that may have brought Wilde to prison, the experience was intense and horrific. *De Profundis*, a letter written to his former lover, covers literary ground from poetry to prayer. It is not hard to point to Wilde's imprisonment as the beginning of the end of his career; and possibly of his life. Given these circumstances, it is ironic that the first complete publication of *De Profundis*—in the early 1960s—was part of a revival of interest in Wilde and his work.—J.W.R.

## Background: Oscar Wilde, Lord Alfred Douglas, and the Marquess of Queensberry

During his American lecture tour of 1882, Oscar Wilde (1854–1900) visited a prison in Lincoln, Nebraska. He remarked, "Poor sad types of humanity.... Little whitewashed cells, so tragically tidy, but with books in them. In one I found a translation of Dante.... Strange and beautiful it seemed to me that the sorrow of a single Florentine in exile should, hundreds of years afterwards, lighten the sorrow of some common prisoner in a modern gaol" (Wilde,

*Letters* 166). Wilde could not have imagined that years later he would be reading Dante in a prison cell and writing his own account of a spiritual journey through a personal Hell.

Wilde's American tour was a triumph (Elmann 158–60). He had left England as a minor poet, and returned as a celebrity. He soon established a reputation in many literary genres: short stories, essays, the novel, and drama. The subject of same-sex desire/homosexuality in his novel *The Picture of Dorian Gray* (1890–1891) raised questions about the author's moral character (M. Holland, *Trial* 39, 77–78, 81, 220–22).[1] This conflation of author and work was not entirely incorrect. In 1891 the thirty-six-year-old Wilde met Lord Alfred ("Bosie") Douglas, the twenty-year-old son of the Marquess of Queensberry. Douglas was captivated by Wilde's wit, Wilde by Douglas' beauty. This relationship placed Wilde in the middle of a family quarrel, and ultimately led to his imprisonment.

John Sholto Douglas, the Ninth Marquess of Queensberry, was best known for establishing the Queensberry rules for fighting. Fighting also was part of his family life. As Ellmann noted, Queensberry was not "a simple brute. In fact, he was a complex one. Insofar as he was brutal, he practiced a rule-bound brutality" (387–88). At first charmed by Wilde, Queensberry became hostile when he heard rumors of the nature of the relationship between Douglas and Wilde. Queensberry was already concerned about his eldest son, Lord Drumlanrig, who was said to be involved in a homosexual relationship with a prominent politician (M. Holland, *Trial* xviii–xix).

While his lawyers would later attempt to portray him as a concerned father, his family situation was hardly ideal. Sibyl, Marchioness of Queensberry and mother of Lord Alfred Douglas, had won a divorce case from the Marquess of Queensberry in 1887 on grounds of adultery. Douglas, who like his father had a temper, was frequently at odds with Queensberry and was not above deliberately baiting him. The more his association with Wilde annoyed his father, the more Douglas flaunted it. Queensberry's middle son Percy tended to side with his Douglas against their father (Ellmann 405, 418; H. Hyde, *Lord* 66). As the judge at Wilde's trial stated in his summation to the jury, "Lord Alfred's family seems to be a house divided against itself" (H. Hyde, *Trials* 263).

The Marquess forbade his son from associating with Wilde—when Douglas refused, Queensberry harassed Wilde. Wilde felt persecuted, and found it difficult to write. In June of 1894 Queensberry appeared at Wilde's home with a prizefighter and threatened the author. Wilde threw Queensberry and his associate out. On February 14th of the following year, Queensberry was prevented from attending the opening of Wilde's *The Importance of Being*

*Earnest*, which the Marquess had planned to disrupt with a basket of vegetables that he intended to throw at the stage. On February 18, 1895, Queensberry left a visiting card at the private gentlemen's club to which Wilde belonged inscribed "To Oscar Wilde posing [as a] somdomite" (In his anger, or out of ignorance, Queensberry misspelled "sodomite").

## *The Libel Trial of Queensberry; The Trials of Oscar Wilde for Gross Indecency*

Disturbed at his home, at the theatre, and at his private club, Wilde decided that legal means were needed to end this persecution by Queensberry. Wilde, with Douglas' encouragement, prosecuted the Marquess for libel. It was an unfortunate and foolish decision, considering Wilde's relationship with not only Douglas but also many other young men. Queensberry's lawyer, Edward Carson, argued that "sodomite" was justified, and questioned Wilde concerning his letters to Douglas and his literary works. Carson prepared to produce in court other young men whom Wilde had entertained. Fearing that their testimony might lead to Wilde's arrest for Gross Indecency, Wilde's lawyer withdrew the libel charge. Queensberry was acquitted (M. Holland, *Trial* 280–283; H. Hyde, *Trials* 144–45).

The Marquess now gave the state prosecutor evidence against Wilde. Gross Indecency was a relatively new crime. Sodomy between males had been punishable in England by death, which in 1861 was changed to ten years to life imprisonment at hard labor. The Criminal Law Amendment Act of 1885 was intended to protect women by raising the age of consent. An addendum (Section 11) to this act also changed the penalties for sexual acts between males. It replaced the term "sodomy" with the vague term "gross indecency," and reduced the penalty to one day to two years' imprisonment, with or without hard labor. Because the term was vague, and punished acts committed in private on the testimony of one of the participants, it became known as the "blackmailers' charter" (Halsall; M. Holland, *Trial* xxxvii).

On the evening of Queensberry's acquittal, Wilde was arrested. From the start of the trial the press was against Wilde and portrayed Queensberry as a concerned father (H. Hyde *Trials* 156). Various young men testified to indecencies Wilde committed with them. Their testimony was somewhat tainted by the fact that most were prostitutes and blackmailers (H. Hyde, *Trials* 174–76, 207–12; Ellmann 475). Wilde denied all charges, and the trial ended with the jury unable to agree. Wilde was released on bail, but the hostility of the public resulted in the end of his book sales and the closing of his plays, cutting off all income. Creditors auctioned off his possessions (H. Hyde *Trials* 164–66, 217–19). Some, including Carson, disputed the necessity of a second trial (H. Hyde *Trials* 223–24). Others claimed that Queensberry had blackmailed the government concerning a homosexual scandal (Gagnier 339, 353–54, 354n6). The evidence against Wilde at his second trial (May 22 to 25, 1895) was the same, but the prosecution was relentless and the judge unsympathetic. After the jury convicted Wilde, Justice Wills shocked the court with his harsh sentence: "It is the worst case I have ever tried ... you ... have been the centre of a circle of extensive corruption of the most hideous kind among young men ... I shall ... pass the severest sentence that the law allows. In my judgment it is totally inadequate" (H. Hyde, *Trials* 239–40, 262–72; Ellmann 474–78). His justification was his "utmost sense of indignation at the horrible charges...." Wills had certainly seen worse crimes, but gave the maximum sentence: two years in solitary confinement at hard labor (H. Hyde, *Trials* 273; Ellmann 477–78).

## *Oscar Wilde in Prison: The Writing of* De Profundis

Wilde's imprisonment destroyed his career, bankrupted him, and quite likely led to his early death. He served his sentence in three prisons: Pentonville (May 25–July 4, 1895; May 18–19, 1897), Wandsworth (July 4–November 20, 1895), and Reading Prison (Reading Gaol/Jail) (November 20, 1895–May 18, 1897). The British prison system at this time was designed to punish rather than to rehabilitate. The food was deliberately inadequate; the labor monotonous. Conversation with other prisoners was forbidden. No personal property was allowed in the ill-ventilated, poorly-lit cells. One letter could be sent and received every three months. Books were limited to religious texts for two months, and afterwards a single book a week from the small prison library. Punishment was frequent and often arbitrary. Insanity was a danger for prisoners in solitary (Gagnier 336–40). The food produced constant diarrhea. The plank beds produced insomnia. Visitors were allowed only four times a year, locked in cages opposite the prisoners three or four feet away (Wilde, *Letters* 1045–49; Hyde, *Trials* 163). A special exception was granted to Constance Wilde, who was allowed to visit her husband in his cell to inform him of his mother's death (Ellmann 492–98).[2]

Wilde's deteriorating condition led to an investigation. As a result, in June of 1895 he was visited by Richard Haldane, a member of parliament who knew him. Haldane obtained permission for him to receive books not available in the prison library, and recommended that Wilde write about his prison experience. His situation again improved after James Nelson became Governor of Reading (summer, 1896) (Wilde, *Letters* 652n1, 653n2, 854, 982–83; Bristow 29; Rose xxxiv–xxxv). Nelson allowed Wilde writing materials, and gave him permission to write a long letter to Douglas. Wilde began the letter in January of 1897, and finished it in March of the same year. This was a book-length epistle, which Wilde called the *"Epistola: In Carcere et Vinculis"* [Letter/Epistle: In Prison and in Chains] (Wilde, *Letters* 683n1, 780–83). His literary executor, Robert Ross, later titled it *De Profundis* [Out of the Depths], from Psalm 130: "Out of the depths I cry to you, O Lord" (Wilde, *Letters* 510–11; Bristow 29). It is by this name that it is known today.

*De Profundis* is a complex and unusual work, in some ways a genre unto itself. Attempts at categorization show how its contradictions have puzzled critics. It has been called a love letter, resistance against prison life, punishment of Douglas, a hymn to suffering, individualism, and Christ, and a rehabilitation. It has also been called a self-serving mythology, an *apologia* and confession, a movement from adoration of Douglas' physical body to adoration of Christ's spiritual body, a refusal to reform, a repudiation of his former life, an affirmation of his former life, and a cynical comedy aimed at deceiving society.[3] That cogent arguments could be made for such apparently contradictory categories, and combinations of these categories, indicates its complexity. That Wilde himself was able to combine apparently contradictory ideas has been noted by scholars. Perhaps classification is too limiting: this essay will illustrate some of its aspects through analysis of selected themes.

## *Lord Alfred Douglas in* De Profundis

First, there is the description of Lord Alfred Douglas. This theme begins the text, and is continued throughout the work. This ranges from what sounds like elevated concern for the welfare of his soul to complaints about his debts (emotional, intellectual, ethical and financial) to Wilde. It is harsh, and often unfair. Douglas is described as shallow, utterly incapable of feeling for others (Wilde, *Letters* 687). His literary and intellectual accomplishments are belittled (Wilde, *Letters* 685, 692–93, 702–03). His scenes and abusive letters make it impossible for Wilde to write. Wilde attempts to leave him about every three months, but is drawn back by letters, tears and threats of suicide (Wilde, *Letters* 691–92, 695, 700–01).[4] Financial debts are relentlessly catalogued, including estimates of weekly and daily expenses (Wilde, *Letters* 688–89, 703–04, 713, 767–68, 775). Douglas consumes Wilde's life: "Having made your own of my genius, my will-power, and my fortune, you required, in the blindness of an inexhaustible greed, my entire existence" (Wilde, *Letters* 690). He is blamed for Wilde's conviction, and for his bankruptcy (Wilde, *Letters* 690–91, 702–04, 775–76).

Douglas treats the imprisoned Wilde horribly. Others offer condolences to Wilde for his mother's death, but Douglas does not write. When Wilde does hear about him, it is that he is intending to publish Wilde's private letters. But he sends no more letters to Wilde. The letter begins with a complaint about Douglas' silence. Wilde repeats this towards the end of the work, suggesting that Douglas reply with a letter of his own and including the instructions "Address the envelope to 'The Governor, H.M. Prison, Reading'" (Wilde, *Letters* 778). This is written by a disappointed lover, and while some accusations are fair many are distorted or untrue. Douglas alone did not bankrupt Wilde, nor was he responsible for Wilde's relations with other young men. He had been discouraged by the Governor from communicating with Wilde, which explains some of Douglas' silence (Wilde, *Letters* 684n1).

Wilde's *De Profundis* goes beyond recrimination and blame to produce an autobiography of his tragedy. There are elements in the portrait of Douglas that make him a sinister figure, if not an anti–Christ. If Wilde represents the world of art and intellect, Douglas is flesh and appetite: "Your interests were merely in your meals and moods. Your desires were simply for ... ordinary or less ordinary pleasures" (Wilde, *Letters* 687). Douglas' lack of responsibility is called his "creed" (Wilde, *Letters* 764–65). Douglas and Queensberry are like the guards who cast dice for Christ's garments: "In your hideous game of hate together, you had both thrown dice for my soul" (Wilde, *Letters* 709). His attempt to publish Wilde's letters is called "a sacrilege" (Wilde, *Letters* 717).

Wilde recalls the doxology ("Through Him, with Him, in Him") of the Christian mass in describing Douglas' role in his imprisonment: "It was through you, for you, and by you that I was there" (Wilde, *Letters* 710). He echoes the language of the Confessional ("in what I have done and what I have failed to do"): "By your actions and by your silence, by what you have done and by what you have left undone, you have made every day of my long imprisonment still more difficult" (Wilde, *Letters* 728). Douglas finally is a false Christ, who transubstantiates bread and water but not into body and blood: "The very bread and water of prison fare you have by your conduct changed. You have rendered the one bitter and the other brackish to me. The sorrow you should have shared you have doubled, the pain you should have sought to lighten you have quickened to anguish" (Wilde, *Letters* 728). Douglas is portrayed as the opposite of Christ, who was the consoling Paraclete (Comforter).

After such a litany of evil, one would think that Wilde would reject Douglas. Yet Wilde cannot stop thinking about him, and while the thoughts are negative they are focused upon Douglas: "the memory of our friendship is the shadow that walks with me here: that seems never to leave me: ... it follows me into the prison-yard and makes me talk to myself as I tramp round: each detail that accompanied each dreadful moment I am forced to recall" (Wilde, *Letters* 706). One suspects, in spite of the language used, that not all the memories Wilde relived were negative or even chaste. He describes the letter in highly emotional terms: "You must take it as it stands, blotted in many places with tears, in some with the signs of passion or pain, and make it out as best you can, blots, corrections and all" (Wilde, *Letters* 770). Wilde reminds Douglas that their relationship is the letter's main subject: "I have now written, and at great length, to you in order that you should realise what you were to me before my imprisonment, during those three years' fatal friendship: what you have been to me during my imprisonment ... and what I hope to be to myself and to others when my imprisonment is over" (Wilde, *Letters* 769–70). He suggests that Douglas reflect on his actions: "I have had to look at my past face to face. Look at your past face to face. Sit down quietly and consider it" (Wilde, *Letters* 775). This implies a kind of sharing between them: as Wilde contemplates his past in his cell, Douglas will sit quietly and consider his past. The shared past will unite them in isolation and contemplation.

This reunion will not only be spiritual. Wilde discusses how they will meet when he is released (Wilde, *Letters* 776). The setting will be a romantic one of his choosing: "when the June roses are in all their wanton opulence, I will ... meet you in some quiet foreign town like Bruges, whose grey houses and green canals and cool still ways had a charm for me, years ago" (Wilde, *Letters* 778). To meet, both must change their names, as the friends in Wilde's *The Importance of Being Earnest* change theirs: "For the moment you will have to change your name ... just as *my* name ... will have to be abandoned" (Wilde, *Letters* 778). In the play, the name change was through baptism and for love. Wilde mentions sorrow and humility in their meeting, but also love: "there is a ... chasm between us now, the chasm of Sorrow: but to Humility there is nothing that is impossible, and to Love all things are easy" (Wilde, *Letters* 778). Wilde ends his letter with a complaint about Douglas' silence, yet again speaks of the power of love. "I waited month after month to hear from you. Even if I had ... shut the doors against you, you should have remembered that no one can possibly shut the doors against Love for ever.... There is no prison in any world into which Love cannot force an entrance" (Wilde, *Letters* 778–79). Wilde has come full circle, and suggests that their friendship may begin again: "Perhaps we have yet to know each other" (Wilde, *Letters* 779). Wilde offers, finally, "to teach" Douglas "something much more wonderful, the meaning of Sorrow, and its beauty" (Wilde, *Letters* 780). The letter ends with an invitation rather than a rejection.

## *Autobiography, Fantasy and Tragedy*

Wilde's description of his own life and career also has an element of fantasy. As Gagnier noted, this is at least in part a prisoner's reconstruction of a past in opposition to prison life (335, 341, 349). Wilde says, "I had genius, a distinguished name, high social position, brilliancy ... I made art a philosophy, and philosophy an art ... there was nothing I said or did that did not make people wonder: ... whatever I touched I made beautiful in a new mode of beauty: ... I awoke the imagination of my century so that it created myth and legend around me: I summed up all systems in a phrase, and all existence in an epigram" (Wilde, *Letters* 729). His ruin seems deliberate: "Tired of being on the heights I deliberately went to the depths in the search for new sensations. What the paradox was to me in the sphere of thought, perversity became to me in the sphere of passion" (Wilde, *Letters* 730). Even his fall brings with it a kind of greatness: "I have come ... from a sort of eternity of fame to a sort of eternity of infamy" and "in the lowest mire of Malebolge I sit between Gilles de Retz and the Marquis de Sade" (Wilde, *Letters* 691, 734).[5]

Wilde's opinion of his "crime" is interesting. Although "perversity" is part of his downfall, his reason tells him "the laws under which I am convicted are wrong and unjust laws, and the system under which I have suffered a wrong and unjust system" (Wilde, *Letters* 732). He describes his relations with young men in a heroic (if Freudian) manner:

> They ... were delightfully suggestive and stimulating. It was like feasting with panthers. The danger was half the excitement. I used to feel as the snake-charmer must feel when he lures the cobra to stir ... and makes it spread its hood at his bidding, and sway to and fro in the air.... They were to me the brightest of gilded snakes. Their poison was part of their perfection.... To entertain them was an astounding adventure. Dumas *père*, Cellini, Goya, Edgar Allan Poe, or Baudelaire, would have done just the same [Wilde, *Letters* 758–59].

What, then, was he guilty of? Only this: "At the end I had to come forward, on your behalf, as the champion of Respectability in conduct, of Puritanism, in life, and of Morality in Art. *Voilà où mènent les mauvais chemins!* [See where the bad roads lead]" (Wilde, *Letters* 758–59). Homosexuality is not to blame for his downfall. For Wilde, the road to respectability and morality is the road to ruin.

He does not spare the society that put him in prison: when he turned to its laws for protection against Queensberry society turned its laws against Wilde. He has no use for people's lack of imagination: "People point to Reading Gaol, and say, 'There is where the artistic life leads a man.' Well, it might lead one to worse places. The more mechanical people ... always know where they are going, and go there.... A man whose desire is to be ... a Member of Parliament, or a successful grocer, or a ... solicitor, or a judge, or something equally tedious, invariably succeeds in being what he wants to be. That is his punishment" (Wilde, *Letters* 753). Society places people in prison and then abandons them upon their release. Wilde contrasts the kindness of the poor, for whom prison is an occasion for sympathy, with the cruelty of his own class, which makes a former prisoner a pariah (Wilde, *Letters* 728).

## *Prison, Revelation and Redemption*

The prison itself becomes a character as well as a setting in Wilde's narrative. It creates its own reality, and confirms existence: for prisoners "Suffering ... is the means by which we exist, because it is the only means by which we become conscious of existing; and the remembrance of suffering in the past is necessary to us as the warrant, the evidence, of our continued identity" (Wilde, *Letters* 696). As Gagnier has noted (335, 341–42) this is part of a prisoner's necessary reconstruction of the world outside. For Wilde, memory is re-creation: "There is nothing that happened in those ill-starred years that I cannot recreate in that chamber of the brain which is set apart for grief or for despair: every strained note of your voice, every twitch and gesture of your nervous hands, every bitter word, every poisonous phrase comes back to me" (Wilde, *Letters* 706). That the re-creation is not entirely true is immaterial: memory, justification, and literary effect are one. In this passage, Wilde recalls an earlier description of Queensberry's "twitching hands"; while his insistent memory of Douglas recalls an earlier vision of the Marquess' face that haunted Wilde in court (Wilde, *Letters* 758). Time itself is without meaning: it moves in circles like the useless exercise in the prison yard. The world moves on, but for the prisoner the past is the present:

> With us time itself does not progress. It revolves. It seems to circle round one centre of pain.... Outside, the day may be blue and gold, but the light that creeps down through the thickly-muffled glass of the small iron-barred window beneath which one sits is grey.... It is always twilight in one's cell, as it is always midnight in one's heart. And in the sphere of thought, no less than in the sphere of time, motion is no more. The thing that you personally have long ago forgotten ... is happening to me now, and will happen to me again tomorrow [Wilde, *Letters* 720].

This drives Wilde to despair: at Wandsworth he wants to die, and at Reading plans to commit suicide on the day of his release (Wilde, *Letters* 735).

Then there is a change, which Wilde ascribes to his spiritual conversion: "The plank-bed, the loathsome food, the hard ropes shredded into oakum till one's fingertips grow dull with pain ... the silence, the solitude, the shame.... There is not a single degradation of the body which I must not try and make into a spiritualising of the soul" (Wilde, *Letters* 732). This also follows an improvement in conditions by Governor Nelson. Regulations are still observed, but the spirit behind them has changed. Wilde begins to appreciate kindnesses he has received. When he is allowed white bread to eat for the first time, the experience is Eucharistic: "I carefully eat whatever crumbs may be left on my tin plate, or have fallen on the rough towel that one uses as a cloth ... and do so not from hunger ... but simply in order that nothing should be wasted of what is given to me. So one should look on love" (Wilde, *Letters* 749). Prison has become revelation.

What exactly the revelation consists of is the subject of debate. This being Wilde, it is hard to pin down what exactly he is talking about: Greek paganism, Christianity, Nature, or some aesthetic combination of them all. The first hint of Wilde's redemption through nature comes with Robert Ross' act of kindness at the bankruptcy court. Here, as Wilde was transferred from prison to the Court past a mocking crowd, Ross raised his hat to Wilde in a silent salute. The memory of this kindness "unsealed ... the wells of pity, made the desert blossom like a rose, and brought me out of the bitterness of lonely exile into harmony with the wounded, broken and great heart of the world" (Wilde, *Letters* 723). Wilde's spiritual journey is described in natural terms: "I have hills far steeper to climb, valleys much darker to pass through" (Wilde, *Letters* 731–32). He looks forward to the spring of his release from prison, when lilac and laburnum will be in bloom (Wilde, *Letters* 777). Nature will bring healing and refuge:

> Society, as we have constituted it, will have no place for me ... but Nature, whose sweet rains fall on unjust and just alike, will have clefts in the rocks where I may hide, and secret valleys in whose silence I may weep undisturbed. She will hang the night with stars so that I may walk abroad in the darkness without stumbling, and send the wind over my footprints so that none may track me to my hurt: she will cleanse me in great waters, and with bitter herbs make me whole [Wilde, *Letters* 777–78].

For Wilde those who understood nature best were the Greeks, who "...loved the trees for the shadow that they cast, and the forest for its silence at noon" (Wilde, *Letters* 776–77). The influence of his Classical education is clear, as he refers to Euripides, Aristotle, Socrates, Plato, Aeschylus, and Sophocles (Wilde, *Letters* 688, 690, 702, 740, 742–43, 745–48, 752, 776). He speaks of the "pomp of the Latin line or the richer music of the vowelled Greek," and quotes Greek directly on several occasions (Wilde, *Letters* 685, 688, 776).

His repeated mention of "the gods" seems like paganism. They have given Wilde his genius and career; they influence his relationship with Douglas and mock traditional ideas of wisdom (Wilde, *Letters* 685, 701, 729, 732). He mentions Apollo and other deities by name more often than he names Christian saints. Nonetheless, he finds the Greek deities too cruel: "The curved brow of Apollo was like the sun's disc crescent over a hill at dawn, and his feet were as the wings of the morning, but he himself had been cruel to Marsyas and had made Niobe childless" (Wilde, *Letters* 746). Most importantly, the Greeks did not believe that the past could be changed—Wilde believed that repentance was "the means by which one alters one's past" (Wilde, *Letters* 752). Wilde rejects classical Paganism, but it is not clear what he would replace it with: "The faith that others give to what is unseen, I give to what one can touch, and look at ... I feel as if I would like to found an order for those who cannot believe: The Confraternity of the Fatherless one might call it, where on an altar, on which no taper burned, a priest, in whose heart peace had no dwelling, might celebrate with unblessed bread and a chalice empty of wine" (Wilde, *Letters* 732).

The image of Christ is complex in *De Profundis*, and is closely linked to the image of Wilde himself. This does not necessarily make it less sincere as a religious meditation and text, but it does raise some questions concerning the connection between the Christ of *De Profundis* and Christianity. Wilde states that except for St. Francis of Assisi, there have been no Christians since Christ (Wilde, *Letters* 753). Wilde identifies Christ's opponents as Philistines, whom he sees as the Jews and the British: "In their heavy inaccessibility to ideas, their dull respectability, their tedious orthodoxy, their worship of vulgar success, their entire preoccupation with the gross materialistic side of life, and their ridiculous estimate of themselves and their importance, the Jew of Jerusalem in Christ's day was the exact counterpart of the British Philistine of our own" (Wilde, *Letters* 751). Wilde's is a Hellenized, not a Jewish, Christ. He claims that the Greek gospels are the exact words of Christ, who "like the Irish peasants of our day," was "bilingual, and ... Greek was the ordinary language ... all over Palestine.... Charmides might have listened to him, and Socrates reasoned with him, and Plato understood him" (Wilde, *Letters* 748–49). Wilde sees in the responses of the servitor at Mass "the ultimate survival of the Greek chorus" (Wilde, *Letters* 743). Christ fulfills and surpasses the ancient Greek ideas: his personality is "infinitely greater than that any made by myth or legend" (Wilde, *Letters* 746). Wilde's Christ is entirely mortal. His miracles are attributed not to the power of God, but to the "charm of his personality," so that "his mere presence could bring peace to souls in anguish ... and men whose dull unimaginative lives had been but a mode of death rose as it were from the grave when he called them" (Wilde, *Letters* 743).

Above all, the Christ of *De Profundis* is an individualist, a poet and an artist (Wilde, *Letters* 740). His life is a poem that surpasses Greek tragedy, his suffering a theme for art beyond compare (Wilde, *Letters* 742, 746). Wilde sees himself, the romantic, in Jesus: "I see in Christ not merely the essentials of the supreme romantic type, but all the accidents, the wilfulnesses even, of the romantic temperament also. He was the first person who ever said to people that they should live 'flower-like' lives" (Wilde, *Letters* 750). Wilde had said earlier in the letter that he was "made for exceptions, not for laws"; he similarly describes Christ: "For him there were no laws: there were exceptions merely" (Wilde, *Letters* 732, 751). Wilde provides a voice for those in prison, just as Christ is a voice for those "who are dumb under oppression and 'whose silence is heard only of God'" (Wilde, *Letters* 746).[6] Christ, like Wilde, goes beyond standards of morality. He is not interested in reforming people, or even relieving suffering. He does not wish to "turn an interesting thief into a tedious honest man.... But in a manner not yet understood of the world he regarded sin and suffering as being in themselves beautiful, holy things, and modes of perfection" (Wilde, *Letters* 752).

This Wildean Christ is described in terms that combine the themes of nature, the Greeks, the artist, and Wilde himself. He speaks the language of Plato and Socrates, yet unlike the Greeks knows that a sinner can change the past through repentance—something the Olympian gods themselves could not do (Wilde, *Letters* 749, 752). His miracles seem "as exquisite as the coming of Spring, and quite as natural" (Wilde, *Letters* 743). Wilde and Christ know humility, yet preach the virtues of nature and of Hellenism. As an artist and an individualist, Christ realizes, as Wilde does, that "Things, also, are in their essence what we choose to make them.... 'Where others,' says Blake, 'see but the Dawn coming over the hill, I see the sons of God shouting for joy'" (Wilde, *Letters* 779).[7] Ultimately, Wilde saves himself: or rather Christ saves Wilde, because Wilde saves Wilde.

## *Wilde After Prison;* De Profundis *After Wilde*

While he was writing *De Profundis*, Wilde referred to it as "the most important letter of my life, as it will deal ultimately with my future mental attitude towards life, with the way in which I desire to meet the world again" (Wilde, *Letters* 678). He was not allowed to send it to Douglas from prison, but the prison authorities gave it to Wilde upon his release. Wilde then gave

Ross the manuscript and told him to have two typed copies made before sending Douglas the original. Wilde's description (written in prison) mixes humor with Roman Catholic religious ceremony:

> The lady type-writer might be fed through a lattice in the door like the Cardinals when they elect a Pope, till she comes out on the balcony and can say to the world "*Habet Mundus Epistolam*" [The World Has an Epistle]; for indeed it is an Encyclical Letter, and as the Bulls of the Holy Father are named from their opening words, it may be spoken of as the "*Epistola: In Carcere et Vinculis*" [Epistle: In Prison and in Chains] [Wilde, *Letters* 782].

Ross ultimately sent a typed copy to Douglas and kept the original. As for Wilde, he does not mention *De Profundis* in his letters after his release from prison. He and Douglas reunited, but were soon separated: by legal threats from both families, by financial difficulties, and perhaps by the inability to reconstruct the past (Wilde, *Letters* 880, 898, 933n1). Wilde's imitation of Christ did not, in later life, extend to poverty: "Like dear St. Francis of Assisi, I am wedded to Poverty: but in my case the marriage is not a success: ... I see no beauty in her hunger and her rags" (Wilde, *Letters* 1145). He remained plagued with financial worries until his death.

Wilde did not repent of his love for Douglas, or for that matter his love of other young men: "A patriot put into prison for loving his country loves his country, and a poet in prison for loving boys loves boys. To have altered my life would have been to admit that Uranian love [homosexuality] is ignoble. I hold it to be noble—more noble than other forms" (Wilde, *Letters* 1019, 1019n3).[8] He continued to have affairs with young men after his release from prison. If society thought prison would teach him a lesson, it was mistaken: "the world is angry because their punishment has had no effect. They wished ... to say 'We have done a capital thing for Oscar Wilde: by putting him in prison we have put a stop to his friendship with Alfred Douglas and all that that implies.' But now they find that they ... did not influence me, they simply ruined me, so they are furious" (Wilde, *Letters* 993). Wilde wrote letters advocating prison reform, and finished *The Ballad of Reading Gaol*, his last literary work. Apparently he never returned to *De Profundis*.

Wilde died in 1900, possibly of cerebral meningitis (the cause of death is still a matter of debate). Ross published selections from the work in 1905, adding more excerpts in 1908. These deleted any references to Douglas, or any indication that it was addressed to him. When Ross and Douglas became enemies (largely over Ross' position as Wilde's literary executor) Ross donated the manuscript to the British Museum with the condition that it remain sealed until 1960 (Wilde, *Letters* 683n1; H. Hyde, *Lord* 150, 183; M. Hyde 211–13). The public at the time saw *De Profundis* primarily as a religious text, from the passages published. The work's popularity was the beginning of the revival of interest in Wilde, and of the rehabilitation of his reputation as a writer— based on an incomplete edition that disguised the nature of his work, an irony he might have appreciated (H. Hyde, *Trials* 315–16; V. Holland 270).

In 1907 Ross showed the typed copy to Wilde's son Vyvyan Holland, who when he read the full text "began to appreciate it at its true value and to understand what an amazing piece of work it is" (179). The public would not know of the complete work until 1913, when Douglas unsuccessfully sued Arthur Ransome and his publisher for libel. Ransome had written *Oscar Wilde: A Critical Study*, which suggested that Douglas was to blame for Wilde's imprisonment, and that he deserted him after this. *De Profundis* was subpoenaed as evidence (H. Hyde, *Lord* 186). Douglas protested that Ross had deceived him. He was unaware of "any connection between the letter you sent me in 1897 (which I destroyed after first reading the first half dozen lines) and the book" (H. Hyde, *Lord* 183). This contrasts with his statements that he never received *De Profundis*. His claim that "Wilde, after his release from prison, only once referred to the letter ... and on that occasion he implored me to forgive him for having written it" is unconfirmed by other evidence and seems unlikely (H. Hyde, *Lord* 183).

The public did not see the complete text of *De Profundis* until 1949, when Vyvyan Holland published Ross' typed copy. When the manuscript was opened in 1960, Wilde's work was first published exactly as he had written it (M. Hyde 213). If not for Wilde's and Ross' foresight *De Profundis* might not have survived at all. The text has created much critical controversy, but it illuminates Wilde's thought and character as perhaps no other of his works does. As a meditation on life, on prison, and on the confinement society imposes upon the artist, it is an eloquent and important document. It criticizes the legal and social persecution of love between men, "the love that dare not speak its name" (H. Hyde, *Trials* 200–01).[9] As a love letter, and a synthesis of Wilde's beliefs (and doubts) it is unique. The work, like Wilde, escapes simple definitions: it combines his suffering, homosexuality, Christianity, Paganism, humor and wit, with a description of his tempestuous relationship with Douglas. *De Profundis* may have been a letter written *in Carcere et Vinculis* (in prison and in chains), but through it Wilde transcended the bonds of scandal and imprisonment to create a powerful and original meditation on life, love, religion, and same-sex desire.

## Notes

1. For the chronology of Wilde's life, see Rose xiv–xxxix.
2. Constance changed the family name to "Holland" in 1895. Wilde's son Vyvyan wrote a memoir of his father, while Wilde's grandson Merlin has edited his grandfather's works.

3. Love letter: Elmann 515; resistance of prison, punishment of Douglas, hymn of praise to suffering, individualism, and Christ, rehabilitation, mythology: Gagnier 335, 341–47, 349; *apologia*, confession, adoration of Christ: Roden, *Same-Sex* 125–26, 145–47; refusal to change, affirmation of former life, cynical comedy: O'Malley176–69 (quoting George Bernard Shaw, Max Beerbohm, and Ellis Hanson).

4. Gagnier notes that the three-month intervals are influenced by the prison schedule (343).

5. In Dante, *Inferno* XVIII–XXX Malebolge is the circle in Hell for those guilty of Fraud. Gilles de Retz (Rais) was condemned for sodomy and murder of children; De Sade was imprisoned for sexual crimes. Both lived long after Dante's death so Wilde's choice of them is a personal one. The lowest depth or tenth bolgia of Malebolge contains notorious liars. Wilde may have in mind one of these, Potiphar's Wife, who attempted to seduce Joseph and then falsely accused him of attempted rape: Genesis: 39.

6. Wilde quotes himself (*Letters* 742) as if quoting from scripture.

7. This is Wilde's version of William Blake's *A Vision of the Last Judgment*; inflected by Job 38:7 (*Letters*, 779n3).

8. Wilde uses the term for homosexuality invented by the sexologist Karl Ulrichs, derived from the Greek "ouranos" (heaven) from Plato's *Symposium*. Uranian, or "heavenly" love was used as a replacement for criminalizing and derogatory terms such as "sodomy."

9. This phrase is from Lord Alfred Douglas' poem "Two Loves." Wilde offered a spirited defense of "the love that dare not speak its name" at his first trial for Gross Indecency. He defined it as "a great affection of an elder for a younger man as there was between David and Jonathan, such as Plato made the very basis of his philosophy, and such as you find in the sonnets of Michelangelo and Shakespeare. It is that deep, spiritual affection that is as pure as it is perfect.... It is pure, it is fine, it is the noblest form of affection. There is nothing unnatural about it. It is intellectual" (H. Hyde, *Trials* 200–01). This was, in typical Wilde fashion, capable of several interpretations. He was on trial for Gross Indecency, a vague term for intimacy between males. His defense of "the love that dare not speak its name" was also vague, perhaps deliberately so. This form of love is described by Wilde as "pure and intellectual" but his love for Douglas was not "pure" in the sense of chaste, and his relationships with the various young men of his acquaintance (including some male prostitutes) was often neither pure nor intellectual. At the trial, the audience reaction was equally ambiguous: "applause ... mingled with some hisses" (H. Hyde, *Trials* 201).

## Works Cited

Bristow, Joseph. "Biographies: Oscar Wilde—The Man, the Life, the Legend." *Palgrave Advances in Oscar Wilde Studies*. Ed. Frederick Roden. New York: Palgrave Macmillan, 2004. 6–35. Print.
Ellmann, Richard. *Oscar Wilde*. New York: Alfred A. Knopf, 1988. Print.
Gagnier, Regenia. "*De Profundis* as *Epistola: In Carcere et Vinculis*: A Materialist Reading of Oscar Wilde's Autobiography." *Criticism* 26.4 (1984): 335–54. Print.
Halsall, Paul. "The Law in England, 1290–1885." *People with a History*. 1997. Web. 11 Aug. 2011.
Holland, Merlin. *The Real Trial of Oscar Wilde*. New York: HarperCollins, 2003. Print.
Holland, Vyvyan. *Son of Oscar Wilde*. London: Robinson, 1999. Print.
Hyde, Harford Montgomery. *Lord Alfred Douglas*. New York: Dodd, Mead, 1985. Print.
\_\_\_\_\_. *The Trials of Oscar Wilde*. New York: Dover, 1973. Print.
Hyde, Mary. *Bernard Shaw and Alfred Douglas: A Correspondence*. New Haven: Ticknor & Fields, 1982. Print.
O'Malley, Patrick. "Religion." *Palgrave Advances in Oscar Wilde Studies*. Ed. Frederick Roden. New York: Palgrave Macmillan, 2004. 167–88. Print.

Roden, Frederick. *Palgrave Advances in Oscar Wilde Studies*. New York: Palgrave Macmillan, 2004. Print.

_____. *Same-Sex Desire in Victorian Religious Culture*. New York: Palgrave Macmillan, 2002. Print.

Rose, David. "Chronology." *Palgrave Advances in Oscar Wilde Studies*. Ed. Frederick Roden. New York: Palgrave Macmillan, 2004. xiv–xxxix. Print.

Wilde, Oscar. *The Complete Letters of Oscar Wilde*. Ed. Merlin Holland and Rupert Hart-Davis. New York: Henry Holt, 2000. Print.

_____. *Complete Works of Oscar* Wilde. New York: HarperCollins, 2008. Print.

# Bertrand Russell, World War I and Analytic Philosophy

### Phil Washburn

## Summary

On the face of it, Bertrand Russell would seem the least likely person to have been incarcerated for political radicalism. But he questioned one of the state's most fundamental powers: the ability to wage war. Given Russell's respected position, this was a serious challenge to the authority of the British government. While *Introduction to Mathematical Philosophy*, written during his imprisonment, does not directly deal with any issues of war or politics, it demonstrated Russell's fearless commitment to finding the truth, regardless of what others may think. It laid the basis for a fundamentally new understanding of mathematics and philosophy. Russell's willingness to challenge accepted conventions in philosophy was integral to his critique of World War I. There are many ways to question the authority of the state, and in a period of raw passions and war propaganda on all sides, patiently investigating the truth was itself a radical act. Although Russell was not an absolute pacifist, he remained an ardent political activist throughout his life, campaigning against war and, later, nuclear weapons.—J.W.R.

## Introduction

On February 9, 1918, almost four years into World War I, Bertrand Russell stood before an angry judge in the Bow Street Magistrate's Court in London. In particular, he had written an editorial in which he said that if American troops were stationed in Great Britain, they would be used to break up strikes by organized labor, as they had done in the United States. Normally expressing opinions would not be a crime in Great Britain. But the government had been stung too often by Russell's vigorous criticisms of it. He was prepared to defend himself at his trial but the judge cut him off, saying his offense was "a very despicable one" (Moorehead 280). He was found guilty and sentenced to six months in prison.

Sending a protester or war resister to jail was not unusual. "About 16,000 men either appeared before a tribunal or absolutely refused to join the war machine," according to Caroline Moorehead (Moorehead 294). The war had become increasingly unpopular through the years, as the number of casualties climbed far beyond anyone's expectations.

On the other hand, sending Bertrand Russell to jail was surprising. In 1918 Russell, 45, was famous all over the world as a philosopher and co-author (with Alfred N. Whitehead) of *Principia Mathematica*, an influential, three-volume treatise on the nature of mathematics and philosophy. He had been invited to teach at Harvard in 1914 and toured the United States that spring giving lectures. In addition to his stature as a scholar, he was a member of one of the most esteemed, aristocratic families in Great Britain. His grandfather was Lord John Russell, twice prime minister under Queen Victoria, and architect of the democratizing Reform Bill of 1832. When Russell's elder brother died in 1931, he became third Earl Russell, i.e., Lord Russell, and took his seat in the House of Lords. He was not an average war resister.

Russell had opposed the war from the beginning in August 1914, and his opposition was fierce, passionate, and energetic. His weapon was his remarkable ability to explain complex ideas clearly in language everyone could understand, and he wielded it effectively in numerous speeches, articles, letters, and editorials. His base of operations during 1916 and 1917 was the No Conscription Fellowship (NCF), an organization of conscientious objectors and pacifists. Besides speaking and writing, editing the organization's weekly *Tribunal*, and holding together the diverse, committed idealists who refused to fight, his campaign included visiting conscientious objectors in jail. Conditions were bad. Inedible food, uncomfortable, cold cells, forced labor, loneliness, and boredom combined to beat down and weaken the young men. Russell tried to encourage them. He needed all of his considerable patience and spirit to hold the group together. His efforts culminated in 1918 when he himself was sent to prison (although under better conditions).

Russell served about five months of his six-month term in the prison at Brixton, and was released early for good behavior. (Other protestors and conscientious objectors served longer terms.) While in prison he wrote *Introduction to Mathematical Philosophy*, which, together with his other works, helped create analytic philosophy, the dominant mode of philosophy in Great Britain and the United States for the remainder of the century. Analytic philosophy is different from the prevalent schools of thought on the Continent, such as phenomenology, existentialism, Marxism, and postmodernism. One writer says, "What unifies all analytic philosophers is their agreement concerning the central task of philosophy," which is "to clarify the meaning of language" (Stumpf 430). Or as Russell says, "the aim of analysis is to make sure that every statement represents an adequate picture of the reality, of the facts, of the world" (Stumpf 434). It is our language itself that causes confusion over philosophical issues, and clarifying or improving our language will help us understand these deep problems. We will examine Russell's particular brand of analytic philosophy below.

After the war Russell continued writing both technical and popular books on an astonishing range of topics. In 1950 he was awarded the Nobel Prize for Literature "in recognition," the committee said, "of his varied and significant writings in which he champions humanitarian ideals and freedom of thought." During the 1950s and 1960s (when he was in his 80s and 90s) he spoke at rallies against the arms race, nuclear weapons, and the American involvement in Vietnam.[1]

How is Russell's prison book related to his opposition to the war? *Introduction to Mathematical Philosophy* is about as far from political activism as one can get. It's a highly abstract discussion of the nature of mathematics. It isn't related to war and peace, or policies, or even people. It's not even about the physical world. In one way, then, we can think of *Introduction to Mathematical Philosophy* as a complete about-face, a flight from the emotional, messy work of persuasion and advocacy into a realm of impersonal, eternal concepts and pure thought. Russell himself spoke of his prison experience as a kind of rest, and his book as a refreshing return to his original vocation of philosophy (Monk 521).

But we can also look at his prison book in a different way. I don't think Russell's personality consisted of two completely different and separated parts—political activism and abstract philosophy. Instead, if we consider his whole career, I think we can see both the energetic opposition to the war and the highly technical theories in the *Introduction to Mathematical Philosophy* as expressions of one basic temperament. Russell was passionately, intensely devoted to the truth, to seeing things and understanding them as they really are. He campaigned tirelessly against Britain's war policies because he believed they were mistaken and wrong. In prison, his intense concentration on the foundations of mathematics reveals the same extraordinary drive to question the popular, superficial answers and find a deeper truth. It's true that sitting alone in a jail cell is very different from organizing meetings and distributing pamphlets on the street, which he had done for the NCF. But the energy devoted to the book, the faith in one's work, the attention to detail, the perseverance in the face of difficulties, are the same.

Russell's activism and his philosophical writing are similar in another way as well. In both he exhibited tremendous courage. When he criticized Britain's war effort, he faced vehement condemnation by virtually his whole society. Cambridge University fired him, close friends denounced him, the government imprisoned him. But he held to his convictions. *Introduction to Mathematical Philosophy* was also a kind of revolt against conventional assumptions in the field of philosophy. Together with G.E. Moore, Russell devised methods and produced results that were completely different from everything they had been taught by the philosophy dons at Cambridge in the 1890s. Many in the philosophy establishment ridiculed the new "analytic philosophy" as trivial wordplay (Barrett 299–300). In 1912 Russell wrote a book in the new style with the comprehensive title *The Problems of Philosophy*. George Santayana, the pragmatist philosopher at Harvard, said that a better title would have been "The Problems which Moore and I Have Been Agitating Recently" (Clark, *The Life of Bertrand Russell*, 200). But Russell was convinced that his approach had promise, and he didn't let the opposition frighten him.

In the next section of this essay I will describe Russell's opposition to the war and the difficulties he faced, culminating in his imprisonment. Then I will explain how *Introduction to Mathematical Philosophy* influenced the growth of analytic philosophy.

## *Russell and the War*

World War I began when Serbian nationalist Gavrilo Princip assassinated Archduke Ferdinand, heir to the throne of the Austro-Hungarian empire on June 28, 1914. The event set off a chain reaction, because of different nations' military alliances with each other. Austria declared war on Serbia; Serbia's ally Russia declared war on Austria; Austria's ally Germany declared war on Russia; Russia's ally France declared war on Germany.

Russell thought the conflict was sheer lunacy, mass slaughter for no reason. Nations went to war in 1914 not to defend lives or property, but for "national pride," he said.[2] The militaries insisted they could not break their agreements. So the civilian governments had to generate public support for war by creating lurid propaganda about "the enemy." Russell naively believed that when Great Britain (France's ally) declared war, most English people would protest. He was shocked when crowds poured into the streets to support the declaration (Monk 368).

In that situation, some people—probably most people—would join the crowds, and find a rationalization for doing so. As Russell wrote in a letter, "it is so hard not to think one *must* be wrong when everyone is against one." (Moorehead, 207) But Russell never wavered, even when his closest friends supported the war. Russell was very close to his co-author of *Principia*, Alfred North Whitehead, with whom he had worked for six years, and who had been his tutor at Cambridge. He was deeply depressed, therefore, when Whitehead told him conscientious objectors were "contemptible," and that Whitehead's son would volunteer (the young man was killed in March 1918). Russell's student and protégé, Ludwig Wittgenstein (who was from Vienna), joined the Austrian army at the beginning of the war.

The pressure on Russell increased as the war intensified. In May 1915, the Germans used two new technological wonders. Their submarines sank the *Lusitania*, a civilian ocean liner, in order to intimidate and cripple Allied shipping (and because they suspected it was carrying munitions). And at Ypres in Belgium, they used poison gas for the first time to kill and maim enemy soldiers. The public was outraged at the Germans but also at any British citizens who did not support the war. Ronald Clark says, "As the fighting went on and casualty lists showed that a confined European war had turned into a national blood-letting, Russell became one of the most hated men in Britain" (Clark, *Bertrand Russell and His World* 51).

To Russell, the atrocities only confirmed his belief that the war was madness, and he redoubled his attempts to bring people back to sanity. He wrote anonymous pamphlets for the No Conscription Fellowship defending the conscientious objectors who had been jailed, unjustly, he believed. When some NCF members were arrested in 1916 for distributing one of his pamphlets, he wrote to the London *Times* revealing his authorship and saying he should be the one arrested. (Clark, *The Life of Bertrand Russell* 283). The government agreed. In March he was convicted of "undermining the war effort" and fined 100 pounds. He refused to pay. The government confiscated the furniture and books from his rooms at Cambridge University, where he taught, and auctioned them to raise the 100 pounds. Some of Russell's friends went to the auction, bought the items, and returned them to him.

Russell's criminal conviction created two more sources of pressure on him, besides loss of friends, public contempt, and criminal prosecution. One was from the government, which used the conviction as a basis for taking his passport to prevent foreign travel, and banning him from entering parts of England. Since Russell was guilty of undermining the war effort, the government asserted, he might make further attempts to aid the enemy. Russell speculated that the government was afraid he would signal submarines from the coast. More seriously he said its real goal was to prevent him from accepting an invitation to the United States to give more anti-war speeches, and to prevent him from giving speeches to anti-war groups around England (Moorehead 258). But he was not intimidated.

The second source of pressure stemming from the conviction was a decision by Russell's employer, Cambridge University. In 1915 Russell's five-year lectureship had ended and been renewed. He asked for a two-year leave of absence to work for the NCF, which was granted. But after the conviction in 1916, the governing board of the university voted to cancel the renewal. He was effectively fired.

Russell endured the pressures from all these sources. The reactions of ordinary people and his friends saddened him, but the actions of the government and the university made him angry. He worked even harder for the NCF in 1917. But in February of 1918 the government turned up the heat by charging Russell with a more serious crime: harming Great Britain's relations with an ally, i.e., the United States, by insulting the ally in an editorial. The Defense of the Realm Act prohibited "impeding recruiting and discipline" and harming Britain's relations with an ally, as well as other things (Monk 521). He was convicted, sentenced to six months in jail, and went to prison in May.

I think Russell showed a special kind of courage in his opposition to the war. What is difficult for some is easy for others, and that is true for courage and fear as well. Some people would be discouraged by the loss of a job more than the loss of friends; for others the opposite would be true. Russell faced an additional difficulty: he was as devoted to truth and understanding as others were to friends, or their jobs. But the issues surrounding the war were exceedingly complex and cloudy. It was very hard to know if one's position was correct. For many, this was not very problematic. Firm conviction was more important than clear understanding. Many readily accepted the government's point of view. Others examined the questions superficially, and accepted answers that felt satisfying, under the pressure of the moment.[3] Neither approach was enough for Russell. He demanded clarity. For him, therefore, sorting out the ambiguous facts and working through all the arguments were more daunting challenges than they were for many other people. One can say that in addition to personal, physical, and moral courage, Russell showed intellectual courage.

Russell's reasons for opposing the war were complicated. He was not a pacifist. He believed that some wars could be justified, but not this war with Germany. The pacifists who opposed the war held a simple, inviolable principle—all violence is wrong—which is easy to understand even if one disagrees with it. But Russell supported the violent Russian Revolution in March of 1917 (Kerensky's revolution, not Lenin's, which occurred in October). Russell resigned from the NCF later that year partly because he believed the violence used to overthrow the Czar was justified, while most other members of the NCF did not. He opposed the war with Germany because of his instinctive horror at the slaughter, but also based on his calculations of relative goods and evils. The "cure" of killing hundreds of thousands of young men was worse than the "disease" of allowing Germany to achieve its objectives, he thought. That is, he did not believe self-defense always justifies violence. He said that if the Germans occupied England, and the British passively resisted, the Germans would soon go home (Ryan 67–69). Nevertheless, he must have had doubts about this proposal at times. Russell wasn't afraid to think long and hard about the most complex problems and take stands on them.

Not only were Russell's motives complicated, but the situation in England was complicated as well. When the war broke out, Russell was against it while most British citizens were for it. (Germans supported their government, the French supported theirs, and so on.) But as Russell protested, additional issues arose. One was the Military Service Bill, adopted in January 1916. Should all physically fit, single men between 18 and 41 be required to perform military service? Or should some be exempt because of their long-held religious beliefs? Russell criticized the draft and supported the conscientious objectors. Some (like Whitehead) condemned Russell for his position on the war *and* his position on the draft. But others agreed with Russell in opposing compulsory military service, even if they disagreed with his view that the war was illegitimate. Opposing the war wasn't a single decision; it required a number of decisions on many difficult questions.

By 1916 a third issue arose: free speech. When Russell was fined for writing a pamphlet, many supporters of the war thought the government went too far in punishing expressions of opinion. Many more felt the same way when he was imprisoned in 1918 for writing an editorial (Moorehead 253). But the issue was divisive. Some thought the punishment was too light. The specific charge was insulting an ally, but Russell himself thought the government was trying to silence him, and to intimidate the conscientious objectors and frighten them into joining the military. Free speech in a war is a complicated problem. Reasonable people can disagree about the philosophical questions as well as the interpretations of events. Russell understood the arguments *against* his point of view as well as his critics did (probably better), and that means he had to struggle mightily in his own mind in order to decide what he should do. For a man like Russell, facing that challenge required as much courage as facing an angry crowd.[4]

## Going to Prison

I have been arguing that Russell's opposition to the war required personal and intellectual courage. His willingness to go to prison is an example of his courage. However, a skeptic could reject this example on the grounds that Russell's stay in prison required no sacrifice at all. On the contrary, it was pleasant and productive, more like a vacation. And going on vacation is not an act of courage.

I think this hypothetical objection is mistaken, but to see its origin, we need to examine British prisons in 1918 and Russell's prison experience. In the British penal system, one could be sentenced to the first division or the second division, comparable to minimum and maximum security prisons in the United States. Russell was sentenced to the first division, where conditions were much better than the second division. As the brother of an earl, and a well-known philosopher, Russell received some privileges that other prisoners could not. His cell was larger than average, he could hire another prisoner to clean it and do other chores, he could have his meals prepared elsewhere and delivered to him, he had unlimited access to books and newspapers. In fact, when he first arrived at Brixton Prison, he was very pleased to have a respite from the frustrating work of political activism. He wrote to his brother,

> One is free from the torturing question: What more ought I be doing? Is there any effective action I haven't thought of? Have I a right to let the whole thing go and return to philosophy? Here I *have* to let the whole thing go, which is far more restful than choosing to let it go and doubting if one's choice is justified. Prison has some of the advantages of the Catholic Church [Monk 527–28].

He had been writing, speaking, and organizing for about three years, and he wanted to return to theoretical philosophy. There were some restrictions, which he found increasingly burdensome. He was limited to one short visit per week by a group of three people. His letters were limited to four pages per week on prison stationary (although Russell got around this by writing in French and telling the warden he was copying historical passages for his professional work). Nevertheless, his imprisonment was more like a scholarly retreat than a punishment, at least for most of the time. During his five months in jail he read a tremendous amount, he wrote the *Introduction to Mathematical Philosophy*, and he outlined another book on the nature of the mind.

However, this objection to the idea that going to prison exhibited tremendous courage fails for a simple reason: when Russell took the risks that he knew could land him in prison, he didn't know that he would be sentenced to the first division. As a matter of fact, he was initially sentenced to the second division. He had visited conscientious objectors in the second division, and he had seen firsthand the terrible wasting effects of poor food, poor ventilation, no exercise, isolation, tedious, maddening work, and nervous exhaustion. Some never recovered their health. Moreover, he thought the age of eligibility for military service would be raised, in which case he could be in prison for much longer than six months. It was only after the court received appeals from many of the most prominent people in England that his sentence was reduced to the first division. But he was willing to risk going to the second division to protest the war. That commitment shows uncommon courage.

## *Introduction to Mathematical Philosophy*

When Russell went to jail in May of 1918, he was relieved to return to technical philosophy. He applied himself to his earlier vocation with his usual energy and focus. He divided his waking hours into three parts: for four hours he wrote, for four more hours he read philosophy, and for four hours in the evening he read history, science, literature and other books that interested him.

*Introduction* is a summary for a popular audience of Russell's and Whitehead's earlier three-volume work *Principia Mathematica*. Though intended for non-specialists, it is still an abstract, detailed, dense book. It is also very interesting and illustrates the beginnings of analytic philosophy. Anglo-American philosophy for the past hundred years has been characterized by an emphasis on clarity, a focus on language, and the method of analysis. I will describe a few notions in Russell's book without attempting to survey the entire work and use those notions to show how his thinking influenced much of later twentieth-century philosophy.

Russell's goal in *Introduction* is to establish clear and firm foundations for the science of mathematics. For him, establishing firm foundations means showing how mathematics depends upon logic or can be derived from logic. So, for example, a key part of the book is Russell's definition of "number"—a mathematical concept—in terms of classes—a logical concept.

Russell begins his book describing a similar attempt to establish a foundation for mathematics by Giuseppe Peano. Peano tried to derive the series of natural numbers (0, 1, 2, 3, etc.) from three primitive concepts and five basic principles. But Russell shows that Peano's concepts are too vague. As an alternative Russell proposes his own definition of "number." He proceeds very cautiously and first explains what he is *not* doing. He is not defining "two," "three," or any particular number, but is defining the concept of number itself. He says,

> Returning now to the definition of number, it is clear that number is a way of bringing together certain collections, namely, those that have a given number of terms. We can suppose all couples in one bundle, all trios in another, and so on.... Each bundle is a class whose members are collections, i.e. classes; thus each is a class of classes [Russell, *Introduction to Mathematical Philosophy* 14].

For example, think of several groups: the three Musketeers, the three Little Pigs, the three Wise Men, and the three Blind Mice. Each of these groups, or classes, has three members. We can imagine all the groups that are similar to these (i.e., all the groups that have three members), which would be a very large group or class. That large group would be a class of classes. A number is a class of classes.

But this doesn't tell us what distinguishes one number from another. Every number is a class of classes. To distinguish numbers, Russell first defines a "one-one relation."

> A relation is said to be "one-one" when, if x has the relation in question to y, no other term x' has the same relation to y, and x does not have the same relation to any term y' other than y [Ibid., 15].

Russell now uses his precise concept of a "one-one relation" to define "similar" classes. Two classes are similar when there is a one-one relation between each of the terms in one class with each of the terms in the other class.

With this groundwork in place, Russell gives the following definition: "The number of a class is the class of all those classes that are similar to it" (Ibid. 18). For example, the number of the class of Three Musketeers is the large class that contains all the other classes that are similar to the class of Musketeers. Russell's definition of a number is not intuitive; he is saying that a particular number, such as three, is actually a class. But he argues that his definition has several advantages. It employs the concept of a class, which is a logical concept and part of the science of logic. Furthermore, as Russell says,

> we naturally think that the class of couples (for example) is something different from the number 2. But there is no doubt about the class of couples: it is indubitable and not difficult to define, whereas the number 2, in any other sense, is a metaphysical entity about which you can never feel sure that it exists or that we have tracked it down [Ibid.].

This passage shows that Russell is not only trying to clarify the fundamental concepts of mathematics, but is also trying to avoid confusing, metaphysical assumptions.

This brief example from *Introduction to Mathematical Philosophy* illustrates Russell's general approach. He goes on to discuss such concepts as a series, different types of numbers, and especially infinity. Russell's project is fascinating in itself, but it is also important for its influence on later philosophy.

Russell was one of the principal founders of analytic philosophy, which dominated philosophical thinking in the Anglo-American world for decades. Analysis means taking things apart, and we can see Russell's desire to do that in his analysis of number. He says "the philosophy I espouse is analytic because it claims that one must discover the simple elements of which complexes are composed, and that complexes presuppose simples, whereas simples do not presuppose complexes" (Moran 16).

One example of analysis is his explanation of counting. Counting seems like a simple process, but in fact it is complicated. Russell says counting the items in a group is actually a comparison: it is a "one-one comparison" of the group with the series of natural numbers beginning with one. The number of items in the group is the last number we come to in the one-one comparison with the number series.

Another example of analysis comes from the German philosopher Gottlob Frege, who also wanted to base mathematics on logic. Frege analyzed "meaning." Like counting, the notion of meaning may seem to be simple. A word has meaning or it doesn't. We understand a word's meaning or we don't. But Frege analyzed meaning into three parts: First, a meaningful word has a reference. "The morning star" refers to Venus. The same term also has a sense. The sense of "the morning star" is a small object in the sky, bright, and occurring in the morning. Finally, meaningful words call up ideas or associations in people's minds. The "morning star" makes some people think of certain images or even feelings they have had. Thus, Frege analyzes meaning into reference, sense, and ideas. (Notice that sense is an objective, publically shared understanding, not subjective images or feelings in one person's mind.) (Kenny 121–22).

Many philosophers in the past have employed analysis. What is different about the movement Russell influenced is the emphasis on language. The British empiricists, for example, claimed that complex ideas could be analyzed into simple ideas, and analytic philosophy is similar. But Frege, Russell, G. E. Moore, Wittgenstein and other twentieth century philosophers shift the emphasis from ideas to words and language. That shift is "the major innovation of the century," according to Christian Delacampagne (Delacampagne 32). In fact, Russell is as much concerned with translation as he is with analysis. In *Introduction* he wants to translate vague and confusing concepts of mathematics into precise, determinate definitions. For example, after painstakingly defining "posterity" in terms of several simpler concepts, Russell says,

> The notion of "those terms that can be reached from 0 by successive steps from next to next" is vague, though it *seems* as if it conveyed a definite meaning; on the other hand, "the posterity of 0" is precise and explicit just where the other idea is hazy.

> It may be taken as giving what we *meant* to mean when we spoke of the terms that can be reached from 0 by successive steps [Russell, *Introduction to Mathematical Philosophy* 22].

Analytic philosophy attempts to uncover what people meant to mean when they said things that were vague and confusing. Russell wants to translate confusing statements into precise and clear equivalents.

In its early form, analytic philosophy was devoted to the creation of an ideal language. Russell says, "In a logically perfect language, the words in a proposition would correspond one by one with the components of the corresponding facts" (Stumpf 434). Facts could be analyzed into the simplest elements of experience, and the philosopher could show how complex thoughts and concepts were built up from simpler ones. In an ideal language, complex expressions could be explained by showing how they were constructed from simple ones. Russell (along with Frege) had helped create a new branch of logic, called "quantificational logic," that was more flexible and precise than the traditional, categorical logic of Aristotle, and that could be the basis of an ideal language. In *Introduction to Mathematical Philosophy* he wanted to analyze mathematics into its simplest, most fundamental axioms, and prove that those could be translated into the new language of logic. Later philosophers such as Rudolf Carnap tried to translate the language of everyday life into a precise, ideal language.

Other analytic philosophers believed the ideal language was the language of science. They believed that our ordinary ways of speaking about physical objects or the self or good and evil only created confusion. The way to dispel the confusion was to translate these ordinary ways of speaking into the clearer, verifiable language of science. Such translation is a kind of analysis, but with an emphasis on language.

The best example of this type of analytic philosophy is Ludwig Wittgenstein's *Tractatus Logico-Philosophicus,* published in 1921. Wittgenstein had been Russell's student in Cambridge and absorbed most of his ideas. But he pushed them in new directions. He agreed with Russell that the "surface grammar" of ordinary expressions is misleading, and the task of philosophy is to discover the underlying, sensible, "logical form."[5] He also agreed that we could analyze statements about the world into simpler and simpler statements until we came to those that refer to "atomic facts." But while Russell's ideal language was quantificational logic, Wittgenstein believed natural science gives us the best form of knowledge and the best language we have.

A group of philosophers in Vienna in the 1920s, known as logical positivists, were strongly influenced by Wittgenstein's book. Like Wittgenstein, they believed natural science gives us our only clear and reliable description of reality. Like Frege, they wanted to define meaning in relation to this reliable description. They proposed the "verificationist theory" of meaning, according to which the meaning of a sentence is the observations that would prove the sentence is true (or false). For example, what does the sentence "Apples are red" mean? We understand the meaning only by knowing what we would have to observe in order to verify that the sentence is true (i.e., we would observe that apples are red).

This positivist theory of meaning has some radical implications. If you cannot say how you would verify a sentence scientifically, then you do not know what the sentence means. "The soul is immortal." What would you observe to prove that that sentence is true or false? In fact, there is nothing you could observe. The logical positivists concluded that all such sentences are meaningless. In a famous short book called *Language, Truth and Logic* (1936) A. J. Ayer claimed that all talk about supernatural beings, the afterlife, beauty, and even moral goodness was meaningless. Most analytic philosophers, including Russell, decided that Ayer and the positivists had gone too far. But the positivists' program of analysis and translation illustrates a fundamental trend of twentieth century philosophy. And Russell's prison book was an important precursor of this trend.

## Conclusion

While *Introduction to Mathematical Philosophy* seems completely divorced from his anti-war activism, I have argued that both were expressions of his devotion to finding the truth, and his courage in the face of criticism. There may be another connection. Russell believed his philosophical work was as valuable as his political work. He explains the value of philosophy in the concluding passage of his earlier book, *The Problems of Philosophy*. He says,

> Philosophy is to be studied, not for the sake of any definite answers to its questions, ... but for the sake of the questions themselves; because these questions enlarge our conception of what is possible, enrich our intellectual imagination and diminish the dogmatic assurance which closes the mind against speculation; but above all because through the greatness of the universe which philosophy contemplates, the mind also is rendered great and becomes capable of that union with the universe which constitutes its highest good [Russell, *The Problems of Philosophy* 161].

### Notes

1. In 1961, at age 88, he was arrested for using a loud speaker at a demonstration in Hyde Park, in violation of the park rules. He was convicted and sentenced to a week in prison

(which he spent in the prison hospital, in deference to his age). Ronald W. Clark, *The Life of Bertrand Russell* (New York: Alfred A. Knopf, 1976), 590.

2. Russell wrote, "All this madness, all this rage, all this flaming death of our civilization and our hopes, has been brought about because a set of official gentlemen, living luxurious lives, mostly stupid, and all without imagination or heart, have chosen that it should occur rather than that any one of them should suffer some infinitesimal rebuff to his country's pride." Ray Monk, *Bertrand Russell: The Spirit of Solitude, 1872–1921* (New York: The Free Press, 1996), 369.

3. The day before Great Britain declared war, H.J. Massingham, the editor of *The Nation*, agreed to print a letter from Russell condemning the war. But the next day, after the declaration, he changed his mind. Ray Monk, *Bertrand Russell: The Spirit of Solitude, 1872–1921* (New York: The Free Press, 1996), 369.

4. People in the United States were imprisoned for actively opposing the war as well. The Espionage Act of 1917 "imposed stiff penalties for antiwar activities," and the Sedition Act of 1918 penalized "anyone who might 'utter, print, write, or publish any disloyal, profane, scurrilous, or abusive language about the form of government of the United States ... or the uniform of the Army or the Navy...' More than a thousand people were convicted under these broad restrictions on freedom of speech." James A. Henretta, et al., *America's History, Vol 2: Since 1865*, 3d ed. (New York: Worth, 1997), 728.

5. Forrest E. Baird, Walter Kaufmann, eds., *Philosophic Classics, Vol. V: Twentieth-Century Philosophy*, 2d ed. (Upper Saddle River, NJ: Prentice Hall, 2000), 159. In the *Tractatus*, Wittgenstein says "Language disguises thought. So much so, that from the outward form of the clothing it is impossible to infer the form of the thought beneath it.... Philosophy aims at the logical clarification of thoughts." Quoted in W. T. Jones and Robert J. Fogelin, *A History of Western Philosophy, Vol. V: The Twentieth Century to Quine and Derrida*, 3d ed. (Belmont, CA: Wadsworth, 1997), 233.

## Works Cited

Ayer, A. J. *Language, Truth and Logic*. London: Victor Gollancz, 1936. Print.
Baird, Forrest E., and Walter Kaufman, eds. *Philosophic Classics, Vol. V: Twentieth-Century Philosophy*, 2nd Edition. Upper Saddle River, N.J.: Prentice Hall, 2000. Print.
Baldwin, Thomas, ed. *The Cambridge History of Philosophy, 1870–1945*. Cambridge: Cambridge University Press, 2003. Print.
Barrett, William. *Irrational Man: A Study in Existential Philosophy*. New York: Anchor Doubleday, 1958. Print.
Clark, Ronald W. *Bertrand Russell and His World*. New York: Thames and Hudson, 1981. Print.
_____. *The Life of Bertrand Russell*. New York: Alfred A. Knopf, 1976. Print.
Delacampagne, Christian. *A History of Philosophy in the Twentieth Century*. Trans. M. B. DeBevoise. Baltimore: Johns Hopkins University Press, 1999. Print.
Henretta, James A., et al. *America's History, Vol 2: Since 1865*, 3d ed. New York: Worth, 1997. Print.
Jones, W.T., and Robert J. Fogelin. *A History of Western Philosophy, Vol. V: The Twentieth Century to Quine and Derrida*, 3d ed. Belmont, CA: Wadsworth, 1997. Print.
Kenny, Anthony. *A New History of Western Philosophy, Vol. IV: Philosophy in the Modern World*. Oxford: Oxford University Press, 2007. Print.
Monk, Ray. *Bertrand Russell: The Spirit of Solitude, 1872–1921*. New York: The Free Press, 1996. Print.
Moorehead, Caroline. *Bertrand Russell: A Life*. New York: Viking, 1993. Print.
Moran, Dermot, ed. *The Routledge Companion to Twentieth Century Philosophy*. London: Routledge, 2008. Print.

Russell, Bertrand. *Introduction to Mathematical Philosophy.* 1919; London: George Allen and Unwin, 1970. Print.
\_\_\_\_\_. *The Problems of Philosophy.* 1912; New York: Oxford University Press, 1959. Print.
Ryan, Alan. *Bertrand Russell: A Political Life.* New York: Hill and Wang, 1988. Print.
Schwerin, Alan, ed. *Russell Revisited: Critical Reflections on the Thought of Bertrand Russell.* Newcastle. UK: Cambridge Scholars, 2008. Print.
Stumpf, Samuel Enoch. *Socrates to Sartre: A History of Philosophy,* 2d ed. New York: McGraw Hill, 1975. Print.
Vellacott, Jo. *Bertrand Russell and the Pacifists in the First World War.* New York: St. Martin's Press, 1980. Print.

# His Majesty's Hotels: Gandhi's *Satyagraha* in South Africa

MARTIN F. REICHERT

## Summary

Mohandas Gandhi was one of the most famous political prisoners of the twentieth century. His lifelong struggle for equal rights, first in South Africa and then in India, made him an iconic revolutionary figure. In *Satyagraha in South Africa*, Gandhi talks about his time in South Africa working against the British colonial government; he also lays out the philosophical principles for political action that he called *satyagraha*. It was this vision of nonviolent political action that set the stage for the conflict in South Africa and in India. It was also picked up by other activists around the world, notably Martin Luther King, Jr., in the United States. It is often forgotten that Gandhi spent two decades in South Africa, honing his political skills and learning how organizations operate, before he returned to India and became involved in the struggle for Indian independence.—J.W.R.

## Gandhi in Jail

It is highly unlikely that many people, besides Gandhi, enjoyed going to jail. In *Satyagraha in South Africa* (1924), he asked his followers "to consider the prisons as His Majesty's hotels" and their own suffering "as perfect bliss" (Gandhi 34: 125).[1] In his cell, he claimed, he found "perfect happiness and peace" (128). Being under arrest afforded him a welcome opportunity for "self-purification" (181). In *An Autobiography, or the Story of My Experiments with Truth* (1925–1929), he largely glossed over his numerous arrests, remarking merely that jail taught him "wholesome rules of self-restraint," notably to give up tea and to finish his last meal before sunset (44: 333f.).

By then, he had gathered plenty of experience. Altogether, Gandhi spent 2,327 days of his life behind bars.[2] Were colonial jails really so peaceful as to be comparable to a *mandir*, a temple, as Gandhi often claimed? Did he perhaps receive special treatment? Or was he just an exceptional individual who somehow managed to transcend reality? Aren't his claims hopelessly idealistic, then, grandiose even, not to mention politically naïve and quite possibly dishonest?

## Conditions in Colonial Jails

In 1908, when describing his first two prison terms upon his release in a series of newspaper articles, Gandhi had sung a different tune. Together with numerous other Indian immigrants, he had been arrested for failing to obey the recently passed Asiatic Registration Act—the so-called Black Act—which forced foreigners to be thumb-printed and carry a certificate, or passport, at all times. Two incidents may illustrate some of the real terrors he and his fellow inmates experienced; both took place during his second stint in jail, in fall of 1908. The first night proved a taxing one for the inexperienced leader of the protest movement. In his newspaper he related how he was lying in bed when a Native—or "Kaffir"—inmate came over; Gandhi could not understand his language, but it was clear that he was being mocked. A moment later, he was accosted by a Chinese inmate who then "went to a Kaffir lying in bed. The two exchanged obscene jokes, uncovering each other's genitals" (9: 256). Both of them were murderers and larcenists. "Knowing this, how could I possibly sleep?" (Ibid.) Another scary incident occurred in the prison lavatory. While Gandhi was using one of the stalls, which had no doors, in came "a strong, heavily-built, fearful-looking Kaffir" who demanded that he get out. Gandhi replied that he was not finished yet. "Instantly he lifted me up in his arms and threw me out." Two of his fellow Indian prisoners who had witnessed the confrontation were weeping whereas Gandhi, who walked away uninjured and smiling, went on to claim that he was "not in the least frightened"; he admitted, though, not without a sense of humor, that he "had no motions for four days" afterwards (270).

It is clear, then, that Gandhi was in no way oblivious to, let alone spared, the terrifying, often brutal reality of colonial prisons, which were set up not so much to punish, let alone rehabilitate or reintegrate, criminals, but to subjugate, infantilize, and dehumanize as well as economically exploit the non-white population.[3] In his newspaper articles, he complained bitterly about some of the abuses, especially the food and the proximity to Native prisoners, accusing the authorities of "callous contempt for the Indian community" (210). Conditions in his native India turned out to be as atrocious as they had been abroad, at least initially. While in South Africa a jail sentence usually meant hard labor, such as pounding gravel, or sewing, in India political inmates were often kept without occupation. Gandhi filled the time with reading, writing, and spinning—his famous spinning wheel had initially been confiscated by the warden whereupon he threatened not to eat if he was not allowed to spin. Daily he was frisked for weapons or prohibited material, such as newspapers or periodicals. Living in almost complete isolation from the outside world, he was allowed one visitor every three months and one letter received and one written during the same period. These quarterly visits and letters could be arbitrarily refused. Gandhi's nationalist movement, incidentally, was soon to lead to improvements in the Indian penal system. With the growing influx of middle-class inmates, prisons became hotbeds of resistance and political agitation, prompting investigations and modest reforms that began in the 1920s, unlike in South Africa of course, where reforms only came with the end of Apartheid.[4]

## *The Book* Satyagraha in South Africa

It is a common misconception that Gandhi began his *Autobiography* while in jail.[5] His most substantial piece of writing from prison is *Satyagraha in South Africa*, a record of his formative years written ten years after his return to India.[6] At the time of writing, Gandhi was serving a six-year sentence, though he was released early in 1924, after about two years, when falling ill with acute appendicitis. The British government was afraid that if he died in custody, his death would spark new riots. By then, he had completed thirty chapters, about two thirds of the book.[7] A fellow-prisoner who happened to be the owner of the Gujarati monthly *Navajivan* offered to write to Gandhi's dictation. The chapters appeared serially in *Navajivan* between April 1924 and November 1925; the book was published in two parts in 1924 and 1925 in Gujarati. The English version appeared in serial form in *Young India*, another weekly published by Gandhi, and in book form in 1928.

Aside from the newspaper articles that were written in 1908, the South Africa book gives us the most detailed record of Gandhi's jail time. We already saw, however, that by now he cast his experience in a gentler light, belittling the hardships he and his followers had suffered. True, he remembers several nonviolent resisters who died in jail (chs. 31, 40, 45); but the language he adopts, when not religious as in the passages highlighted above, tends to veer toward the humorous or the gently self-mocking, as when he describes his experience as a defendant in the same court where he plied his business as a lawyer (34: 125); the shock he and his compatriots suffered when finding themselves in "the Negro ward"; their indignation when they were made to dress in clothes assigned to Native convicts; their complaints about the boredom, the lack of hygiene, and the unsalted mealie pap (126f.)—obviously upsetting for the Indians, whom Gandhi presents as rather finicky, what with their dietary restrictions and their concerns about caste purity. If the point of the book was, as he states in the Preface, to reassure himself and his reader that "victory is absolutely certain" in the current struggle in India and that there was "no ground whatever for despair in the fight that is going on" (4f.), should not the author have made more of his first-hand experiences to rile up potentially seditious Indians against the British? Why did he downplay the severity of the conditions? Wasn't he passing up an opportunity to draw more bodies into the anti-colonial struggle?

I argue that Gandhi was by no means blind to the reality of British imperialism and violence; rather, what appears as starry-eyed idealism is actually a hardnosed disillusionment that occasionally veers toward the apocalyptic. Before going into details, a few words about Gandhi's life and the circumstances of his imprisonment.

## *The Early Years*

Mohandas Karamchand Gandhi was hardly born a fearless leader. Little Mohan first saw the light of day on October 2, 1869, in Porbander on the Indian Ocean. His family belonged to the Gujarati merchant caste, the third of India's four major castes. Even though his grandfather and father had been *diwans* (advisors and administrators) to the local prince, we know from his autobiography that Mohan was a shy boy who showed hardly any promise in school. In the South Africa book his early life is not mentioned at all. The reader therefore does not get to enjoy any of the often hilarious, sometimes shocking revelations of which biographers have made much: his excessive fear of darkness; his marriage in 1882 at age twelve to a girl his age; his taste for meat; the death of his ailing father—while Mohan was in bed making love to his teenage wife.

The first important decision of his life was to go to London, against the objections of the elders of his caste, to study law; he hoped to become successful as a professional in India. In 1891, after three years of studies in London during which Gandhi tried hard to turn himself into an English gentleman, wearing Western suits and taking classes in dancing, French, elocution, and the violin, he took the bar and returned home. His attempts to make a living as a barrister in Bombay failed, however. He was unfamiliar with the Indian legal system, and when he finally took up his first case, he found himself completely tongue-tied in court so that he had to refund the fee to his client. He was also turned down for part-time work as a high school teacher. When his brother lined up a temporary job for him in Durban in Natal, he sailed off to South Africa in 1893, leaving behind his wife and children. He ended up staying for twenty-one years, leading the movement against discrimination by colonial government through nonviolent activism and realizing in the process, as he put it later, "my vocation in life" (276).

## South Africa

The two decades spent in South Africa were formative in several respects. For one thing, they confronted him with a facet of Western civilization that he had been able to ignore in the genteel, cosmopolitan environment of London, namely that it was founded on violence, exploitation, and racism. For another, South Africa afforded him an opportunity to mix with Indians of various backgrounds—in terms of caste, profession, class, religion, and gender—to an extent that would have been difficult at home, so that when he eventually returned he was able to see with different eyes. It also helped him conceive of Indians as a nation working together rather than pursuing limited self-interests. Finally, it provided him with invaluable experience as a lobbyist dealing with colonial administrations in Natal and Transvaal and with the imperial government in London.

The first encounter with the racist underbelly of the glittering Empire came as a shock. This incident, immortalized near the beginning of Richard Attenborough's famous movie *Gandhi*, is emblematic of this experience. Gandhi had a first-class train ticket, but when a white passenger complained about the presence of a "coloured" man, he was evicted from the train by a policeman and spent a freezing night in Maritzburg station pondering whether to return to India or follow his duty in South Africa. This episode, dramatized at length in Gandhi's autobiography, is dealt with only cursorily in the South Africa book. In any case, it was not his own misfortunes but the abuses of others that mobilized him to oppose the repressive measures of the British rulers. Initially, he was retained to look after the interests of the Indian merchants, mostly Muslims from his home state, Gujarat.

In the 1860s, Indian laborers had been imported by the South African government to work on plantations and in coalmines, and Indian merchants had followed them in hopes of making a fortune abroad. Their presence was deeply resented by Boers and British alike. The situation in South Africa was tense to begin with. The British had seized control of the Cape area in 1795, driving the earlier Dutch settlers—the Boers: "farmers"—further north. Native peoples, particularly the Xhosa and Zulu, were forced to submit or to move. Tensions only increased when gold and diamonds were discovered inland during the nineteenth century. These frictions escalated during Gandhi's time, and within a few years both the Afrikaners—in the Boer War (1899–1902)—and the Zulus—in the Zulu Rebellion (1906)—were brutally crushed by the British. Discriminatory laws were passed to check immigration and restrict the upward mobility of non–European settlers. When Gandhi's protests on behalf of his clients proved ineffective, from 1906 on he began to adopt more confrontational measures, such as the burning of registration certificates. At a community assembly on September 11, 1906, Gandhi took an oath "before God and man" (89) to stand firm in the face of violence and abuse, to suffer patiently without resorting to retaliatory violence but also without cowing down to the laws he perceived as unjust. If the Indians followed him along, at least initially, it was because they were driven by their mercantile interests, not by moral motives. Not surprisingly, when confronted with imprisonment and deportation, the merchants' initial enthusiasm for noncooperation gradually waned.[8]

It was only in 1912, when Gandhi took up the cause of the working class, that he was able to mobilize a more substantial and more committed army of supporters. They had much less to lose than the merchants in the fight against the government. Most of them were indentured laborers; as members of the Commonwealth they could not be enslaved, but in Natal they were subject to a Poll Tax which, considering their small income, was exorbitant and condemned them to perpetual servitude. Under Gandhi's leadership, they willingly broke the law through walkouts, illegal border crossings, and similar acts of civil disobedience. Faced with a mass movement, the government at last started to make concessions and in 1914 reached an accord that repealed the Poll Tax. Proclaiming victory, Gandhi left South Africa for good and returned to his homeland. His claim that the struggle had a "happy ending" (276) glosses over the shallowness and short duration of the compromise he achieved. With Gandhi out of the way, the repressive colonial politics in South Africa were quickly resumed.

## *India*

Back home, Gandhi soon took up his struggle against the Raj—the British colonial power—with a series of nonviolent campaigns on a local scale.

These were largely successful. In 1919, he announced a Non-Cooperation Movement, the first campaign on a national level. At the time the Indian majority was held in check by an astonishingly small number of British Civil Service officers: a few thousand of them commanded 76,000 British troops, and 129,000 Indian troops (Heathcote 381f.). Gandhi's call for a nation-wide strike resulted in sporadic outbreaks of violence, however. In 1922, during the worst incident, twenty-two policemen, trapped inside their station during a protest in a town called Chauri Chaura, were burned to death by a mob that chanted the Mahatma's name. Gandhi took full responsibility and, even though the violence had been fairly isolated, immediately called off the entire campaign; his belief that the Indian people were ready to bring about peace by nonviolent means had been a "Himalayan blunder," he realized in the Preface to *Satyagraha in South Africa* (34: 4). He was put on trial and, as mentioned, sentenced to six years in prison.

Some biographers have read the book on South Africa, which was written during that time, as an attempt to come to terms with the spectacular failure of nonviolence in India. By claiming victory in the past, he could comfort himself and his followers in the present struggle. Such arguments miss the point. Gandhi's conceptions of failure, of fight, and of victory were different from the common notion. Having maintained lively contacts with many members of the Indian community in South Africa, and having a son permanently settled there, he was very much aware of the predicament of the Indians in South Africa: "They are still fighting" (7), he acknowledged in the preface, and later in the book he indicated that their situation had actually deteriorated since his departure (277). The reason for his counterfactual claim, the reason for downplaying the violence he suffered at the hands of the British, the reason for calling prison "a holy and happy place," does not lie in faulty memory, nor is it a rhetorical ploy or idealization. Rather, it lies in his belief in a force he called *satyagraha*.

## *Satyagraha*

Satyagraha (stressed on the second syllable: suht-YUH-gruh-huh) was a term Gandhi coined with the help of a follower; it roughly translates as "truth force," "firmness in truth," or "soul force." Existing terms, he felt, were insufficient to express what he conceived of as essential. The term "passive resistance," used by suffragists in England, failed to capture the active, creative, courageous engagement with an opponent that he found crucial in his campaigns. "Nonviolence" was a doubly negative term and did not take into account the willingness of the practitioner of Gandhi's methods to suffer violence. As Faisal Devji has pointed out very astutely, in Gandhi's thinking violence plays an ambiguous, even paradoxical role. On the one hand, a violent response to a violent act only increases the violence and destruction already in the world. On the other hand, if nonviolence were to mean simply the avoidance of violence, it would be equivalent to cowardice. In Gandhi's view, the world is saturated with violence. Even basic life-sustaining measures, such as eating or lovemaking, he held, involve violent aspects. Caught between violent retaliation and cowardice, what should a satyagrahi (practitioner of satyagraha) do? His followers, Gandhi reasoned, needed to be trained like soldiers to look death in the eye willingly and bravely, without flinching, but also without returning the violence. Such courage in the face of suffering, he believed, would have a deep impact on the enemy; it could not fail to win over his heart, transform his violence. In order for this conversion to nonviolence to take place, then, the opponent must be provoked to commit violent acts, indeed atrocities.

To resist having recourse to violence in the face of violence was, of course, an entirely counterintuitive notion, rooted more in Christian gospel—mediated by Tolstoy's writings—than in conventional political wisdom. It was also far removed from the meek, turn-the-other-cheek preconception one often finds associated with Gandhi and his "passive resistance." The Mahatma left no doubt that in the absence of a creative, nonviolent response to oppression he much preferred violence to the inaction of the coward. His goal, though, was to convert rather than defeat and vanquish the enemy, and in order to do so he was willing to risk the death of thousands of satyagrahis. Satyagraha can certainly be thought of as a spiritual practice, but it is a spirituality that remains firmly rooted in reality, in the physical body of the satyagrahi who has been trained to overcome the fear of prison and suffering, of violence and death.

While the status of violence in satyagraha is a critical and troubling issue, another is the role of religion. To the extent that satyagraha has immediate political consequences, it infuses politics with religion. Gandhi considered the very existence of satyagraha to be God's doing. This led him to rethink the classic concept of *dharma-yuddha*, a Sanskrit term meaning "righteous struggle." The ancient court adviser Kautilya, for instance, in his *Arthashastra* from the fourth century BCE, had distinguished "open" forms of fighting—waged on a battlefield—from "treacherous" ones that entailed guerrilla warfare; his distinction was purely pragmatic: winning was all that mattered. Gandhi, by contrast, infused the notion of *dharma-yuddha* with a religious dimension so that it came to mean "holy war" or "just war."

That is the beauty of satyagraha. It comes up to oneself; one has not to go out in search of it. This is a virtue inherent in the principle itself. A *dharma-yuddha* in which there are no secrets to be guarded, no scope for cunning and no place for untruth, comes unsought; and a man of religion is ever ready for it. A struggle which has to be previously planned is not a righteous struggle. In [a] righteous struggle God Himself plans campaigns and conducts battles. A *dharma-yuddha* can be waged only in the name of God, and it is only when the satyagrahi feels quite helpless, is apparently on his last legs and finds utter darkness all around him, that God comes to the rescue [5].

The twenty-first-century reader cannot but be struck by Gandhi's prescience. With its rhetoric of jihad, of righteousness, of God and truth, of apocalypse, the passage is an eerie anticipation of the contemporary situation when politics has come to be dominated by morality, by religion, by concerns and movements that lie beyond its pale. Gandhi's vision of the end of politics, of a world obscured by darkness in which violence has become endemic, which leaves the reader with no reassurance at all. Does the end mean the breakdown of binary friend-enemy oppositions, the cessation of violence and injustice? Does it mean global annihilation and death? A charge frequently leveled against Gandhi's satyagraha is that it is impractical, unrealistic, impossible. In light of the above passage, to call him an idealist or a dreamer would be to miss the mark entirely. Gandhi made no false promises about the possible outcome of nonviolence; but unlike most people, he had actually experienced the contagious logic of violence, its mimetic escalation to extremes, and he had no delusions about its deadly outcome. His gaze into the abyss of violent conflict was unflinching.

## *Textual Analysis*

Few contemporaries of his were ready to gaze with him. *Satyagraha in South Africa* records his attempt to train some of them to do so. The early chapters are devoted to laying out the geography and history of South Africa and to chronicling the settlement of the Indians there. The author appears chatty and long-winded. "Africa is one of the biggest continents in the world," reads the first sentence (7). The reader who manages to look past generalizations and platitudes will discern an indictment of modern Western civilization and Christendom, as in this passage about the Dutch settlers: "The Boers are simple, frank and religious.... Every Boer is a good fighter.... I have stated above that the Boers are religiously minded Christians. But it cannot be said that they believe in the New Testament. As a matter of fact Europe does not believe in it" (17). The argument, then, is more subtle than it appears at first; stylistically, it frequently hinges on tensions or contradictions marked by "and yet," "but," "nevertheless," which are among Gandhi's favorite expressions, especially when it comes to describing human nature.

In other area as well, Gandhi's book poses certain challenges to "the patient reader" (85). The list of characters who make an appearance is long, but highly selective. Compared with the autobiography, his wife and four sons are dealt with only cursorily. Maganlal Gandhi, a remote cousin and most devoted follower to whom the book is dedicated, is mentioned only a few times in passing; it was he who helped coin the word "satyagraha." The omission by name of any Africans he met is certainly striking. Even Indian supporters make only episodic appearances; few of them are mentioned repeatedly. Many, maybe most, are severely flawed, either in their character or in their commitment to the fight. There is, for instance, a publicly celebrated satyagrahi who lost courage and secretly abandoned the movement rather than risk going to jail again (118). Another, a "lion-like" (196) community organizer whose "invaluable qualities had shone forth like jewels," suffers from such "irritability," "anger," and "rashness" that these traits eventually "eclipsed his good qualities" (124). A visiting Indian dignitary by name of Gokhale, the closest thing Gandhi ever had to a mentor, comes off as fussy and pampered. Ambiguities abound: "All this notwithstanding, many Indians remained perfectly firm. Many more however weakened" (183). A particularly startling moment in the book is the introduction of a "hero," over one third of the way into the work. The occasion is one of the mass meetings that led to the burning of the registration certificates in August 1908. One speaker at the rally was Ahmad Muhammad Kachhalia, "the hero, not of this chapter alone, but of the present volume" (112). What are Kachhalia's qualifications for this epic role? At the meeting he gave "a very short speech" in which he swore "in the name of God" that he would rather be hanged than submit (Ibid.). And shortly before the bonfire of certificates he resisted the pressure from his European creditors to drop out of the struggle and, because of this show of "firmness and courage" (162), was made Chairman of the Transvaal British Indian Association. These are the only two passages of any substance where Kachhalia is mentioned. Gandhi did not refer to him by name in the autobiography, and in *Satyagraha in South Africa* he finally admitted that Kachhalia was a rather "obscure hero" (113). The term "hero" seems to be used rather loosely. At any rate, the Indians, despite their plight as colonialized people, hardly come off as morally superior to the British.

One of the few recurring characters is Gandhi's main antagonist, General Jan Smuts, a leading politician in the Transvaal. The title of the chapter that discusses Smuts's reneging on a promise to the Indian community is marked with a parenthetical question mark—thus: "General Smuts' Breach of Faith (?)"—and Gandhi comments: "I am ashamed of writing the caption of this chapter as well as the chapter itself, for it deals with the obliquity of human nature" (158). What happened was that after Indians had flooded the jails, Smuts promised to revoke the already mentioned discriminatory Black Act provided that the Indians registered voluntarily. Gandhi had been warned by many English friends that the general could not be trusted, but he decided nevertheless to lead his community to the registration offices. He realized too late that Smuts had no intention of making good on his promise. From the distance of a decade and a half, Gandhi evaluated Smuts's actions. "Even today," he wrote, he considered the incident "a breach of faith from the Indian community's standpoint" (Ibid.). "However"—here is that favorite formula again—however, "the General's action did not perhaps amount to an intentional breach of faith." In that case, "[i]t is quite possible" that Smuts "was not guilty of a deliberate breach of faith" (Ibid.). Gandhi then devoted a lengthy chapter to analyzing Smuts's character. His conclusion was highly ambiguous: "First, he has some principles in politics which are not quite immoral. Secondly, there is room in his politics for cunning and on occasion for perversion of truth" (165). Gandhi was not above depicting Smuts in a negative light; toward the end of the struggle, when Smuts was forced to give in to the demands of the Indians he had harassed for so long, Gandhi compared him to "a snake which has taken a rat in its mouth but can neither gulp it down nor cast it out" (263). In other places satyagrahis are encouraged "never to be afraid of trusting the opponent," even if he plays them false twenty times, but "to trust him for the twenty-first time" (133). So the issue of trusting one's opponent is not neatly resolved. Satyagraha is, after all, an experiment; the latter word, which anticipates the title of the autobiography written a year later, recurs frequently throughout the South Africa book. Gandhi is visibly wrestling with its practice, and he expects his reader to do the same: to maintain an uneasy distance toward conventional—epic—expectations of good and evil, friend and enemy, us and them. Given the obliquity of *all* human nature, opposites coincide and differences collapse.

One of the most interesting aspects of *Satyagraha in South Africa* is the glimpse the reader gets inside Tolstoy Farm, the second of the four alternative communities Gandhi founded in his lifetime. Sociologically speaking, these ashrams, as he called them later, were reckless experiments—and perhaps most difficult to tolerate for the only people who had not followed him there of their own free will: his wife and children. Aside from his family members, the other settlers of Tolstoy Farm, who spent much time together in manual labor and prayer, were composed of members of different religions, ethnicities, castes, ages, and cultural backgrounds. In retrospect, the mature author can only marvel at his lack of worries. How could he ever send "mischievous" boys and "innocent" girls to the spring to bathe together (201)? How could he be so firmly convinced that dietary changes or fasting alone could cure any disease? The doctor was never called, he reports, nor were drugs ever used. Snakes presented a different kind of danger. Apparently they were to be found everywhere on the grounds of the settlement. Gandhi announced to his shocked followers that it was a sin to kill snakes and any other animal. Hermann Kallenbach, a German Jew who lived with Gandhi for many years, took this verdict to the extreme by attempting to tame a huge cobra. Again, years afterwards Gandhi could only breathe a sigh of relief that no one was ever bitten. He admitted that it was difficult for him personally to overcome his fear of snakes. Nevertheless, "[a] person who fears snakes and who is not ready to resign his own life cannot avoid killing snakes in case of emergency" (208).

This, of course, brings us back to the question of satyagraha and the cultivation of soldierly courage in the face of violence and death. Gandhi was not at all blind to the realization that one's fearlessness and self-sacrifice might be neither perfect nor sufficient to melt the opponent's heart and thus to transform reality. He warned that the sufferer should not have the expectation that suffering will necessarily work. The adversary might continue to take advantage of one's trust; hard labor will not be magically lifted from the prisoner's lot; the "wicked warder" might never cease his harassment; a motley bunch of self-interested Indians might never come together as a community, let alone a nation. To have any such expectations would make the satyagrahi's suffering just another form of coercion and violence. In this sense, satyagraha is offered for the "virtue inherent in the principle itself"; it is indifferent to its outcome. By contrast, violence "works," at least in the short run, and that is what makes it so immediately plausible and contagious; its long-term effect, however, is disastrous as both sides get swept away in its frenzy. Writing years later, at the beginning of World War II, Gandhi saw very clearly that the Allies could defeat the Nazi; but in order to do so, he argued, they "would have to out–Hitler Hitler" (79: 235). As the war progressed—and came to an end with Hiroshima and Nagasaki in August 1945—he saw his words fulfilled.

Satyagraha is not a political tool, then; it is not an instrument for the resentful revolutionary, for the striking worker, for the uprising colonized masses to get what they want. Gandhi knew from first-hand experience that even those who thought of themselves as opponents of the Empire could still be caught up in the Empire's principles and values. They continued to speak the Empire's language, to wear its clothes, to play by its music. Something more was needed than courage. How to break out of the endless cycle of violence and retribution, what René Girard calls the mimetic relationship with the enemy-model? Of utmost importance was the realization that violence originated in the self: "I have observed the roots of evil deep down in my own nature" (Gandhi 34: 200f.). Gandhi was the first to remind himself and his followers of his own shortcomings. His refusal, often against all evidence, to see his adversary as an enemy was rooted in the recognition of his own implication in the violent structure of the world. The opponent was no different—and, against all appearances, no more evil—than himself: "All men are imperfect" (118). The fight against violence, then, starts within the self, with the renunciation of one's own violent desires, including the desire to survive at the cost of others. Gandhi's famous vow of brahmacharya (chastity) at the age of 36, his dietary quirks and fasts may seem bizarre in our promiscuous, consumerist society. For Gandhi they were as important to the transformation of reality as the cultivation of soldierly fearlessness.

As the leading public figure in India between the wars, he devoted his boundless energy to a number of issues that radically—though not necessarily successfully—challenged the political status quo of his nation. He fought to end poverty, untouchability, and, late in life, the Hindu caste system; he tried to establish women's rights and better relations between Hindus and Muslims; and above all he strove for independence from Britain. It took several more campaigns, notably the 1930–33 Civil Disobedience Movement (the Salt March) and the 1942–43 Quit India Movement, and several more stints in jail to drive the colonial government out of India and secure independence. When it finally came, in August 1947, the actual result—the partition of India and Pakistan and the outbreak of communal violence in various parts of the subcontinent—was far from what he had hoped for. But one need only remember his apocalyptic musings to realize why he was not very surprised by this outcome either. On January 30, 1948, he was assassinated by a Hindu who thought the Mahatma was making too many concessions to the Muslims. Half a century after his murder, one century after his fight in South Africa, it is apparent that Gandhi's unsentimental assessment of a world of violence could not be more timely.

## Notes

1. For the sake of convenience, I cite all of Gandhi's works from the—controversial—online version of the *Collected Works of Mahatma Gandhi* with the volume number preceding the page number.

2. My count differs from Homer Jack (516), who claims that Gandhi spent 2,338 days in jail, and from Louis Fischer, who concurs with Jack: "Altogether, he spent 2,089 days in Indian jails, and 249 days in South African prisons" (394). Presumably the discrepancy arises from counting the beginning and ending day separately, thus adding eleven days to the total.

As it pertains to the topic of this volume, here is a list based on references in the *Collected Works*:
*In South Africa (215 days):*
- 10–30 January 1908 in Johannesburg Jail (arrested for failing to register and refusing to leave the country; sentenced on Jan. 10 to two months' simple imprisonment; served 20 days);
- 7 October–12 December 1908 in Volksrust Jail ("King Edward's Hotel"), Pretoria (arrested for failing to produce registration certificate; sentenced on Oct. 14 to two months' imprisonment with hard labor; served 66 days);
- 25 February–24 May 1909 in Volksrust, then Pretoria Central Goal (arrested for refusing to produce registration certificate and to give fingerprints; sentenced on Feb. 25 to three months' imprisonment with hard labor; served 88 days);
- 6–8 November 1913 in Palm Ford (arrested for having brought unauthorized persons into the Transvaal and released on bail; served 2 days);
- 9 November–18 December 1913 in Heidelberg Jail, then Dundee Jail (both near Johannesburg), then Volksrust, then Bloemfontein, Orange Free State (arrested for inducing indentured immigrants to leave the Province; sentenced on Nov. 11 to nine months' imprisonment with hard labor, then on Nov. 14 at Volksrust to a further three months' imprisonment; served 39 days).

*In India (2,112 days):*
- 10–11 April 1919 (arrested and released; served 1 day);
- 10 March 1922–5 February 1924 in Sabarmati Jail, Ahmedabad, then Yeravda Jail (now Yerawada Central Jail), Poona (now Pune), then Sassoon Hospital, Poona (arrested for sedition; sentenced on Mar. 11 to six years imprisonment; served 697 days);
- 5 May 1930–26 January 1931 in Yeravda (arrested under Regulation 25 of 1827 "for removal of inconvenient persons without assignable reasons" (Gandhi 54: 369), which authorized detention without trial; served 266 days);
- 4 January 1932–8 May 1933 in Yeravda (arrested under Regulation 25; no trial; served 490 days);
- 1–23 August 1933 in Sabarmati Central Prison, then Yeravda, then Sassoon Hospital (arrested for disturbing the public peace; released on Aug. 3 and rearrested within an hour for disobeying an order of the Government to remain within Poona city limits; sentenced on Aug. 4 to one year imprisonment; served 22 days);
- 9 August 1942–6 May 1944 in Agha Khan Palace, Poona (arrested under Defense of India Rules for the purpose of public safety; no trial; served 636 days).

3. See Bernault who shows that South African jails played an important economic role from the 1880s onward by drawing upon the mostly African detainees as cheap labor; racial discrimination and segregation emerged at around the same time. See also Peté and Devenish who discuss corporal punishment, specifically flogging, in colonial jails as part of the emergence of a discourse of race.

4. For the reforms in India, see Barker, who advised the Indian Jails Committee during the 1920s. Arnold discusses the Indian prison as the "material adjunct to a colonial system of economic exploitation and political control," a system that defined itself as civilized and modern vis-à-vis the cruelty and barbarism of India's history, religion, and social practices. For the conditions in South Africa, see Mandela (8f.) whose experiences were very similar to those of Gandhi.

5. See, e.g., Jack 514. The roots of this faulty assumption no doubt lie in an ambiguous phrasing in the 1925 "Introduction" to the autobiography. There Gandhi wrote that he "should indeed have finished the autobiography had I gone through my full term of imprisonment at Yeravda [jail], for there was still a year left to complete the task, when I was discharged" (Gandhi 44: 89). The Gujarati original renders the passage differently: "But it would be still

one year before I could take up the task. I could in no circumstances even start writing the autobiography before then. The work, therefore, remained unattempted" (44: 470). The autobiography was written and published serially, in weekly installments, starting in late 1925.

6. With the exception of *Satyagraha in South Africa*, the pieces he wrote for publication in prison were all short, like the articles for his newspapers. There was a *Primer* (1922, published posthumously in 1951), offering lessons for school children; *From Yeravda Mandir* (1930, published in 1932), a short treatise on the ashram vows every member of Gandhi's household had to obey; *Ashram Observances in Action* (1932, published in 1948); and *Key to Health* (1942, published in 1948), which is concerned with dietary questions, sex, and other addictions.

7. The time of writing can be determined fairly precisely. On November 26, 1923, Gandhi noted in his jail diary: "Today commenced writing the history of Satyagraha in South Africa" (26: 450). By the time he was released on February 7, 1924, he had completed 180 pages, with about 100 left to go. In an interview with *The Bombay Chronicle* on March 27, 1924, he announced that the book would soon be published (27: 120), and a few days afterwards, on April 2, he was preparing the preface (147).

8. See Maureen Swan's revisionist reading of Gandhi's South African years. She argues that the Indian minority can hardly be said to have rallied as a body behind Gandhi's leadership. For one thing, they were far from unified to begin with, being split into three large groups that were looking primarily after their own interests: the merchant elite, the young professionals, and the indentured workers. For another, it was the people—the merchants at first, the workers later on—who politicized Gandhi, not the other way round.

## Works Cited

Arnold, David. "The Colonial Prison: Power, Knowledge and Penology in Nineteenth-Century India." *Subaltern Studies VII: Essays in Honour of Ranajit Guha*. Ed. David Arnold and David Hardiman. Oxford: Oxford University Press, 1994. 148–87. Print.

Barker, F.A. "Twenty Years of Penal and Prison Reform in India." *The Howard Journal of Criminal Justice* 6.1 (1941): 52–59. Print.

Bernault, Florence. "The Politics of Enclosure in Colonial and Post-Colonial Africa." *A History of Prison and Confinement in Africa*. Portsmouth: Heinemann, 2003. 1–53. Print.

Devji, Faisal. *The Impossible Indian: Gandhi and the Temptation of Violence*. London: Hurst, 2012. Print.

Fischer, Louis. *The Life of Mahatma Gandhi*. New York: Harper & Row, 1950. Print.

Gandhi, Mohandas K. *The Collected Works of Mahatma Gandhi*, Vol. 98. New Delhi: Publications Division, Government of India, 1999. Web. 19 July 2013.

Girard, René. *The Girard Reader*. Ed. James G. Williams. New York: Crossroad, 1996. Print.

Heathcote, T.A. "The Army of British India." *The Oxford History of the British Army*. Ed. David G. Chandler and Ian Beckett. New York: Oxford University Press, 2003. 362–84. Print.

Jack, Homer. *The Gandhi Reader*. New York: Grove Press, 1956. Print.

Mandela, Nelson. "Gandhi the Prisoner: A Comparison." *Mahatma Gandhi: 125 Years*. Ed. B.R. Nanda. New Delhi: Indian Council for Cultural Relations, 1995. 8–17. Print.

Peté, Stephen, and Annie Devenish. "Flogging, Fear and Food: Punishment and Race in Colonial Natal." *Journal of Southern African Studies* 31.1 (2005): 3–21. Print.

Swan, Maureen. *Gandhi: The South African Experience*. Johannesburg: Ravan, 1985. Print.

# Jawaharlal Nehru's *Discovery of India*: The Writing of History, Fighting for Freedom in Ahmandnager Jail

TILOTTAMA THAROOR

## Summary

Jawaharlal Nehru is another combatant against the English Colonial system known for his long struggle for national self-determination. Like Gandhi, and other twentieth-century anti-colonial revolutionaries—some famous, some not—he was educated in the colonial home country at the best institutions; in Nehru's case, Cambridge University and the Temple Inn Bar. This experience of English "civilization," India's suffering and predicament as a subject nation and the injustices of foreign rule, prompted him to political action—action that led to his confinement in His Majesty's Prisons for a total of nine years. He was then elected prime minister of a newly independent India just two years after getting out of prison. *Discovery of India*, written during his longest prison stay, is a panoramic view of the country—its history, people, politics, and future.—J.W.R.

## Introduction

On a sweltering August pre-dawn in 1942, the 52-year-old Jawaharlal Nehru was abruptly woken in his sister's house in Bombay and informed that the police had arrived to arrest and take him to jail. Neither surprised nor alarmed, he took his time to shave and write a few letters, before accompanying the police to Bombay's railway station, the Victoria Terminus, where a special train conveyed him and many others to an old medieval fort in the western town of Ahmadnagar. This was to be his confined space for the next three years till his release in June 1945. This was where he completed perhaps his most famous book, *The Discovery of India*.

Jawaharlal Nehru was no stranger to prison. From his first arrest and conviction in 1921, he was jailed eight times and spent a total of nine years incarcerated. Each time his jailer was the British government, which ruled India at that time; on each occasion, his offence was blatant and deliberate opposition to that foreign rule with the intention of ending it. For Nehru was amongst the most illustrious of Indian freedom fighters, a prominent member and leader of the Indian National Congress, immersed in its efforts to obtain India's independence from the British. He led and participated in agitations, protests, acts of civil disobedience, consistently and energetically defying British authority for more than twenty years. In response, the British arrested and detained him—and many others, including Mahatma Gandhi—in a variety of Indian jails. Freedom was eventually won in August 1947 and Jawaharlal Nehru became independent India's first Prime Minister. By then he had also published several books, mainly produced behind bars.

*The Discovery of India* was the last of his three most distinguished books, prior to which were *The Glimpses of World History* (written in the form of letters to his daughter, Indira, in 1934) and the 1936 *An Autobiography*. There is a discernible development of themes and preoccupations through the three books, and *The Discovery of India* is a culmination of Nehru's explorations of history, India and himself, and a preparation for India's self-governance and his assumption of power. In "discovering India," he was delineating its past, dissecting its colonial present and determining its independent future.

## *Biography and Political Beginnings*

Jawaharlal Nehru was born in 1889 into an affluent, upper-class Brahmin family of Allahabad, a culturally and politically vibrant northern Indian city. His father, Motilal Nehru, was a self-made, successful lawyer, who joined the Indian National Congress to challenge British rule. Yet he had many English friends who enjoyed his lavish and convivial hospitality. Motilal's liberal social views, his rejection of caste restrictions and his genial agnosticism, encouraged a lively, open formative environment for the young Jawaharhal. But as the only child for almost ten years before the birth of his two much younger sisters, he experienced a loneliness that seems to have remained a part of his temperament even in his most tumultuous political days.

He was initially taught at home by European governesses and tutors, and at the age of fifteen travelled to England for his education in the most elite English institutions from 1905 to 1912: first at the exclusive private school, Harrow, then at Cambridge University for a degree in science. This contributed to his life-long appreciation of a scientific outlook and scientific achievements, and complemented his love of literature, history, even sociology, as reflected in his writings. His biographers have noted that in college he encountered the ideas of progressive intellectuals, such as Bertrand Russell, John Maynard Keynes and George Bernard Shaw, studied about the Italian revolutionary Garibaldi and the French and American revolutions, and was attracted to the English Fabian Socialists' views, which advocated a gradual and reformist form of socialism. He also followed closely the developments in India regarding calls for *Swaraj* (the movement for more Indian involvement in governance) and *Swadeshi* (the movement to promote Indian products and boycott imported British goods).

Jawaharlal completed a law degree, passing the London Bar exam, and finally returned to India in 1912 to enter his father's flourishing legal practice, and marriage to Kamala after overcoming reservations about an arranged marriage to an unknown bride. Though Kamala suffered frail health, she participated in the freedom struggle and was jailed on one occasion. She died before Indian independence, and *The Discovery of India* begins with poignant descriptions of her final illness and death.

Motilal, eager to devote more time to Indian nationalist politics, delegated much of his successful legal practice to his 23-year-old son. But legal cases never engaged Jawaharlal's interest as he wrote, "I felt I was being engulfed in a dull routine of a pointless and futile existence" (Wolpert 29). And the biographer Stanley Wolpert writes, "the only diversion Jawaharlal could find for his unused energy and intellect was Indian politics ... [it] offered him an arena of conflict, one sufficiently diverse to invite intellectual dissent ... in this impossible imperial Raj" (Wolpert 29–30).

Jawaharlal attended his first political meeting of the Indian National Congress in December 1912, after which his commitment to the freedom struggle became all-consuming. Working for and leading the Congress party, he developed a close association and partnership with Gandhi: Gandhi seemed "the only person giving effective reply to the brutality of the British," writes Nehru expert S. Gopal (787). In the campaigns against British rule, Nehru also embraced the Non-Violent Civil Disobedience informed by the Gandhian principles of Satyagraha (which literally translates as "insistence on truth"). The tactics of Satyagraha—strikes, protests, pickets, deliberate infringement of British laws—were aimed at asserting the "truth" of Indian rights, exposing and countering the venality of colonial laws, challenging British authority, and weakening the capacity of colonial institutions to function effectively. Retribution—from beatings to arrest and imprisonment—was inevitable, and its endurance was integral to the Satyagraha doctrine as explained by Gandhi: "a vindication of truth by the infliction of suffering not on the opponent, but on oneself." Non-violently combating the inequities and iniquities of British rule was an honorable duty; unflinchingly accepting the brutal brunt of the law, injury and imprisonment, and continuing the struggle were also an indictment of British injustice.

Nehru's Satyagraha activism began in 1919 when the British imposed measures suspending all civil liberties of Indians, including the right to peaceful assembly. In response the Congress party authorized nation-wide strikes and protests which Nehru supported with alacrity as "a way out of the tangle, a method of action which was straight and open and possibly effective. I was afire with enthusiasm ... I hardly thought of the consequences—law-breaking, jail-going" (Wolpert 40). When British troops massacred civilian families gathered in Amritsar city's Jalianwalah Bagh, Britain's moral authority to rule collapsed and India erupted in outrage and protests. Nehru travelled around villages mobilizing Satyagraha actions, and seeing rural India for the first time, he records, was "a revelation. We found the countryside afire with enthusiasm and a strange excitement. Enormous gatherings would take place at the briefest notice by word of mouth" (Wolpert 46). The ubiquitous abject poverty, a legacy of colonial neglect, presented a "new picture of India ... naked, starving, crushed and utterly miserable," shamed his "easy-going and comfortable life" and "filled me with a new responsibility." Many years later, *The Discovery of India* evoked the degradation he witnessed and its urgent remedies: to eradicate the failed British rule, and advance a socially just independent future.

## *Jail Terms*

By 1921, the year of Jawaharlal's first jail term, he had "become wholly absorbed and wrapt in the movement," experiencing with his co-workers, "a kind of intoxication ... the happiness of a person crusading for a cause," untroubled "by fear or hesitation." He "gave up all my other associations and contacts, old friends, books, even newspapers," except when they dealt with the "work at hand." Later, somewhat remorsefully, he recalls how he "almost forgot my family, my wife" and infant daughter, as he "lived in offices and committee meetings and crowds," and felt the "thrill and power of influencing the mass" (Wolpert 49–50).

Nehru's first jail sentence in December 1921 was for protesting against the visit to India by the Prince of Wales, an extravagantly ceremonious symbol of imperial rule. Nehru and his father were arrested while addressing a large crowd, and Motilal proclaimed it "a high privilege to serve my motherland by going to jail with my only son" (Wolpert 50). Father and son in Lucknow jail were hardly alone—30,000 protesters against the Prince were His Majesty's jailed "guests" across the country.

Released three months later in March 1922, Jawaharlal was back in jail in May after he had organized pickets against merchants selling foreign cloth. The charges were "intimidation and abetment of an attempt to extort" and the sentence two concurrent jail terms of nineteen months. After Jawaharlal entered Naini Jail in April 1930 for illegal salt manufacture, a symbolic breaking of British salt monopoly, his 69-year-old father Motilal soon joined him on sedition charges. Jawaharlal's major concern was for his ailing father crammed into an 11 feet square cell. The family's eminent position kept them supplied with abundant fresh fruit and good food otherwise not available in prison. Motilal recorded his appreciation of Jawaharlal's solicitous care in a letter: "he anticipates everything and leaves nothing for me to do. I wish there were many fathers to boast of such sons" (Wolpert 114).

Jawaharlal Nehru returned alone to prison in January 1931, sentenced to two years rigorous imprisonment for inciting peasants not to pay taxes, followed by arrest in 1940 for sedition. But his final incarceration in 1942 in the remote, rugged barracks of the converted Ahmadnagar Fort, was the longest, and possibly harshest. Nehru and the entire Congress party leadership landed in jail when they launched the uncompromising "Quit India" movement, refusing to support the British World War II effort without assurance of Indian self-governance. And in Ahmadnagar jail he completed *The Discovery of India*.

When not in jail, Nehru plunged into the unceasing political work of organizing, negotiating, public speaking. He also traveled abroad, including to Spain during its Civil War and the Soviet Union. In Europe he visited labor organizations, mines and factories and attended a Congress of Oppressed Nationalities in Brussels, strengthening his socialist, anti-imperialist proclivities. In the Soviet Union, he was "impressed by the tremendous changes" produced by the Russian Revolution, and recognized that "socio-economic emancipation" needed to accompany the political change pursued by the Indian nationalist movement, writes political scientist L. S. Rathore. However, David Kopf insists that Nehru was "not seduced by Communist propaganda," and B. G. Gokhale claims that Nehru's early enthusiasm towards the Soviet Union for "one of the mightiest experiments in history" was later "tempered by the events of the Stalinist era." Moreover, argues Gokhale, "the Gandhian influence on him was so deep and pervasive that Nehru could not subscribe to the violence implicit" in Soviet brutalities, and his Liberal Humanist sympathies rejected Soviet-style coercions, regimentation and suppression of freedoms. Not surprisingly, Nehru fiercely abhorred the Fascism emerging in Europe and unequivocally declined invitations from Mussolini's Italy and Nazi Germany in 1936 and 1937.

## *Jail Experience*

During his nine years in jail, Nehru celebrated several birthdays, but also suffered the deaths of his father and wife. The conditions of these jail terms varied from comforts such as "rickety furniture" provided by kind jail staff to deprivations of reading, writing and family visits, mosquito and bug infestations. Accommodation could be a single cell or one shared with another inmate, often a political colleague or on two occasions his father. At Ahmadnagar he was disconcertingly first housed in a large space with several other political prisoners, though eventually he had a more private space.

Nehru had a variety of responses to these enforced periods in jail. He invariably used the actual arrest, trial and sentencing to make some of his most flamboyantly defiant speeches, repudiating British rule, proclaiming imminent Indian triumph, welcoming his arrest as an honor and glorifying jail "as a heaven for us ... a holy place of pilgrimage," (Wolpert 56). During his 1922 conviction, he exulted in sedition as the "creed of the Indian people (Wolpert 56). In 1930, he declared he had "no other profession, no other business ... or aim than to fight against British imperialism and drive it from India," willing to pay the price in bloodshed and suffering" to realize "the India of our dreams" (Wolpert 118). Following his 1942 arrest, Nehru is reported to have quoted Oliver Cromwell's defiance to the English monarch: "You have sat too long here for any good you have been doing. Depart, I say, and let us have done with you" (Kennedy 155).

Release from prison was also attended by statements fiercely denouncing "the larger prison that is India today," and anticipating the time when "we will demolish all the prison walls that encompass our bodies and minds, and function freely as a free nation" (Wolpert 297).

Incarceration, writes Stanley Wolpert, would "become the highest form of Nehru's national service" (57), though S. Gopal argues that a "thrill" and "emotional nationalism" are more evident in Nehru's earlier jail-related letters and diaries (Gopal 788).

For most part, Nehru seemed to adjust to the rigors of prison life, writing to his sister about waking at 3:30 in the morning, and following an orderly routine of reading, writing, running and walking, as well as the spinning and weaving which Indian nationalists undertook as acts of resistance to the imported British fabrics that had destroyed the Indian textile industry. "Life in prison," he acknowledged in a letter to his sister, "is not exciting, about as eventful as the existence of the average turnip" (Wolpert 112), claiming that imprisonment seeks to "remove all traces of humanity ... to subdue even the animal element" and reduce him to "the perfect vegetable" (Wolpert 112). "Blind obedience" is considered the "only virtue" and "spirit a sin," so Nehru was determined to preserve his spirit, even by sustaining a "creative tension ... as a method of keeping in form and an incentive to continuous effort" (Wolpert 113).

Sometimes the forced inaction of prison brought relief, and he wrote in letters about "slowly developing a measure of serenity, poise, strength of purpose" (Fisher 371), and that "prison life has one sovereign virtue ... teaches one detachment and the capacity to see things in their proper perspective." But he also complained about being "bored, fed up, angry with almost everything and everybody ... my companions who get on my nerves, with the country in general for not being aggressive and active as it might, with the British Empire and above all, with myself" (Wolpert 135).

When conditions were tightened, he was denied family visits and banned from writing, his thoughts were plaintively bleak: "Same round day after day, nothing to distinguish one day from another," an "occasional missed meal" seeming like a "remarkable event." Books came to his rescue: "what would one do without these to escape from ennui and depression" (Wolpert 138). While prison afforded him respite from the frenzy of political action and a sanctuary to think and write, yet he was frustrated, almost agonized, by his separation from ongoing political actions, deliberations, negotiations and important decisions.

This was definitely the case during his three years in Ahmadnagar prison when he wrote *The Discovery of India*. In the outside world major decisions were being made regarding India's future—especially intense debates about Muslim demands for a separate state—from which he felt excluded. His co-prisoners did include other Congress party notables, such as Sardar Vallabhai Patel and Maulana Abdul Kalam Azad. In addition to his own writing, he read books such as Plato's *Republic*, Proust, and Lin Yutang's *With Love and Irony*.

His greatest mode of relaxation seemed to come from gardening, and he created and worked every day on a rose garden with gardening equipment provided by the prison administration and the help of non-political prisoners. A badminton court was also built by the prison authorities and the political prisoners' leisure time was often occupied by games of badminton. In between the blossoming roses and badminton games, he finished *The Discovery of India*.

The accumulated convictions and understandings from his varied experiences, travels, political engagements, prodigious reading and writings are processed and refined in *The Discovery of India*. Nehru's biographers and analysts usually remark on his complex, often contradictory, world-views and intellectual affiliations: "half-Liberal, half–Marxist view of history," contends S.Gopal (305); "intellectually rooted in European Enlightenment, but also in Hindu Vedantic philosophy" (Mathur 528); a scientific rationalist, but not a dogmatic atheist (Rathore 460). "The study of Marx and Lenin," wrote Nehru, "helped me to see history and culture in a new light" (Mathur 530), and he adopted aspects of a Marxist theoretical approach: "the dialectic of continuous change by evolution" (Gokhale 313), the interplay of economics and politics, of imperialism and capitalism, and the role of impersonal world forces, class conflicts and social struggles in historical narratives and political action. However, Nehru's passionate humanism "rejected a mechanical view of human nature" (Gopal 789), writing history not just of impersonal masses, but of individuals as "singular creatures ... of spirit and dignity, involved in endless struggle ... suffering repeated martyrdom ... also rising again and again and triumphing over every adversity" (Gokhale 316).

## *The Book* The Discovery of India

Among the early reviewers of the book, Benjamin Schwartz in 1947, described it as an "indispensable book for understanding India ... mature, lucid, eminently readable," and in a 1991 article, historian David Kopf endorsed it as "a brilliant exposition of Indian cultural change and continuity over five millennia," and "not only a history of India, but a superb comparative history of India and the world" (62). Nehru began work on it during his 1940–1941 incarceration in Dehra Dun jail, and continued after 1942 in Ahmadnagar. But in the Introduction he confesses an ambivalence about the project: "During all these months I have often thought of writing, felt the urge to do it and at the same time a reluctance.... My friends took it for granted that I would write and produce another book, as I had done during previous terms of imprisonment" (34). Yet he hesitates, anxious that it won't be "of particular significance," distanced from the events swirling in the outside world, "what would my poor writing of a past and vanished age be worth then" (34)? He plans to discard the existing pages as "stale and uninteresting" and envisions a different way to assemble his narrative of "the debris of a half-forgotten past" (35).

This new narrative would address the questions that are raised at the beginning of the chapter titled "The Quest": "What is this India apart from her physical and geographical aspects? What did she represent in the past? What gave strength to her then? How did she lose that old strength, and has she lost it completely? Does she represent anything vital now, apart from being the home of a vast number of human beings? How does she fit into the modern world" (49)?

In answering these questions, Nehru composed a book that comprises history, social analysis, autobiographical details and intellectual explorations, in a combination of the modes evident in his earlier *Glimpses of Human History* and *An Autobiography*. This book focuses on the making and renewing of India: its diverse, multi-religious, multi-ethnic cultural and economic history, its contemporary predicament under British rule, existing problems and their future solutions in an independent Indian nation. A major purpose is to understand and explain the causes, circumstances and consequences of India's colonization by the British. Despite multiple conquests and disruptions in the past, India and its people had prospered and advanced. By contrast, India under the British is reduced to degraded, abject subjecthood. It is to retrieve India from this subjecthood that he fights against British rule, goes to prison and writes his book.

Two other important aspects of his imprisonment also direct the narrative, especially the latter sections of it: one, to explain why he and the Congress Party had refused to support the Allied war effort (in spite of his unwavering anti-fascism) unless India was free. Second, his evident dismay and alarm that while he and the Congress leadership were in prison, the Muslim League and its leader Jinnah (a former Congress leader) were free to pursue their goal of a separate Muslim state which Nehru strenuously opposed.

## A Book Description and Analysis

It is curious that the book, intended as an exploration of a complex national history, starts with a very personal account of the last years of his wife's illness and death. He describes how during his previous internment in 1934, he was briefly released so he could visit his wife, a tuberculosis patient in a sanatorium in the German Black Forest. She briefly recovered, but died some years later and he dedicated his second book, *An Autobiography,* to her. Then, after this brief foray into personal grief and remorse, he launches into aspects of his prison life and his book's subject.

India's history is traced from the 5000-year-old advanced civilization of Mohenjo Daro, through successive dynasties and kingdoms, invading armies, settling powers, and the strengths and weaknesses of different periods are appraised. Nehru particularly values India's capacity to absorb and accommodate diverse, enriching influences. Central Asian tribes, Afghan and Mongol conquerors all arrive, mingle, assimilate, and contribute to the eclectic cultural ethos. India, he writes, "was like some ancient palimpsest on which layer upon layer ... had been inscribed ... yet no succeeding layer had completely hidden or erased what had been written previously" (59). The diversity, furthermore, doesn't preclude a "tremendous impress of oneness" that "has held us together" (59). This "oneness" is sometimes vague mystification; sometimes evoked through illiterate village folks' familiarity with the same stories from ancient epics. A distinguishing feature of the oneness is a consistent record of "cultural fusion and synthesis" which first began between migrating Aryans and local Dravidians (73). "Basic Indian culture," he insists, is defined by "the astonishing inclusive capacity to absorb foreign races and cultures," and the concomitant willingness of foreign arrivals (whether people or ideas) to enter into the synthesis and fusion. This notion of the Indian identity gives Nehru the greatest personal satisfaction, enables him to argue that Muslims in India don't need a separate homeland, and defines the vision of a secular, pluralist India.

He situates India in a wider international context by emphasizing the close ties and vital contacts from ancient times with Sumeria, Persia, Egypt, Greece, Rome, Arabia, China, and Indian commercial and cultural influence in East and Southeast Asia. In this pluralist, inclusive India, religions coexist, classical and vernacular languages flourish, science and mathematical concepts are developed and disseminated in a wider world. Golden ages of artistic brilliance and economic vitality do not end when Islam arrives: new forms are invigorated, new splendors conceived, but India's scientific legacy suffered.

Nehru documents all the mathematical and scientific achievements up to the 8th century CE, and then laments the decline of scientific enquiry. He particularly faults the Mughals (the last imperial rulers before the British) for neglecting scientific pursuits and areas such as ship-building (even though he notes that Indian-built ships were used in the Napoleonic wars) and ceding scientific progress to Europe from the 16th century onwards, which propelled European domination in the subsequent centuries. There's particular chagrin that Europeans came to India for Indian manufactured products, such as textiles; then acquired the power to destroy the industry. As the industrial revolution flourished in England, colonial policies stifled any prospect of industrial growth in India. Nehru locates Indian subjugation and inferiority in its current industrial backwardness, and therefore his vision for the Indian future emphasizes the revival of science and industry ... almost a return to a past glory.

In this ebullient narrative of hybridity and harmony, of strangers settling and adapting, of the indigenous enriched by the imported, only the British are an anomaly. They are conquerors who control but reject India as home; they exert superiority rather than civility; as blatant colonialists they exploit, extract and deplete India's resources. To create "a classic colonial economy" India was reduced to a supplier of raw materials and a market for England's industrial goods (299). British plunder, heavy duties and neglect disfigure and ruin Indian lives: impoverishment and unemployment for the industrial and artisanal class, multitudes forced into agriculture, fragmentation of land, rise of landlords and moneylenders, debts and taxes, breakdown of traditional group life and education, and appalling poverty (99).

The latter pages discuss the emergence and rise of the freedom movement and the role of Gandhi. Even though Nehru had some disagreements with Gandhi—e.g., Nehru favored greater industrial development than Gandhi—he eulogizes the latter as seeming to "emerge from the millions of India, speaking their language ... incessantly drawing attention to their appalling condition" (358), and admires Gandhi's "notion of India in which all communities shall live in perfect harmony and gender equality" (363). He opposes the sectarian divide between Muslims and Hindus fostered by the British, and the growing clamor for a separate Muslim state in independent India that offends his fervent faith in India as a secular democracy. He expresses consistent sympathy for the Allied cause in World War II, even though he was jailed because his party had denied support to the war effort, since as Nehru writes, "Western democracies fight not for a change, but for the perpetuation of the old order" (481).

## The Book's Challenges to Existing Western Narratives

A major significance of *The Discovery of India* is its explicit and implicit countering of prevailing Western, especially English, notions and contentions about India, often constructed and perpetuated to justify colonial rule. Renowned post–Independence historian Romila Thapar declares such "nationalist" history-writing vital to retrieve the Indian past from colonial biases and assumptions (Thapar 212). For instance, Nehru rejects the narrative of an unchanging, despotic Indian past, popularized in John Mill's *History of India*, presenting India instead as dynamic and creative, containing local forms of administration within monarchies and empires of the past.

He also challenges the self-serving British argument of the ameliorations of colonial rule. The British may have possessed a more efficient political and military organization, which together with "a succession of fortuitous circumstances and lucky flukes" gave them power in India following the break up of the Mughal empire (276). But the entire period of conquest and plunder only produced "misery and violence" analogous to Central Europe during the 30 Years' War (281).

He denies the British complete credit for introducing modernity and progress in India, claiming instead that the British elevated the obscurantist, traditional structures (i.e feudal princes), in their administration, and allied with "reactionary elements" (330), installing feudal landownership and creating landlessness. They also suppressed Indians' freedom to pursue industrial growth and were reluctant to advance reforms in education and health care, except under enormous pressures from educated Indians. He concedes that "English education put Indians in touch with current western thought" (Gokhale, 317), but celebrates the progressive ideologies and reform efforts of Indians such as Ram Mohan Roy, Tagore, Vivekananda, culminating in his hero, Gandhi.

Nehru crucially complicates the dominant western image of India as singularly spiritual and religious, revealing his own complex position on religion. He writes: "Religion as I saw it practiced and accepted even by thinking people, whether it was Hinduism, or Buddhism or Christianity, did not attract me" (26), particularly its superstitions and dogmatic beliefs. But he accepts that it offers a "set of values," that, occasionally harmful, "are still the foundation of morality and ethics" (26). Nehru is especially moved by Gandhi's definition of Hinduism: "Search after truth through non-violent means; A man may not believe in God and still call himself a Hindu.... Hindusim is a relentless pursuit after truth" (75).

Nehru further contests that Hinduism promotes "other-worldliness," instead maintaining, "probably semitic culture, as exemplified in many religions that emerged from it, and certainly early Christianity, was far more other-worldly." The Indian past that he privileges "produced all manifestations of a vigorous and varied life": "an intense joy in life and nature, a pleasure in the art of living, the development of art and music and literature and song and dancing and painting and the theatre, and even a highly sophisticated inquiry into sex relations" (82). He quotes Arrian, a Greek historian of Alexander's campaign in North India, as impressed by Indian "lightheartedness": "No nation is fonder of singing and dancing than the Indians" (119).

In a 1929 speech Nehru had wondered whether though "born a Hindu," he was justified in "calling myself one or speaking on behalf of Hindus" (Gokhale 314). In *The Discovery of India*, he extensively explores disparate Hindu texts, from systems of logic to Vedantic abstraction. Invariably he highlights those features of Hindu philosophy that support his view of the culture's openness, inclusiveness and tolerance: the Upanishads, "instinct with a spirit of inquiry" (89), that continuously "attempt to harmonize social activity with spiritual adventure" (90). He refutes a Western perception that non–Western cultures subordinate the individual by quoting from the Upanishads, "There is nothing higher than the person," (90) and from a prayer to the sun, "O Sun of refulgent glory, I am the same person as makes thee what thou art," and commends, "What superb confidence" (91). Nehru seems to seek and discovers an individual authority and an empowering humanism in Hinduism as reinforcement against the defeats and humiliations inflicted by colonialism. He finds confirmation of an eternal desire for freedom in the Upanishads: "The question is: 'What is this Universe? From what does it arise? Into what does it go?' And the answer is 'In freedom it rises, in freedom it rests, and into freedom it melts away'" (92).

Such freedom clearly has profound resonances for someone in prison; for someone from a subjugated land. Books and his writings offer Nehru a measure of freedom in prison. But, perhaps concerned that his intellectual wanderings may seem isolated from reality, he records that when he was free he discovered a lot of India by actually travelling around different places, recreating the mountains, rivers, monuments, pilgrim sites, which also gave him insights into the past (51). Self-conscious about his elite status, concerned about being considered removed from the masses, he effuses about visits to the villages, mostly for political purposes, addressing rallies and exhorting freedom. He sometimes writes about villagers with an embarrassing, almost Orientalist flourish: "I grew to know the sturdy Jat of the northern and western districts, that typical son of the soil, brave and independent looking" (58), and excruciating generalizations: "Many a sensitive face and many a sturdy body, straight and clean-limbed; and among the women there was grace and suppleness and dignity and poise and, very often, a look of melancholy" (67–68). But he invariably registers the abject poverty to indict British colonial economic and agricultural policies that impoverish the villages (68) and justify his struggle.

Thus the book discovers the past, records the present and projects, both overtly and implicitly, into the future. After his release from Ahmadnagar prison, Nehru participated in the final freedom negotiations with the British, and was the elected prime minister of India's parliamentary democracy from 1947 till his death in 1964. Political writer Ramchandra Guha recently asserted, "We live in a world shaped by him and his colleagues. Adult suffrage, a federal polity, the mixed economy, non-alignment in foreign policy, cultural pluralism and the secular state—these were crucial choices made by the first generation of Indian nation-builders ... made collectively, but with the consent and justification of one man above all ... Jawaharlal Nehru" (1961).

*The Discovery of India* has glimpses of policies and Constitutional provisions that would be adopted by independent India under Nehru's prime ministership. The secular nationalism, industrialization and poverty alleviation that constituted India's "modern" identity are formulated in the book. Coexisting Socialist and Liberal impulses envisioned a planned, "mixed economy" (combining private enterprises and state-owned industry), to ensure that development benefitted the poorest. India's secularism, which constitutionally guarantees equal rights and freedoms to all religions, is often ascribed to Nehru's pluralist, inclusive vision. India's future internationalism, its non-aligned equidistance in the Cold War, relations with China and the non–Western world are intimated in the book. The India discovered, to become India advanced, had first to be a free India. The past was not a foreign, nor another, country. It was the same country, awaiting a new future.

## Works Cited

Fisher, Margaret W. "India's Jawaharlal Nehru." *Asian Survey* 7.6 (June 1967): 363–73. Print.

Gokhale, Balkrishna Govind. "Nehru and History." *History and Theory* 17.3 (Oct. 1978): 311–22. Print.

Gopal, S. "The Formative Ideology of Jawaharlal Nehru." *Economic and Political Weekly* 11.21 (May 22, 1976): 787–92. Print.

———. *Jawaharlal Nehru: An Autobiography*. Cambridge: Harvard University Press, 1976. Print.

Guha, Ramchandra. "Verdicts on Nehru: Rise and Fall of a Republican." *Economic and Political Weekly* 40.19 (May 7–13, 2005): 1958–96. Print.

Kopf, David. "A Look at Nehru's World History from the Dark Side of Modernity." *Journal of World History* 2.1 (Spring 1991): 47–63. Print.

Mathur, A. B. "Jawaharlal Nehru's Political Ideals." *The Indian Journal of Political Science* 51.4 (Oct.–Dec. 1990): 527–39. Print.

Nehru, Jawaharlal. *The Discovery of India*. New Delhi: Oxford University Press, 1986. Print.

Rathore, L.S. "Political Ideas of Jawaharlal Nehru." *The Indian Journal of Political Science* 46.4 (Oct.–Dec. 1985). 451–73, Print.

Schwartz, Benjamin. *Middle East Journal* (Jan 1947). Print.

Wolpert, Stanley. *Nehru: A Tryst with Destiny*. Oxford: Oxford University Press, 1996. Print.

# Drifter's Escape: Adolf Hitler and the Writing of *Mein Kampf*

ROLF WOLFSWINKEL

## Summary

The most disturbing figure in this volume, Hitler is proof that initial obscurity is not necessarily a bar to political victory and historical infamy. His ascension to power is almost a cautionary tale of right-wing politics in a democracy. *Mein Kampf*, written while Hitler was in prison, was part of this process. While not taken seriously at first, Hitler became the mouthpiece for ideas held in secret by high-ranking political and business officials. He played on long-standing nationalist and racist ideas and identities. He was also able to bring together disparate reactionary political elements. Hitler's national political career began with the absurd action of jumping onto a table, firing a pistol, and declaring "the revolution" had begun. This failed "revolution" landed him in jail (a very comfortable experience compared to those of others in this book) and gave him the opportunity to write *Mein Kampf*. Germany's political circumstances were ripe to give a figure like Hitler prominence, and place him on the national stage. While most are familiar with the history of the Third Reich from 1933 onward, this essay offers insight into the undistinguished, prefamous Hitler. *Mein Kampf* also exploited the "stabbed in the back" myth of German history that helped fascism to rise in the 1930s.—J.W.R.

## A Career Out of Nowhere: 1889–1923

When the doors of the prison fortress of Landsberg-am-Lech, 40 miles west of Munich, closed behind Adolf Hitler on November 11, 1923, it appeared that he had suffered another blow in a long series of failures. Two days earlier he had tried to seize power in the so-called "Bierkeller Putsch." It had resulted in a fiasco. Sixteen Nazi demonstrators and three policemen had been killed, many were injured and Hitler, who had first fled, was arrested two days later. The future looked bleak, but then life for Adolf Hitler had never looked promising from the start. First he had tried during his student days in Vienna to be admitted to the Academy of Fine Arts and after having been rejected there, he had tried his luck at the School for Architecture. He was turned down there as well, because he did not have the required matriculation certificate. In 1914 he had volunteered to serve in the 16th Bavarian Infantry Regiment (the List-regiment) and during four long years in the trenches of Belgium and France he had never been promoted. Now the attempt to "become a politician" had also suffered a serious setback. It seemed that whatever he set out to do he always ended up on the losing side. Adolf Hitler was born on April 20, 1889 in the Austrian border town of Braunau-am-Inn, where his father, Alois, worked as a customs official. Hitler's early years are the subject of much speculation, due to the fact that his own book is virtually the only source. Consequently there are all kinds of, sometimes titillating, rumors swirling around his ancestry. Did his paternal grandmother, Anna Maria Schicklgruber, indeed become pregnant, while serving in a Jewish household in Graz? Did she even work in Graz? Or did she work in Vienna in the household of Baron de Rothschild? Was he possibly the grandfather? There is a great number of these speculations, none based on verifiable facts. The only thing we know for certain is that Hitler's father, Alois, was born in 1837 (d. 1903) and that a certain Johann Georg Hiedler would later admit to being his father. In 1876 Alois therefore changed his name legally from Schicklgruber to Hiedler, which was written as Hitler since 1877. Some sources quote Hitler as saying this name change was the only good thing his father ever did.

Alois Hitler died in 1903, his wife Klara (Pölzl) in 1907, leaving Adolf an orphan at 18. He was not destitute, at least not initially. Until his 21st birthday he received an "orphan allowance" from the state of Austria, which enabled him to share a room in Vienna with a friend from Linz, August Kubizek. In his book about the time they spent together (August Kubizek, *The Young Hitler I Knew,* Greenhill Books, 2006), Hitler comes across as serious and passionate, not yet thinking about a career in politics, but considering himself an artist. Indeed, he would never abandon the bohemian lifestyle of those early days in Vienna, preferring to stay up late into the night and to sleep late into the day, much to the despair of his staff. After he could no longer afford the rent and he and Kubizek had parted ways, Hitler tried to make ends meet by painting and selling postcards on the streets of Vienna, living in a homeless shelter. Another homeless man, Reinhold Hanisch, also down on his luck, became his associate, until they had the almost inevitable fall-out.

Sometime in 1912 or 1913 Hitler moved from Vienna to Munich. There is some uncertainty about the date. Initially he seems to have tried to escape Austrian military conscription. As an artist he obviously looked down upon the constraints of army life, but when he was arrested in Munich and extradited to the Austrian military authorities, he was rejected as "medically unfit."

In any case he was back in Munich, when the First World War broke out. Through a remarkable coincidence a photograph has been preserved, taken on the 1st of August 1914 in front of the Feldhernnhalle in that city. A proclamation is being read, announcing the outbreak of war. Thousands of people are beside themselves with joy. Similar scenes are also known from Berlin, Vienna, Paris and London. But with the help of a magnifying glass Hitler can be seen in the crowd in Munich. He is not cheering, like so many others, but his face looks happy, almost radiant. Two days later he volunteered for the German (!) army and joined the 16th Bavarian Reserve Infantry Regiment. There is some controversy around Hitler's citizenship. Some authors maintain that by joining the German army in 1914, he automatically lost his Austrian citizenship, acquired by birth. However, there is no record of this. He officially renounced his Austrian citizenship in 1925, but did not become a German citizen until February 1932. For those seven years he was therefore stateless.

On October 21, 1914, his regiment was moved to the trenches of Flanders, where it immediately took part in the First Battle of Ypres. It was largely annihilated. In December of that year Hitler earned the Iron Cross 2nd Class. In August 1918 he would be decorated again, this time with the Iron Cross 1st Class, an unusual decoration for a soldier, who was not an officer. There is no reason to belittle these decorations, or his bravery, as is sometimes done. To survive four years of trench warfare is remarkable enough, to survive four years of trench warfare as a dispatch runner—the dangerous job of carrying messages from regimental headquarters to battalion headquarters and vice versa— is almost a miracle. To be among the survivors, where so many had died, may have contributed to the idea that he was destined for greater things. In the same way that Mussolini saw himself as "L'Uomo della Providentia" (The Man of Providence), Hitler must likewise have thought he was chosen by Providence to accomplish a higher task.

From accounts of his comrades quite a lot is known about Hitler's behavior in Flanders. He is seen as a loner, seldom writes or receives letters, doesn't drink, doesn't smoke, doesn't talk about women, all of which will not have made him popular. He is sometimes drawn into political conversations, talking about "evil Marxists" or "nefarious Jews," but not more so than others. All in all, he seemed to have liked his soldier's life. There is no mention of him having been lazy or a shirker. It may well have been the happiest time of his life. In an unverifiable story, told to this author by the late Andre Bequart of Wytschate in Flanders, Hitler is said to have returned to the area, where he spent four happy years, on his way back from France, after the capitulation in 1940. Bequart was the owner of a small trench museum in Croonaert Wood between Messines and Wytschaete, where Hitler earned his first Military Cross in 1914, and he showed me the places where he had taken Hitler at his request. According to him the Führer had been visibly moved by his own memories. Later, in Mein Kampf, he will call his participation in the war "the greatest and most unforgettable time of my earthly experience," which boils down to the same thing.

That ambivalence of never having felt so alive and with the constant presence of random death all around might explain the observation that "only by understanding the *Fronterlebnis* (the front experience) can one understand National Socialism" (Ekstein 307). It is a sentiment that Hitler shared with many others. All too frequently the war had become the most formative period of their lives. Gottfried Feder, another leading Nazi of the early days, remarked: "National Socialism is, in its truest meaning, the domain of the front" (Ekstein 309). In many ways it is similar to what is called in England "the fellowship of the trenches," in Italy Mussolini would talk about "*trincerocrazia*" (trenchocracy), and Germany would have its "*alte Kämpfer*," a term of endearment for "old soldiers," except that these "old" soldiers were in their early twenties.

The defeat in November 1918 was hard to accept. There are many contemporary accounts of feelings of betrayal, despair and abandonment. The German army had won the war on the Eastern Front a year earlier, it stood as yet undefeated in France, how could they suddenly have lost the war, without some politicians at home having stabbed the soldiers in the back? Most guilty among these politicians were the socialists and communists, with their dreams of internationalism and pacifism, and many of these were Jews. There are grounds to believe that Hitler's later virulent anti–Semitism was fed from here on and not earlier, as is sometimes believed. For instance, Hitler received the Iron Cross First Class at the recommendation of a Jewish officer of the List-regiment and some sources even have that same officer, Hugo Gutmann, putting the decoration on his uniform in August 1918. It was the only decoration he would wear at all times.

In his own bombastic way he would later describe the sense of futility the Armistice had left him with:

And so it had all been in vain. In vain all the sacrifices and privations; in vain the hunger and thirst of months which were often endless; in vain the hours in which, with mortal fear clutching at our hearts, we nevertheless did our duty; and in vain the deaths of two million who died. Would not the graves of all the hundreds of thousands open, the graves of those who with faith in the fatherland had marched forth never to return? Would they not open and send the silent mud- and blood-covered heroes back as spirits of vengeance to the homeland which had cheated them with such mockery of the highest sacrifice which a man can make to his people in this world? Had they died for this, the soldiers of August and September, 1914? Was it for this that in the autumn of the same year the volunteer regiments marched after their old comrades? Was it for this that these boys of seventeen sank into the earth of Flanders? Was this the meaning of the sacrifice which the German mother made to the fatherland when with sore heart she let her best-loved boys march off, never to see them again? Did all this happen only so that a gang of wretched criminals could lay hands on the fatherland [Hitler 205].

An analysis of this short fragment leads to a number of interesting observations: apart from the narcissistic, quasi-literary style, there is in the first place the reference to the "silent mud-and blood-covered heroes," whose graves are about to open. German military lore is full of references to fallen comrades. One of the most revealing is the popular soldier song: *"Ich hatt' einen Kameraden"* (I had a comrade-in-arms), written in 1809 (!) by Ludwig Uhland, in which a dead comrade is addressed as *"ein Stück von mir"* (a part of me). The SS slogan *"Die toten Kameraden marschieren mit"* (Our dead comrades are marching along) should be seen in the same light of soldier bonding.

But the most interesting part of the quote is in the last sentence, where he talks about "a gang of wretched criminals." Also sometimes referred to as 'November criminals' he is pointing to those politicians he considered responsible for signing the humiliating cease-fire agreement of November 11, 1918. The last emperor of Germany, Wilhelm II, had fled to The Netherlands a few days earlier, leaving the country virtually without a government. The Social-democrat Kurt Ebert was appointed chancellor, but his government was far from generally recognized. Germany was in turmoil and in no position to continue the war. The military High Command, with generals von Hindenburg and Ludendorff at the top, recognized that only too clearly, but they were reluctant to shoulder the blame. Leftist politicians played straight into their hands by taking the position that the military had lost all credibility. It had not been particularly helpful that the Allies (France, Britain and the U.S) had widely publicized the condition that they would only negotiate with 'true representatives' of the German people. National-liberals and *Zentrum* Catholics were largely tainted because of their support for the war effort, so it was left to the socialist party (SPD) and other left-wing groups to enter into talks with the Allies. It is true that the leader of the German delegation during the armistice talks was the (Catholic) Center Party politician, Matthias Erzberger, but he was on the left wing of that party. Maybe more significant is that he was killed in 1921 by a member of a right-wing organization for his role during these negotiations.

So it was left to a civilian delegation to seek the best terms for an armistice. The negotiations took place at a remote artillery railway emplacement, in the forest of Rethondes, near the village of Compiègnes, which could accommodate two trains side by side. It would be hard to illustrate the potency of symbols more clearly than by the fate of the railway car the Armistice was signed in. This car, Wagon-Lits 2419 D, went back into regular service for a few years after 1918, but from 1921 to 1927 it was exhibited in Paris. In 1927 it became the centerpiece of a small memorial on the very same spot in the forest, where the Armistice was signed. On June 22, 1940, Adolf Hitler, accompanied by Hermann Göring, Joachim von Ribbentrop, Wilhelm Keitel and other high-ranking Nazis returned to the forest and there, instead of in Paris, he dictated the terms of surrender to France. After that ceremony the railway car was brought to Berlin and exhibited there. The memorial in the forest was destroyed. When at the of end of 1944 and the beginning of 1945 American and British bombardments on Berlin intensified, Hitler ordered the car to be taken to a secret place (Crawinkel in Thuringia). SS troops were ordered to destroy it late March or early April 1945. However, the original site in the forest of Compiègnes was rededicated in 1950, by order of the French authorities, an exact replica of Wagon-Lits 2419 D was found, Wagon-Lits 2439, also built in 1913, and renumbered 2419 D. That's where it is today, fully refurbished. A potent example of reconstructed history.

The German delegation was led by Matthias Erzberger, a left of center member of the catholic—*Zentrum*—party, who became the symbol of what was seen as backstabbing politicians. His assassination in August 1921, followed by the murder of Walther Rathenau in June 1922, should be interpreted as a clear sign that the right wing was gaining in strength and confidence.

In two successive paragraphs of *Mein Kampf,* Hitler refers to the Armistice three times in a row: he calls it "the greatest villainy of the century," "something repulsive," and "the calamity" (204–05). For him the war would indeed never end.

## *The "Drummer to Germanism"*

Part of his anger may have been inspired by questions about his future: he was thirty years old and apart from his four years in the army he had never had a job. For four years he had incessantly been in the front line, but the end of the war he experienced in a hospital near Stettin, temporarily blinded by an English mustard gas attack. The rumors about an armistice he picked up there, he described as "sinister."

At the end of Chapter VII he would write that the shameful events of the Armistice made him decide to become a politician, but he had no idea how to go about it. Instead of staying in Munich, which was in a state of virtual civil war, offering many opportunities for budding politicians, he became a guard in a camp for prisoners-of-war in the small Bavarian village of Traunstein and would only return, after the camp was disbanded, in early April 1919. Munich was in the throes of a chaotic and bloody period of confusion, in which, it seemed, everybody was arresting everybody, but again Hitler abstained from any political action. Living in army barracks he was no more than a spectator. But in the summer of that year the private who never got promoted received an order to become a "liaison man." He had to follow a course in "civic thinking"; among his teachers were captain Ernst Röhm, later leader of the SA (Sturm Abteilung), and Gottfried Feder, a man with a chaotic and undisciplined mind, but his ideas about breaking the "interest slavery" made a deep impression on Hitler. It was becoming clear to him that both capitalism and communism seemed enemies of the "true" Germany, something he would later refer to as his "great discovery."

In his new capacity—collecting information about radical movements—he went to a meeting of a group, calling itself the "German Workers Party," and he met the chairman, called Anton Drexler, a railway machinist. It was a small and rather unimpressive collection of disgruntled men, but Hitler liked what he heard and decided to join. In his *Adolf Hitler* (1976) John Toland argues that Hitler joined the DAP at the instigation of general Ludendorff, which would explain why a soldier, let alone an "intelligence officer," would be allowed to join a political party. Toland writes: "So, in a sense, Hitler was ordered to do what he had already decided to do" (94). His membership number was 55. Actually he was given number 555: in order to make enrollment appear more than it was, membership registration started at 500.

At the next meeting he was asked to join the Board as Board Member number 7, with as special duties: "propaganda and recruitment." The man without a future had stumbled upon his niche. He found he had a way with words, or better that he had an intuitive knowledge for what his audiences wanted to hear. Increasingly he spoke for more and more receptive audiences, his reputation as somebody who said what everybody else was thinking spread rapidly. Membership of the DAP grew exponentially and before long Hitler felt confident enough to issue the hapless chairman Anton Drexler an ultimatum: he wanted to take over the party and the leadership. The Board saw no other solution and appointed Drexler vice-chairman. On March 31, 1920, Hitler resigned from the Army.

One of his first official deeds in his new function as "Führer" (Leader) of the party was to suggest a name change: the DAP would become the NSDAP (National-Socialist), a prefix that in itself was not very significant, but it would quickly become abbreviated to Nazi party (from *National*, the first four letters in German are pronounced *Nazi*). In this way he made clear that unlike Bolshevism with its vaguely international ring, the only true socialism was "national" socialism. In his public speeches an image of a new enemy began popping up more and more: "International Jewry." He also designed a flag for the movement: bright red with a white circle in the middle, in the circle a black swastika. After having written the program for the new party, the so-called "25 Points," Hitler would from now on refer to himself as an "author," using language to drum up support for the national reawakening of Germany and German "values."

In his speeches for larger and larger audiences Hitler would always come back to these two topics: Germany needed to be woken up. The stamp of shame and national humiliation embodied by the Weimar Republic and in particular by left-wing parties like the SPD (Socialists) and the KPD (Communists), had to be eradicated. The other theme that he would increasingly turn to was the threat of what he called "international Jewry." International Jewry was seen as the antithesis of national *German* values. There is no doubt that both subjects resonated well with his audiences, they kept turning up in bigger and bigger numbers.

During 1920 and 1921 he spent much time building up the party, surrounding himself with dubious characters like Ernst Röhm, Dietrich Eckhart, Hermann Göring and Rudolf Hess. Eckhart, a mediocre Bavarian poet, is often considered one of the main influences on Hitler's career. Robert Wistrich refers to him as the "spiritual godfather" of National-Socialism. The second volume of *Mein Kampf* has a dedication to him on the last page.

These men had very little in common, except a hatred of Marxism and strong nationalist sympathies. The parliamentary methods of the Weimar Republic created nothing but scorn in them, but it was unclear what political results the party hoped to achieve. Hitler often spoke about the use of force and of an overthrow of the Jewish-Marxist cabal in Berlin, but he never made clear how he was going to accomplish that.

All that changed in 1922. In Italy Mussolini's March on Rome at the end of October of that year had given him and his party virtually dictatorial powers. His success made a deep impression on Hitler and his paladins. The idea of a "March on Berlin" became a hotly discussed topic, especially when the central government appeared weak and irresolute in the wake of the French occupation of the Ruhr in January 1923.

Bavaria was not like other German states. Or maybe I should say there were more German states like Bavaria, but Bavaria was the most extreme. Until 1918 it had had its own army, with its own uniforms and its own General Staff, Bavarian officers swore an oath of loyalty to their own Bavarian king. The republican government in Berlin was viewed with suspicion and hardly concealed hostility. If anywhere, a movement to topple the Weimar Republic had the best chance in Bavaria. Mussolini's act of bravura of October 1922 had made a deep impression on many here. Hitler and his Nazi party were probably the most outspoken, but there were others who felt the same, some even in positions of high authority. First among these was the Bavarian prime minister, Gustav von Kahr. He was generally seen as the man who would pave the way for the return of the old monarchy in Bavaria, embodied in the person of Crown Prince Rupprecht. Together with General Otto Hermann von Lossow and Chief of Police Hans von Seisser he successfully undermined and even sabotaged directives from the government in Berlin. They had a large following. It has been said of the Weimar Republic that it was "a democracy without democrats," and that was certainly even more true of Bavaria. All this is to say that Hitler's attempt to seize power in November 1923 must have met with the tacit approval of many, not only Nazis.

The actual events have a slightly operatic air to them. On the night before—November 8, 1923—the march to the center of Munich was planned to take place, Hitler and a large entourage infiltrated a nationalist meeting in an establishment called the *Bürgerbräukeller*, where all three men were to speak. Hitler acted in a most dramatic fashion, jumping on a table, producing a pistol, firing into the ceiling, and declaring: "The National Revolution has begun, the government in Berlin must abdicate." The triumvirate of von Kahr, von Lossow and von Seisser were sufficiently intimidated by the roar of approval from the crowd to go along with the momentum of that evening. It was agreed that the next morning there would be a march to the seat of government in Munich. They would be joined by the very symbol of Imperial Germany, Field-Marshall Erich von Ludendorff.

The next day, November 9, 1923, the three aristocrats had changed their minds, having had sufficient time to think things over. Prince Rupprecht had made it clear he thought the Putsch foolish, von Lossow had ordered—in the middle of the night—loyal army battalions in Augsburg and Regensburg and other nearby army barracks to be ready to come to Munich by rail immediately.

The "March on Berlin" quickly turned into a farce and should have been the end of Hitler's ambitions to do in Germany what Mussolini had done in Italy. In despite of having been warned that an armed police cordon was waiting in front of the Town Hall, about two thousand marchers began their demonstration: on the *Odeonsplatz* in the center of town shots were fired and chaos erupted. When people to the left and right of Hitler began to fall away, either being hit or—like Hitler himself—forced to take cover, only von Ludendorff continued to march forward. Folly or heroism, he believed nobody would dare to shoot at him. And nobody did. Once he had marched straight through the ranks of firing policemen and had arrived at the back of their line, a police officer arrested him. Nineteen people were killed, many more injured, and most of the leaders were arrested either there or in the days after.

## *A Memoir at 34*

Initially Hitler had fled the scene in an ambulance; his left arm and shoulder were slightly injured. On November 11 he was arrested and taken to the prison fortress of Landsberg. The party was in disarray: with the exception of Hess and Göring, who had managed to flee to Austria, all Putsch leaders had been taken into custody. The future seemed bleak. The "treason" trial began on February 24, 1924, and would last until April 1. In those five weeks of court proceedings Hitler went from obscure local politician, hardly known in Munich, let alone outside, to national celebrity. But now all his practice in long monologues, his hours of public speeches and his tried and trusted way of turning arguments of his opponents to his own advantage were finally paying off. The accusation of high treason he rejected with contempt. High treason was what the Marxist and Jewish politicians had committed, in 1918, when they stabbed the soldiers at the front in the back. If he was guilty of high treason, then certainly von Kahr, von Lossow and von Seisser—all three had turned witnesses for the prosecution—should be standing next to him. The problem was not whether Hitler was wrong or right, the problem was that most people in the courtroom, including the judges and the jury, actually agreed with him. The verdict therefore was not surprising: a five-year prison sentence, with the possibility of parole after six months. The *Times* of London commented drily: "The trial has at any rate proved that a plot against the Constitution of the Reich is not considered a serious crime in Bavaria." Of course, Landsberg-am-Lech was not an ordinary prison, as Hitler was not an ordinary prisoner. Apart from cells for convicted criminals, it also had a 'protective custody' section. As political prisoner Hitler enjoyed certain privileges:

his accommodation was spare, but consisted of two reasonably comfortable rooms, he could receive visitors at all times and he could work on his book. He could not leave, though. After the 2nd World War Landsberg was in use for awhile to house Nazi War Criminals.

It seems that he came up with the idea of writing a book about his life, soon after the beginning of his sentence. After having written the 25 Points Program of the NSDAP, he considered himself an author. Now he had the time for a more expansive work. His publisher, one of his earliest admirers and his former company sergeant major, Max Amann, expected a work about the intricacies of the failed 'Putsch.' He based those expectations on the working title he was given: "A Four and One-half Year Struggle against Lies, Stupidity, and Cowardice: Settling Accounts with the Destroyers of the National Socialist Movement." Initially Hitler meant the book to be a support for the party members, while he was in prison. He wanted to give details about the program and about why the attempt to seize power had failed. But soon he was thinking in broader terms, nothing less than his life and his struggles would be the topic. He therefore wanted "Mein Leben" (My Life) as the title, which Amann later changed to "Mein Kampf" (My Struggle). The subtitle of the first volume, "Eine Abrechnung" (Settling Accounts) still referred to the original idea, but by now had lost its meaning.

*Mein Kampf* is a strange book. This may partly be due to the fact that Hitler didn't actually write it by hand himself, but dictated it to two or three of his devoted scribes. Among these Rudolf Hess was probably the most dedicated. It had also been Hess, who had introduced Hitler at a party meeting in 1922 as *"Der Führer."* It was published in two volumes: the first volume in the fall of 1925, the second came out in December 1926. Part autobiography, part political pamphlet, part rant and part hysteria, *Mein Kampf* is never entertaining. Maybe due to its incoherent and chaotic structure it was not an instant success, not even among the party faithful. Its almost 900 pages proved too much for many.

Of course, later, after Hitler became Chancellor in 1933, it would become an almost required present at weddings, birthdays, work anniversaries and graduations, and it would make him a millionaire. But even then it remained doubtful how many people actually read it. Due to the density of very much of it most readers will have restricted themselves to the more pragmatic parts of the book, partly because it is easier to see what the author means. One example: writing about Marxism, Hitler describes this "doctrine of destruction": "I again immersed myself in the theoretical literature of this new world, attempting to achieve clarity concerning its possible effects, and then compared it with the actual phenomena and events it brings about in political, cultural, and economic life" (154). Joachim Fest concludes: "Behind the front of bold words lurks the anxiety of the half-educated author that his readers may question his intellectual competence" (Fest 202).

Konrad Heiden, who wrote the introduction to the English translation and author of a well-received biography of Hitler, remarked: "The essential parts of the book do not concern questions of foreign policy or military geography, but of race, propaganda, and political education" (Heiden xviii). It is not easy to summarize such a book, but two main topics can be seen to run through the many chapters: First there is his rabid hatred of Jews and his eulogization of its counterpart, the "Aryan race." Anti-Semitism was not a new phenomenon: the end of the 19th century had seen a surge of Russian, French and German outbursts of anti–Semitic racial hatred. Hitler went a step further, when he writes that in the end there will only be two races left, which are engaged in a fight to the finish. Proudly he speaks of *"meine große Entdeckung"* (my major discovery), when he states that capitalism and communism only appear to be each others enemies, but that in reality they both conspire together to destroy Germany. Behind Wall Street and the Kremlin he sees a conspiracy of "international Jewry" to climb to world domination. Only the Germans stand between the Jews and the realization of that objective. In the final conflict Germany has to win or go under.

The second large theme is the need for *"Lebensraum im Osten"* (living space in the East). Writing about "the East" he means Eastern Europe: Poland, Ukraine, Russia, the Baltic States, traditionally seen as 'the bread basket of Europe.' Hitler believed that the growing Aryan nation would need more space to provide for its surplus population. War with that part of Europe is therefore inevitable. The people living there would either become laborers for the Germans or be destroyed. It is true, Slavs were not Jews, but they were just as inferior to the Aryan race, and therefore expendable.

After Hitler's suicide and Germany's collapse in 1945, the book would be banned in many countries. In some cases this ban continues, often in the form of a ban on publishing as opposed to possessing it. That is the case in Germany, for instance. Towards the end of 1924 the possibility of early parole came up. The state prosecutor requested a report on Hitler's behavior in prison. It was written by prison warden Leyhold and contained sentences like "He is easily content, modest, and desirous to please. Makes no demands, is quiet and sensible, serious and quite without aggressiveness, and tries painstakingly to abide by prison rules" (Fest 218). Clearly a model prisoner. The state prosecutor saw therefore no reason not to grant him parole. On December 20, 1924, Hitler walked through the doors of the fortress in Landsberg-am-Lech a free man.

But the Germany of 1925 was a different Germany than a year earlier: Hitler found the party in disarray, the government in Berlin had acquired some respectability, both nationally and internationally, and the willingness of many to try a path outside the law had strongly diminished. That included Hitler. He set out to rebuild the party and to prepare it for "the legal revolution" as opposed to "an illegal one."

From 1924–25 to 1929 it seemed as if there was a future for the Weimar republic; Germany was allowed to join the League of Nations in 1926, economic recovery plans like the Dawes plan of 1924 and the Young plan of 1928 did much to restore faith in the German economy, Germany was invited to rejoin the International Olympic Committee and granted the Games of 1936. In the general elections of 1928 Hitler's reconstituted Nazi Party managed to gain 12 seats out of more than 430. Again the future looked bleak. All that would change after the crash of the New York Stock Exchange in October 1929. Once again Hitler began to think of seizing power, this time democratically with the help of the ballot box. It would end on January 30, 1933, when he was appointed chancellor of Germany with almost 50 percent of Germans having voted for him. The gamble to "become a politician" that he had taken in 1919, had paid off: the aimless drifter of 1923 had found his way in jail.

## Works Cited

Fest, Joachim C. *Hitler*. New York: Harcourt Brace Jovanovich, 1973. Print.
Heiden, Konrad, and Adolf Hitler. Introduction. *Das Zeitalter Der Verantwortungslosigkeit: Konrad Heiden*. Zürich: Europa-Verlag, 1936. n.p. Print.
Hitler, Adolf, and Ralph Manheim. *Mein Kampf*. Boston: Houghton Mifflin, 1971. Print.
Toland, John. *Adolf Hitler*. Garden City, NY: Doubleday, 1976. Print.
Wistrich, Robert. *Who's Who in Nazi Germany*. London: Weidenfeld and Nicolson, 1982. Print.

# Antonio Gramsci's *The Prison Notebooks*: A Humanist Reconstruction of Marxism

### Brendan Hogan

## Summary

Antonio Gramsci's imprisonment, during which he wrote *The Prison Notebooks*, is the classic story of a political radical and state persecution. Through an active career as a writer, an organizer, and a politician, Gramsci made a significant impression. It was an impression that threatened the political status quo of Italy in the 1920s and '30s. *The Prison Notebooks* offer a critique of capitalism and political organizations, as well as of social and political power. Much of Gramsci's theoretical approach has been adopted in different areas of academia and political analysis. Like many of the figures in this book, he was singled out for special political and criminal persecution, and—again, as with others in this book—the persecution backfired. The attempt to silence Gramsci was a spectacular failure, especially given the fact that the Italian fascists have wound up in the dustbin of history while Gramsci's work and ideas remain alive and vital.—J.W.R.

## Biographical Sketch

Antonio Gramsci was born into a family of a respectable social lineage in Ghilarza, Sardinia, in 1881. While his family was not wealthy in his early years, it did not, at first, suffer the harsher effects of widespread poverty throughout Sardinia at that time. Still, severe poverty made its way into their lives when his father fell upon disgrace through a local scandal. Francesco Gramsci lost his administrative post and the entire family was brought into dire straits. Poverty was a scourge that would haunt Gramsci's life up into his adulthood. This hardship was exacerbated by a spinal aberration that appeared in Gramsci's childhood and developed into a permanently hunched back. The causes of this condition were not fully understood, though his mother attributed it to him being dropped as a child. At any rate, he remained of smaller than normal physical stature his entire life. Gramsci's health fell into compromised states at various points throughout his life and experiences of extreme physical and nervous distress were not uncommon due both to his physiological and his economic hardships.

Gramsci excelled in his schooling enough to earn scholarships that allowed him to leave Sardinia for mainland Italy where his political consciousness would awaken to the variety of struggles so characteristic of industrialized nations. While in Turin, Gramsci continued to succeed in school, impressing his teachers and student colleagues. He was rewarded with just enough scholarship and aid to complete his course of study, though desperate poverty permeated his experience. He became involved in political organizing and quickly became a well known figure in the socialist movement in Turin and from there gained a national reputation through his journalism and political activities. Gramsci rose to prominent international recognition in the Italian Communist Party (CPI) and served in the Italian Parliament as a deputy of the Communist Party. He was arrested on November 8, 1926, in Rome, was moved to various prisons over the course of eleven years, and finally died in custody in 1937.

## *Historical Background*

"We must stop this brain from working for the next twenty years!" So declared the Fascist prosecutor of Antonio Gramsci at his official trial in 1928 following his arrest Fascist police under the direction of Benito Mussolini (Motilio 600).

On the evening of November 8, 1926, Gramsci was arrested while walking in Porta Pia, in Rome. Fascist dictator Benito Mussolini had just ordered that the Communist party members who sat as deputies in the Italian parliament should be "added to the list" of those who were to be expelled for "abandonment of parliamentary work." The list of expelled parliamentarians had been created as punishment for setting up an alternative government known as the Aventine Secession, in protest to the increasingly authoritarian and dictatorial methods of Mussolini. Up for specific targeting were those groups who championed the causes of worker rights and organized labor, often self-proclaimed socialists and communists, and those who had criticized the Fascists. Gramsci had been hounded and followed by police for several years by the time of his arrest. This crucial inclusion of parliamentary deputies on the list of those to be arrested suspended the law of immunity from prosecution that was the recognized legal precedent at the time. With this act, Gramsci's fate was sealed. He was accused of "conspiracy, of instigation of civil war, of justifying criminal acts, and of fomenting class hatred" (Fiori 230). Contrary to the wishes of the minister quoted above, Gramsci's imprisonment allowed him to compile one of the most significant theoretical works of Marxist thought in the twentieth century. With the ongoing adoption of several of Gramsci's key concepts and arguments in these writings, across a variety of disciplines, the *Prison Writings* ranks as one of the greatest works of twentieth century social and political thought.

Italy, at the time of Gramsci's arrest in 1926, was experiencing severe social and political repression due to a confluence of forces, most importantly among them industrialization, the consequences of World War I, and the seizure of political power by the Fascists. Since the unification of Italy in 1871 the forces of modernization had been unevenly distributed and, as in many other European countries, there was a growing conflict between workers and the industrialists. Increasingly force was being used both by the state and by privately hired paramilitaries to curtail worker movements, some of which also resorted to violent actions on occasion. Gramsci had been at the heart of these political struggles and debates since his university days in Turin.

His first interest in terms of political problems was the use, abuse, and marginalization of the south of Italy by the northern establishment. His political sensibility was rooted in his earliest experiences in Sardinia, leading to deep sympathies with the cause of Sardinian nationalism. His studies led him to understand that Italian unification had done very little to bridge the material disparities between the rich north and the poor south. This understanding was reinforced as Gramsci came into touch with the work of northern intellectuals who espoused eugenicist and racist explanations of the South's condition. Specifically, northern Italian academics were promulgating explanations that attributed the uneven development of Southern Italy to genetic characteristics, understood as defects in the "race" of Southern Italian peoples. In Gramsci's youth, this regional racism and oppression of the south and Sardinia in particular, had awakened not only nationalist passions, but also a sense of injustice and exclusion from the entire Italian project.

Turin was a city known for its strong labor movement and a wide variety of political perspectives on how workers could get a more legitimate share of the goods of industrialization. Gramsci's experience as a student organizer and a participant in the political struggles of the day led him to a broader view of the injustices he had witnessed in the distribution of the benefits of modernization in Italy. Through connections made by his older brother, Gennaro, Gramsci became very active in the labor movement in Turin. Gramsci was both an organizer and a writer, creating journals with fellow activists organized around addressing the political struggles of the day. Crucially important, too, was that Gramsci knew the cultural life of Turin as a drama critic and was a critic of culture more generally. This activity reflected Gramsci's lifelong belief that the press, in all of its manifestations, was necessary for the education of the masses as to their real self-interest with respect to economic matters as well as their cultural enlightenment. His emphasis on the education of workers through mediums of a more *quotidienne* variety also informed his understanding of what was required in Italy, given the stage of modernist and capitalist development it had achieved.

This is reflected in Gramsci's life. In addition to his activities in the press, Gramsci also took his educational activities to the workers and youth of Turin. During this time, Gramsci became well known through worker education programs, lectures, and dialogues. Gramsci spent a great deal of time with workers and students discussing their interests and offering his interpretation of the conditions in their struggle for a better life. This was part of a larger vision of just economic production led by factory councils of workers who had collective ownership of the means of production, in contrast to the managerial capitalist model that prevailed at that time. It was Gramsci's popular writings and coordination with others that he became a nationally known figure. He was soon drafted into electoral politics as a member of the PCI, the Communist Party of Italy. His participation in the communist party led to connections with the revolutionary forces in Russia after 1917 and he even traveled there as an Italian representative of the communist party.

His regional frame of analysis, the Italian North's exploitation and mendacious characterization of the Italian South, expanded and deepened. He connected this view to a more inclusive understanding of the forces at work in the processes that combined economic and political power to shape the destiny of Europe, and indeed, anywhere capitalism prevailed.

The crisis of World War I from 1914 to 1919 only reinforced these conflicts and highlighted for Gramsci the need for an even more intensive effort to educate and empower the working class. The failure of the emergence of an international working class organized to meet their collective interests across European national borders was partly responsible for workers choosing nationalism over class based solidarity and slaughtering each other in the millions in World War I. This presented a deep problem for many who agreed with the socialist and communist ideas of Gramsci's cohort. This led Gramsci to rethink some of the pillars of Marxist thought. However, a successful worker's movement modeled on the Russian Revolution of 1917 never materialized in interwar Fascist Italy. It should be remembered that the strategies and activities of the communists and socialists in Italy were a major social force and constituted a significant part of the political context for Gramsci's activities. These groups were powerful enough to be systematically targeted and repressed with physical beatings, intimidation and imprisonment, as in the case of Gramsci and many others.

## *The Book* The Prison Notebooks

Gramsci's prison notebooks are a collection of notes, writings and longer commentaries on a large variety of topics and problems. Their subject matter is wide ranging and in this sense does not constitute a "book" in the traditional sense. However, read together, the three published volumes provide the basis for general conclusions about Gramsci's views on a variety of philosophical, economic, political, literary, and cultural subjects. The challenge is to select the central ideas that Gramsci formulated and had the most influence since the notebooks have made their way to the light of day.

Before getting to these main influential concepts, however, the conditions of Gramsci's imprisonment bear some mentioning. Specifically, Gramsci's fragile health worsened while he was in prison. He was kept in a cell close to the guards' quarters and so he had trouble resting as well due to the disturbance of the round-the-clock presence of the guards. However, he was also in communication with other political prisoners and while he was not allowed to write at first, he exercised his legal right to reading materials and used the law to the greatest degree possible to alleviate his suffering without indicating he was in any way capitulating to the desired outcome of the Fascist government: that he renounce his position and admit that he was wrong. For many months at first, Gramsci was not allowed to write and his reading materials were strictly controlled during his imprisonment. His contacts, such as the famous Italian economist Piero Sraffa, later provided reading materials he requested and he was able to exchange with other prisoners lessons in history, politics, and the study of languages, thus learning to translate German while incarcerated. All the more amazing then is Gramsci's ability to recall much of what he was writing on while in prison from earlier studies. In addressing problems of political organization, questions of philosophy and methodology, as well as political and military movements during the unification of Italy, in the nineteenth century, Gramsci's memory served him extraordinarily well as later editors of his works attest.

In addition, it is useful to remember that Gramsci's letters and writings were subject to censors, and thus much labor has been exercised in interpreting his works. As stated earlier, in order to do this with a collection of comments, fragments, and variety of arguments, it is best to lift out the main conceptual elements of the work. With these biographical and historical details in mind, the stage is set to explore Gramsci's innovative contributions to the tradition of political thought he was a central part of, Marxism, and then examine some specific arguments that had the most lasting impact in discussions of political and cultural theory since his death.

## Gramsci's New Historical Materialism

At Gramsci's time, one of the most significant historical events was the development of Russian communism and the Russian Revolution of 1917. In fact, as we shall see, the concept of "hegemony," one of Gramsci's most important contributions to political theory, has its roots in late nineteenth century Russian socialist thought. The success of the revolution and its decline into a particularly violent and contentious regime were significant lessons that Gramsci drew upon to articulate a view of the status and struggles of the working classes against exploitation under capitalism. Specifically, Gramsci was interested in rethinking the main interpretation of history and the progress of the human species that had informed the Russian debates about "what is to be done" and what happened following upon the deeds of the revolutionaries.

One of the main points of contention Gramsci had with the architects of the revolution was the status of Marx's theory of history. Gramsci was interested in examining this in two ways. First, he was concerned with the account of human society as a theory, in terms of its claims to general truth and validity. Second, Gramsci wanted to extend Marx's own reflections on the practical character of human activity, its transformative and creative nature, into the activity of political theory itself.

Marx claimed he had scientifically determined, the laws of the development of the history of human societies. This provided a scientific explanation of what is responsible for driving the change and progress that society had experienced over the centuries. Crucially, Marx declared that what drives history are not the ideas of individual Great Men or Women, but rather the material forces that allow the human species to meet its physical needs, ones that are analogous to the needs of other animal species. The history of the human species, for Marx, was explained by two major forces: the labor power of the human animal and the technological means at their disposal at any given time in history. Marx theorized that humans meet their material needs by creatively transforming their wider natural environment through these two forces, giving rise to entire societies in all of their differences. Marx referred to these dynamic drivers of human history as the "forces of production."

This is what fundamentally distinguished the human animal from other animals who, while driven by their own material needs also reproduced their species through what the environment provided, did not change the "world" in which they lived. Species of bees continually make the same structure of hive they always have, with very minor variations. Beavers construct the same types of dams, and birds the same type of nest. For example, there are no transformations from Bauhaus style structures to Art Deco in meeting their fundamental need of shelter. Humans, however, exhibit the all-important distinguishing feature of creativity through their material culture.

Humans also, being social animals, meet their needs in conjoined, cooperative activity with other members of the species. The consequences of this theory of history, then, most commonly referred to as historical materialism, is that the social arrangements of laws, educational institutions, religious worldviews, moral norms, forms of government, even the ruling philosophical ideas of any age, are the result of the more fundamental biological metabolism by the human creature of its environment. All human beings are born into a mix of political, cultural, and religious institutions, practices, and rituals. Thus they are subject, not just to the effects of a materially determined mode of production based upon labor power and technological development, but also to the ruling ideas of that age. These ruling ideas are embodied in the institutions that govern and direct the practices of any given human society. These are called the 'relations of production' in the historical materialist vocabulary. To illustrate, a quote from Marx: "The windmill gives you society with the feudal lord; the steam mill, society with the industrial capitalist" (Marx, "The Poverty of Philosophy" 38). We can trace the distinctions in different historical periods to differences in our labor power and technology.

It is important to go into some detail about the theory of historical materialism that Gramsci inherited because it had ossified, in his view, during the Soviet Marxist revolutionary experience. This is not to say, of course, that there weren't significant disagreements among the Russian revolutionaries themselves. The history of pre- and post-revolutionary Russia is rife with major debates and polemics being solved with force rather than words. Think of the exile of Leon Trotsky in Mexico as just one example of this conflict. At the time, however, specific interpretations of human history, and what to do were becoming dominant. This had major effects on proposals for political action to be undertaken as part of a revolutionary international movement.

Gramsci focused in particular on two pernicious developments in revolutionary thought. The first, scientific positivism, was something Gramsci covered extensively in *The Prison Notebooks*. Scientific positivism had its own rich and varied history, but held that events in the natural world are governed by scientific laws expressible by cause and effect statements. At Gramsci's time and in the decades prior to the turn of the twentieth century, the social sciences flourished. The dominant approach to the study of human beings in their social interactions and political life, in many leading research programs, held that social sciences should aim at determining the laws governing human history just as the laws of physics, chemistry, and astronomy had been explained in the natural sciences. In embracing positivism as its model for scientific truth, those studying human phenomena could be guaranteed that their prejudices, political dispositions, and moral values would not "color" the claims made in the name of social science. For any description of human action to be free from class ideology, then, it must embrace this conception of scientific laws and Mikhail Bukharin, the Russian revolutionary, had done just this, under the science of "sociology." However, what this conception of the "laws" of society did, as expressed by Bukharin, is eliminate human freedom in terms of political struggles from his analysis. If history is governed by laws analogous or reducible to those that govern the natural world, then deliberate, free action based upon the right grasp of the historical situation on the part of individual agents or parties becomes moot. Communist society would come about regardless of human freedom, as sure as the moon orbits around the Earth, and this did not seem to accurately reflect the state of history and events at the time.

The second pernicious intellectual development was the reduction of human beings into merely economically determined creatures. Gramsci's term for this mistake is "economism," and might also be called "*homo economicus*." This error reads the materialist theory of history or theory of human nature in too reductive a way, and is one that both the liberal critics of communist ideas *and* the communists themselves were guilty of falling into. Thus, these opposed ideological camps missed the importance of the fundamental power of human political action, in roughly the same way. Gramsci emphasized the creative capacity of humans to shape events based upon their understanding of the forces at work frustrating human emancipation. This creativity could not be reduced to mere utilitarian self-interest. The similarity of his interpretation of human nature to a revelatory text of Marx's found in 1930, the *Economic and Philosophic Manuscripts of 1844* is striking. Gramsci had no access to these essays, though their emphasis on the creative power of the human agent aligns with his criticisms of Soviet contemporaries. Gramsci saw the Soviet Marxists making mistakes that impeded the articulation of a mode of political praxis (Gramsci's term for political action) that acknowledged the open-ended, multi-faceted, and creative dimension of humanity. In other words, the Soviet Marxists were actually getting in the way of workers finally losing their chains and living an emancipated life in a free society, Marx's (and Gramsci's) ultimate goal.

Gramsci, in contrast, articulated a vision of Marxist analysis that was more nuanced in its grasp of the laws of historical development. Rather than reading a simple one-way causal direction from the forces of production to the relations of production, Gramsci thought that political struggles were not merely adjunct to a technologically determined relation of production. Rather political struggle could transform the forces of production, the basis for society. What was required was an analysis that did not reduce contemporary social and political phenomena to surface appearances indicative of some deeper mechanical law of society at work, or rely on an overriding economic model of human action. The simplistic concepts that Soviet Marxists like Bukharin embraced as a kind of demystifying codex, were abstractions to Gramsci. They reduced all social action and struggle to the economic interests of class, governed by a law of historical development understood in a positivistic manner. They were conceptual schemes habitually applied without unraveling the specific elements at work in any given situation. Gramsci believed an additional set of concepts was required to actually combine the aim of complete emancipation with scientific explanation for how society was functioning. It is worth considering these conceptual innovations as they have created a good deal of intellectual debate and informed many political programs since their appearance.

Gramsci wanted to make a distinction between what he called the *organic* elements of a situation, and those that were simply *conjunctural*. Gramsci is distinguishing here between the essential and more permanent features of a situation, the organic, from the accidental, or at least the merely incidental or *conjunctural* characteristics. By making this conceptual distinction, Gramsci believed he had developed tools for figuring out the essential elements of the economic and political situation of his day. This distinction has a corresponding sociological determination.

In order for Marxism to remain scientific and not to devolve into ideology, Gramsci focused on the central role of intellectuals in social order. Intellectuals, according to Gramsci, were a key element in any society, defending and rationalizing the status quo of any regime of production through a kind of social pedagogy. Intellectuals articulated and expressed and reinforced the main mores, norms, rules, and ethos of a society. Their role was to offer a deeper story about the functioning of society that made sense of its behaviors, cultural patterns, and the deep habitual bedrock of any society that cooperates to function and reproduce successfully. In this function, traditional intellectuals mistakenly conceived of themselves as neutral, apolitical, seekers of knowledge, when in fact their work served to legitimate a social order and culturally indoctrinate a people into consenting to it.

Critical or organic intellectuals, however took a diagnostic stance towards the practices of their society. They were able to identify those elements of the regime of production that were part of the permanent, overarching, structure of society that enabled domination by one group over others. In addition to illuminating the deep structure of a society's functioning, intellectuals were also agents of political change. The enlightened intellectual was responsible for engaging in wide social and public education of those who were oppressed by the arrangement of force, power, and the distribution of goods in a society. The hope was that *organic* intellectuals, through political education and activity, would establish an alternative, democratic, self-directed and emancipated culture of individuals who coordinated the means of existence in a nonexploitative way. The interesting thing about achieving such an arrangement, is that it would explode some of the larger myths propagated by the *conjunctural* or traditional intellectuals who legitimated the existing order. In this sense, intellectuals combine both theory and practice in disproving the ideology of the ruling class by replacing the ruling class through educating and motivating the people to assert themselves, become self-directing and unexploited, thus making life better for all.

Gramsci, following as he did Marx's call to engage in the "ruthless criticism of everything existing," was also interested in the specific stage of the historical materialist development of the human species as it stood at his time (Marx, "Letters"). Much of his analysis in the *Prison Notebooks* consist in historical exercises that describe different historical struggles and revolutions such as the French Revolution and the reunification of Italy. He then used the lessons provided in these analyses to illuminate the current situation in Italy and wider Europe with respect to the struggle for emancipation of the entire population from the abuses of the capitalist mode of production.

One of Gramsci's most lasting contributions to political theory is his discussion of *hegemony*. Gramsci developed this concept from the Russian tradition, and used hegemony to describe the situation of domination by one class over an entire society. Hegemony also referred to the overarching social forces at work securing consent to the existing order of things in a society. In Marxist terms, hegemony exists when the social experience of the members of a society conditions them to accept as given the paths of life offered to them. Gramsci was adamant a hegemonic ordering of society according to a fundamental vision and way of life was also carried out in the sphere of culture as much as in economic life.

## *Legacy and Impact*

One of Gramsci's great legacies is the articulation of the cultural aspects of hegemony, and how it operates on the consciousness of the main actors in the drama of national and international life. In addition, Gramsci made distinctions, echoing his experience in Sardinia, between the dominant class and those groups that were what he called "subaltern." The subaltern are those groups subject to the ruling power's initiatives and are classified as either threats, marked as inferior, or in some way dominated and categorized as "below" and "outside" the more powerful agent groups in a society. Alternatively, one could articulate the subaltern as located on the "periphery" of a society as opposed to its "center." The subaltern becomes an important extension of how to discuss the non-dominant groups in society and widens the palette of social analysis beyond the more common groupings of "capitalist," "proletariat," "peasant," and so on.

By highlighting the creative power of the human species, Gramsci directed the tradition of revolutionary Marxism away from vulgar conceptions of human nature. Gramsci interjected a humanist element into theorizing the complicated forces in society. He recognized the possible flaws in all intellectual activity and assertions, and widened the scope and practice of Marxist thought to include cultural practices, scientific dispute and democratic dialogue as he saw them as constitutive elements for transforming society precisely because of the exclusion of those subaltern groups by hegemonic forces.

Gramsci's *Prison Notebooks* are widely variegated, yet precise, comments addressing fundamental texts, literary analyses (both famous and obscure works), historical analysis, and textual exegesis. There is also a profound rethinking of a variety of theorists, economics, and political problems. His concept of hegemony has had wide application in a variety of disciplines; in international relations, education theory, post-colonial studies, and political theory. Concomitant with this concept, the subaltern, those subjugated and categorized as "lower" or "lesser" or "insignificant" by hegemonic forces, has been enlisted in articulating structures of oppression and misrecognition in a variety of social scientific fields. Most specifically in analyses which contrast the Global North and the Global South as descriptive categories to understand the forces and flows of globalization today. His analyses of "Fordism," a particular formation of the capitalist mode of production exemplified by Henry

Ford's automobile factories, has served many analyses of the development of consumer capitalism as not only an economic but also a cultural phenomena.

Gramsci's influence and legacy are still being determined. After a huge concentration of intellectual labor in the 1970s, Gramsci's texts are again becoming prominent for their prescience and scope in analyzing politics, economics, and political theory. For example, questions regarding the levels of inequality and the failure of economics and political science to provide state actors with prescriptions that solve social problems have revived Gramsci's analysis of intellectuals, both organic and conjunctural. Unemployment, poverty, and lost life opportunities as an outcome of economic cycles have critics analyzing the possibility that various intellectual disciplines are actually justifying power structures as opposed to questioning proposals and explanations of government action and inaction in a truly scientific manner. The power of the market across the globe and the transformation of societies into consumption-based cultures has critics rethinking Gramsci's notion of hegemony, now on a global scale, under the moniker of "neoliberalism."

This is to say nothing of the influence this profound and iron-willed thinker and actor had upon Italian politics in his own life and-through his writings in prison-from his death onwards. Gramsci's thought and inspiring example framed party debates in the Italian Communist Party, and political questions in Italy more generally, long after his death.

That *The Prison Notebooks* has garnered such attention, both by the first generation of scholars who cast eyes upon them, and now a new generation facing the unquestionable power of market forces on a global scale, is a testament to the vitality of his thought.

## Works Cited

Fiori, Giuseppe. *Antonio Gramsci: Life of a Revolutionary*. Trans. Tom Nairn. London: Verso Press, 1990. Print.
Gramsci, Antonio. *Prison Notebooks, Vols. 1–3*. Ed. Joseph A. Buttigeig. Trans. Joseph A. Buttigeig and Antonio Callari. New York: Columbia University Press, 1992. Print.
Marx, Karl. *The Economic and Philosophic Manuscripts of 1844 and The Communist Manifesto*. Trans. Martin Milligan. Amherst, NY: Prometheus Press, 1988. Print.
_____. "The Poverty of Philosophy." *The Thought of Karl Marx: An Introduction*. By David McLellan. London: Macmillan, 1971. N.p. Print.
_____. "Letters to Arnold Ruge." May and September 1843. *Karl Marx: Selected Writings*. Ed. David McLellan. Oxford: Oxford University Press, 1977. N.p. Print.
Motilio, Anasta. "Antonio Gramsci (1881–1937)." *Prospects: The Quarterly Review of Comparative Education* 23.3–4 (1993): 597–612. Print.

# Jean Genet: *Our Lady of the Flowers* in Prison

AFRODESIA E. MCCANNON

## Summary

Jean Genet is another of this book's outliers. He was not a well-known figure or particularly political; he had been in jail for petty theft and similar crimes when he began writing. His most famous novel, *Our Lady of the Flowers*, was written in prison, and is about prison life. Genet, like Cervantes, gives us a literary work full of characters telling stories and spinning fantasies that intertwine to become part of a larger narrative, creating a hyper-real effect. Genet's novel takes the time and care to let the reader know that even society's most marginalized person, in this case a homosexual prisoner, is human—with human desires, loves, fantasies, needs, hurts, and wants. This itself was revolutionary. As with some of the other authors in this volume, Genet's novel treats prison, to some degree, as a space away from the pressures of life outside the prison walls. While the book is a work of fiction, the portrayal of prison life—including graphic scenes of discipline and dehumanization—is starkly real.—J.W.R.

## Biography

Jean Genet (1910–1986) owes his literary reputation to his plays, but his first major work was a novel, *Notre-Dame des Fleurs—Our Lady of the Flowers*—written in prison. Even a cursory look into Jean Genet's biography reveals him as a troubled foster child whose run-ins with the penitentiary system might seemed justified, though the offenses were petty crimes. He was born in Paris the son of a Camille Gabrielle Genet in December 1910 who gave him up to a foundling home less than a year later. His father was unknown. Two days after he was given up and became a ward of the state, Genet was put into a foster home in Alligny-en-Morvan, a small rural village in Burgundy known for taking in abandoned children from Paris (assumed to be the offspring of prostitutes). He was raised by Eugenié and Charles Régnier, local artisans, who baptized him, gave him a Catholic upbringing, and promised to raise him until the age of thirteen. From all accounts, though he felt ostracized and rejected by the villagers, Genet had a pleasant upbringing. He had no further contact or connection with his mother, as was the law, but for his name.

Alligny-en-Morvan became almost a mythic village that generated many of the stories and characters of his works. For example, the imagery and vocabulary of the Catholic Church—a major part of his experience in the village—permeates his work as he plays with the figures of priests and angels; even the title of the work he wrote in prison, *Our Lady of the Flowers,* is both a serious and tongue-in-cheek reference to the Virgin Mary. In the village, he knew several children whose names appeared in his work. A boy name Cullafroy—another foundling—becomes Culafroy, the true name of the main character of *Our Lady of the Flowers* and a girl he befriended, Solange also appears, in the work, then re-appears as one of the main characters in his later play, *The Maids* (White, *Genet* 17–19). The local gentry, the village abbey, and several other characters in *Our Lady of the Flowers* are thinly veiled fictionalized versions of people he knew in the village.

Genet was an excellent student, though apparently a pale and effete child who seemed "Parisian" and unfit for the agricultural surroundings in which he found himself. Drawn to literature, he said would find the solitude to read in the family's outhouse. The association between the corrupt and the sublime that might come from reading high literature amidst the smells of an outhouse become one of the thematic engines of *Our Lady of the Flowers* and perhaps engendered his own interest in the relationship between disgust and beauty.

The death of his foster mother, Eugenié Régnier, when he was twelve began a nomadic phase in Genet's life. After having been falsely accused of stealing, he began to commit some petty thefts in the village. He began to run away from all the opportunities afforded him because of his intelligence and academic record. In 1925, at fourteen, he found himself again in the child welfare system in Paris and underwent his first psychiatric analysis. He was found to have a "psychiatric weakness" though he ran away from treatment. He was arrested by police and returned to treatment only to flee again. Caught again, he was held in prison. Paroled to a farm, he ran away. Caught a third time he was eventually sent to the "Children's Prison" of Mettray—an agricultural labor prison for minors—from which he eventually escaped but only to be found and returned again.

From the age of nineteen to twenty-five (1929–1936), to avoid Mettray, he signed up for the military and re-enlisted several times. His ability to stay in the military for such an extended period of time, suggests that there he found home and comfort among the male camaraderie and regimented hierarchy of the armed forces. In the army and on furlough, he traveled to Spain, Syria, and Morocco. In the colonial army he gained a lasting connection to the Arab world and sympathy for the Arab people. He failed to show up at a final re-enlisting in 1936 and, having been declared a deserter, fled from one country to another with falsified documents. He vagabonded through Italy, Albania, Greece, Yugoslavia, Austria, Czechoslovakia, Poland, Belgium and Germany. Genet finally returned to France where he continued his life as a thief. In 1941, during the sentence arising from his tenth arrest (his arrests were mostly for vagrancy and theft, often of books), Genet wrote *Our Lady of the Flowers*.

A significant contribution of this work is his frank depiction of queer life. Rather than shunning or suppressing his homosexuality, Genet would ally himself intellectually and socially with other queer writers who served as mentors, though none of them would deal as frankly with sexuality as Genet. Though at odds with the politics of T. E. Lawrence (Lawrence of Arabia), Lawrence's homosexuality (never admitted) and familiarity with the Arab world made him a natural literary ally. Genet emulated Proust's literary style, although Proust dealt with queer France only from a distance and remained closeted throughout his life. He visited and wrote to André Gide, who himself had written a tract, *Corydon* (1924), in defense of homosexuality. Later, his literary alliance with the openly gay Jean Cocteau would prove to be essential for his literary career which was initiated with the publishing of *Our Lady of the Flowers* in 1944.

## *Social and Political Context*

One of the notable aspects of *Our Lady of the Flowers* is the lack of a sense of historical context. Jean-Paul Sartre, in *Saint Genet*, remarked that "Genet lives outside of history, in parentheses" (Sartre 5). This may be because Genet was a champion of the margins and a denizen of the slums of the countries he visited; things were always dismal where he lived and somehow outside the flow of bourgeois historical time. Yet, in the years before he wrote *Our Lady of the Flowers,* the Great Depression blighted Europe, followed by the beginning of World War II. Genet began writing *Our Lady of the Flowers* in 1941 from a prison in occupied Paris then under the Vichy regime. The historical context seems a dim buzz in the background of the text. The narrator smiles "lovingly" at a German pilot of a plane he hears flying over the prison (Genet, *Our Lady* 52). One line of German is heard in the bar the transvestite, Divine, the work's protagonist, frequents (Genet, *Our Lady* 193). Divine briefly falls in love with a German soldier, Gabriel, who dies in the war: "German soldiers buried him where he fell, at the gate of a castle in Touraine. Divine came and sat on his grave, smoked a Craven there.... We recognize her sitting there, with her legs crossed and a cigarette in her hand, level with her mouth" (Genet, *Our Lady* 151).

Along with this romanticizing of the fallen soldier is a "provocative and ambiguous sympathy for collaborators and Germans," for they too are anti-French (White, 243). Genet's complicated psychic relationship with France led him to cheer on the occupiers and dulled any sympathy for Hitler's victims. In a rare interview Genet expresses an uncomfortable (for the interviewer) appreciation for Hitler's army: "Look, when Hitler gave a thrashing to the French, oh, yes! I was happy, I was happy with this attack.... [I]t wasn't a question of the German people or the Jewish people or of the Communist people who could be massacred by Hitler. It was a question of the corrective the German army gave to the French army" (Genet, "Interview with Bertrand Poirot-Delpech." *Declared Enemy* 200). As someone who felt an outsider from his birth and professed an open hostility to his own nation, his attraction to German Nazis accords with "his emotional rejection of France [but also with] his attraction to a certain masculinity that coincides with a fascist aesthetic" (Gaitet 76). Brutal, authoritative men who are tinged with femininity (like the blond-haired young Nazi soldiers) pepper Genet's texts. Even within his non-fascist characters Genet expresses an appreciation for a masculinity in which "hardness is equivalent to virility" (Genet, *Our Lady* 180). Importantly, though, Genet's positive reaction to the occupiers was not based on a political predilection for fascist ideology or an interest in the historical moment. An understated awareness of historical context in *Our Lady of the Flowers* reflects this political and historical indifference.

## *The Book* Our Lady of the Flowers

*Our Lady of the Flowers* narrates the fantasies of a man, Jean Genet, incarcerated in a French prison. The main character of this fantasy is Divine (born Louis Culafroy) an aging (going on thirty) drag queen and sex-worker who lives in the Montmartre neighborhood of Paris. She lives with her lover *Mignon*, which translates to "Darling." Divine's story is populated with queers of all ilk: other queens (Mimosa, Castagnette, Monseigneur), tough guys and pimps (Darling, Gorgui, Marchetti), and young boys (Our-Lady of the Flowers, Archangel Gabriel). The drama that unfolds takes place on the seedy streets of Paris and in Divine's apartment, the "garret," through which several of the characters float. Many of the characters themselves end up in prison.

By choosing to focus on the life of a community of queers in 1930s Paris, Genet immediately showed himself unfazed by the project of focusing on the abject, that is, the rejected, the untouchable, the filth, the marginal. Genet, as a queer, a thief, a prostitute, and a vagabond belonged himself to the marginal and rejected elements of society. He embraced and made poetic that which is outside the bourgeois norm and forced it into our view, normalized it, made it triumphant. For example, when Divine, the transvestite, wakes beside Darling, the tough queer, who has come to live in the garret, she writes, "[T]he rain begins to fall, liberating within her a sudden happiness so perfect that she says aloud, with a deep sigh, "I'm happy." She was about to go to sleep again, but the better to attest her married happiness there come back to her, without bitterness, the memories of the time when she was Culafroy" (Genet, *Our Lady* 94). New found domestic bliss contrasted with the sadness of childhood memories is a fairly relatable moment to readers outside of Divine's world.

Yet, this end product normalization and embracing of the abject is not always so comfortable. In the work, the character Genet engages with that which is rejected and marginal on several levels. For example, he embraces the smell of his own farts with a relish that works to push the reader to disgust:

> I have already spoken of my fondness for odors, ... above all, the odor of my farts, which is not the odor of my shit, a loathsome odor, so much so that here again I bury myself under the covers and gather in my cupped hand my crushed farts which I carry to my nose. They open to me hidden treasures of happiness. I inhale, I suck in. I feel them, almost solid, going down through my nostrils [Genet, *Our Lady* 166–67].

Perhaps, it is a secret of humanity that many are comfortable with the odor of their flatulence and some may even secretly like it. But this reveling in his own foul odor, pushes the limits of the normative behavior and "def[ies] us to take [Genet] seriously" (Bersani, 18). The image of a solidified fart being ingested takes the reader, purposefully, almost playfully, to the edge of nausea. The narrator, though, can create a relation between disgust and pleasure that, he furthers and ennobles through Genet's considerable talent as a writer. Darling, Divine's lover, also farts, and yet, we are not disgusted:

> If [Darling] says, "I'm dropping a pearl," or "A pearl slipped," he means that he has farted in a certain way, very softly, so that the fart has flowed out very quietly. Let us wonder at the fact that it does suggest a pearl of warm orient: the flowing, the muted

leak, seems to us as milky as the paleness of a pearl, that is, slightly cloudy. It makes Darling seem to us a kind of precious gigolo, a Hindu, a princess, a drinker of pearls [Genet, *Our Lady*, 80–81].

The prettified even clever description of the tough guy's fart as well as his unexpected delicacy makes Darling's farts sublime. The fart, even though made precious, is still a product of the anus. As if to contrast our pedestrian lives with those of his subjects—as with the fart as pearl—through his manipulation of disgust Genet glorifies and yet keeps the life of those living in Divine's cramped apartment abject and separate from his readers: "Our domestic life and the law of our Homes do not resemble your Homes. We love each other without love. They do not have the sacramental character. Faggots are the great immoralists" (Genet, *Our Lady* 110).

The Divine's blissful married domesticity cited above is rudely disassembled and reassembled with a revolving cast of characters. Darling wordlessly disappears, other come. Just as their homes are not our homes, Genet's beauty is not our beauty. Divine's lasting memento of Darling is a sculpture, but not a bust on a mantelpiece:

Of the tangible him there remains, sad to tell, only the plaster cast that Divine herself made of his cock, which was gigantic when erect. The most impressive thing about it is the vigor, hence the beauty, of that part which goes from the anus to the tip of the penis [Genet, *Our Lady* 60].

Beauty is redefined in the way that language is re-invented in this context as well. Genet introduces us to 1930s Montmartre queer slang, poetic and foreign, central in the text but marginal in the society: *tantes-filles, tantes-gars, tapettes, pédales, tantouzes, macs, macquereau* (girl-queens, boy-queens, aunties, fags, nellies, pimps, hustler). The same applies to prison slang where "to flatten the pages" means to make one's bed. Genet breaks down the boundaries between this foreign abhorrent world (he assumes we are horrified and scandalized by all these queers) and the bourgeois standard by making us familiar with it, yet still uses the potency of the scandalous to remind us that "we" are not like "you." This confrontational queerness might seem dated in the current era when same-sex relations are increasingly recognized and normalized, but the culture war over homosexual relations is far from over. Genet's differentiation between the "we" and "you" seems a still fitting reply to the conservative contemporary argument that "they" (queers) are not like "us." His is a glorification, if an ambiguous one, of the marginal.

It is in this context and from this vantage that the larger discussion of prison takes place. As with much in this text, Genet reverses expectations in seemingly embracing the horrifying marginal space of prison. For the narrator, the prison cells are a space of reprieve after the "monstrousness" of arrests. They are, the narrator, says the "sweet prison cells ... which I now love as one loves a vice" (Genet, *Our Lady* 103). Prison allows for self-exploration: "[T]he solitude of prison gave me the freedom to be with the hundred Jean Genets glimpsed in a hundred passers-by" (168). A place to revisit one's life, relive memories of childhood long forgotten: "The atmosphere of the night, the smell rising from the blocked latrines which are overflowing with shit and yellow water, stir childhood memories which rise up like a black soil mined by moles" (Genet, *Our Lady* 97–98). Most of all, it is a place to give life to Jean Genet's imaginary fantasy world of Divine, Darling, and others. These fantasies are often sexual fantasies that occur as he animates the characters at night:

> During the day I go about my petty concerns. I am the housekeeper, watchful lest a bread-crumb or a speck of ash fall on the floor. But at night! Fear of the guard who may suddenly flick on the light and stick his head through the grating compels me to take sordid precautions lest the rustling of the sheets draw attention to my pleasure [Genet, *Our Lady* 55].

The prison inspires the imaginary world he creates at night, gives him masturbatory sexual fantasies and literary inspiration. The childhood memories, stirred by the smell of the latrine, help the narrator accurately place Culafroy—Divine as a young boy—in a Mettray-like Colony for Child Correction (Genet, *Our Lady* 56). The title character, Our-Lady of the Flowers, is based on young inmate Maurice Pilorge. Genet's Black cell-mate, Clement Village, allows the narrator to create a character in Divine's story, Seek Gorgui, who comes to live with Divine and Our Lady in the garret and usurps the youth's attention (Genet, *Our Lady* 166). Darling's experiences as a thief, finally picked up by the police, come out of Genet's own experiences with law enforcement.

Strikingly, Darling's arrest included an invasive, humiliating, and fully narrated cavity search which serves to reveal another layer of Genet's narrative—the reality and horror of prison (Genet, *Our Lady* 247). For all the rhapsodizing of the cell as a sweet, inspirational, and eroticized space, the depressing day to day shuffling of prison is exposed in the interstices of the work. The desperate need for inmates to communicate is reduced to scratchings on bricks: "In that prison, which I shall not name, each convict had a little yard, where every brick of the wall bore a message to a friend" (Genet, *Our Lady* 97). Genet's own manuscript of *Our Lady of the Flowers*, his own attempt to communicate, was confiscated and destroyed by prison guards. He was writing it on paper that he was supposed to use to make paper bags, but, as Genet recounts it, he managed to re-write it again from memory (Genet,

"Interview with Nigel Williams," *Declared Enemy* 261). The freedom that the life of Divine affords our narrator belies the sense of confinement or perhaps grows from being penned into a small dusty space. Darling too, as extension of Genet, is shut in his cell: "With the whisk-broom he sweeps up ashes and dust. The guard comes by, opening the door for five seconds to give the men time to put out the sweepings. Then he shuts it again" (Genet, *Our Lady* 250). Genet, the character, rarely mentions that door, but Darling's experiences mirrored his own; there was a door that opened quickly and shut. He is in prison.

In the novel, the relationship to the prison guards is complicated but grows more and more hostile. Darling, a projection here of Genet, is awed by their authoritarian stature as Genet was by tough-guys, but Darling too is ambivalent about them: "In the presence of the guards, Darling felt like a little boy. He hated and respected them" (Genet, *Our Lady* 255). The guards are part of the System and though the narrator is often ambivalent about their role, a sense of disgust with them rises from the text:

> In this story, the guards also have their job. They are not all fools, but they are all purely indifferent to the game they play.... Recently they have been wearing a dark blue uniform which is an exact copy of aviators' outfits, and I think, if they are high-minded, that they are ashamed of being caricatures of heroes [Genet, *Our Lady* 252–53].

Their indifference, ignorance, mocking allusion to real wars and real men leave them as empty though powerful beings.

From the interaction of prisoner and guard come several predictable sexual fantasies: "I had already wondered what would come of the meeting of a handsome young guard and a handsome young criminal. I took delight in the following two images: a bloody and mortal shock, or a sparkling embrace in a riot of [cum] and panting" (Genet, *Our Lady* 254). Genet, in an interview, describes this dialectic of attraction and hatred: "I've never liked policemen in their role as policemen but I may have been sexually attracted by policemen. One has nothing to do with the other" (De Grazia 312). The fantasy which could go either way, bloody or sparkling, turns violently erotic, as is rare in the text, once the narrator sees from his cell a particular guard on which to focus: "My hatred and horror of that breed must have given me a still stiffer hard-on, for I felt my tool swelling under my fingers—and I shook it until finally ... [*sic*]—without taking my eyes off the guard, who was still smiling pleasantly" (Genet, *Our Lady* 254).

The masturbatory fantasies in the work arise mostly from imagined larger than life pleasurable sexual encounters, but the blood, "hatred," and "horror," of this fantasy is its erotic engine. Genet seems no longer in control of the fantasy as a deep well of dark emotion fuels his erection. The word "horror" is important here because the guards take part in a central monstrosity of the work on which Genet focuses but one that might get lost in drama and eroticism of the text. Prison is horror. The narrator describes another prison he was in where long, geometrical corridors dwarfed the prisoners. He would walk down the corridors reading labels on the cell doors:

> The first labels read: "Solitary confinement"; the next: "Transportation"; others: "Hard labor" ... I was never at the end of the corridor, for it seemed to me to be at the end of the world, at the end of all, and yet it made signs to me, it emitted appeals that touched me, and I too shall probably go to the end of the corridor. I believe, though I know it to be false, that on the doors can be read the word "Death" or perhaps, what is graver still, the words "Capital punishment" [Genet, *Our Lady* 167–68].

Capital punishment is worse than death, for it happens at the hands of a state that dare kill its citizens. Of all the faces that parade through the narrator's cell, the ones that haunt and disturb him most, the ones that are the most precious yet the most unapproachable are the faces of the executed. The narrator tells us that his narrative has not gotten to the crux of the matter: "I wanted to make this book out of the transposed, sublimated elements of my life as a convict. I am afraid that it says nothing about the things that haunt me" (Genet, *Our Lady* 187). One of the things that plagues him is the death of the young Maurice Pilorge: "To come back to Pilorge, whose face and death haunt me: at the age of twenty he killed Escudero, his lover, in order to rob him of a pittance. During the trial, he jeered at the court; Wakened by the executioner, he jeered at him too" (Genet, *Our Lady* 123). The book is dedicated and written in honor of the young men, some still children, executed by the French government for murder. Pilorge's attitude towards the court and executioner reflect Genet's own defiance. This murderer, all murderers become his heroes and our narrator hangs their pictures on his cell wall:

> I managed to get about twenty photographs, and I pasted them with bits of chewed bread on the back of the cardboard sheet of regulations that hangs on the wall. Some are pinned up with bits of brass wire which the foreman brings me and on which I have to string colored glass beads [Genet, *Our Lady* 54].

The decorations he places on the photos indicate that they compose a kind of shrine rather than a gallery of photos. They become his saints and their lives and deaths gain a sacred character. These men and the crimes they committed to put them on the executioner's block are the understated subject of the Genet's work: "And it is in honor of their crimes that I am writing my book" (*Our Lady* 51). These men come to Genet like ghosts, as Divine and Darling do, in the middle of the night, but his reaction to them is much different:

These murderers, now dead, have nevertheless reached me, and whenever one of these luminaries of affliction falls into my cell, my heart beats loudly my heart beats a loud tattoo, if the tattoo is the drum-call announcing that a city is capitulating [Genet, *Our Lady* 52].

They bring him terror and his heart pounds the drum-call of surrender. So much of *Our Lady of the Flowers* and the fantasies found within it are about a triumphal confrontation with the bourgeois norm, but these deaths seem to disarm Genet and stun his literary powers. When he worries that what he wants most to say is going unsaid, I think it is these young men's stories and the horror they represent. They come to his cell, but he is unable to weave them into fantasy. Speaking of them, Genet writes, "My mind continues to produce lovely chimeras, but so far none of them has taken on flesh. Never. Not once" (Genet, *Our Lady* 122). They do not become flesh but remain ghostly and unapproachable. Shame makes him bow his head at thought of giving them existence in his fantasies as if these men are too sacred to be figures in Genet's imaginary world. It is by no coincidence that the executed murderer he creates in his fantasy bears the name of that most holy and sacred of women, Mary, Our Lady of the Flowers. And the flowers? They are the other executed men who inspired the work (Genet, *Our Lady* 52).

*Our Lady of the Flowers* seems less focused on eroticism and more on escaping, yet reconciling with, the horror in Genet's world by running towards it: "The only way to avoid the horror of horror is to give in to it" (Genet, *Our Lady* 84). A strategic "psychic process ... that transforms passive victims into active agents" and allows Genet to have some control in a situation where all freedom of action is threatened (Gaitet, 76). By the end of the work, Divine is dead, "holy and murdered—by consumption" (Genet, *Our Lady* 8) and the praise of the prison cell and it potential gives way to our narrator's thoughts of possible moving beyond hell: "What if I were free tomorrow? (Tomorrow is the day of the hearing.) Free, in other words, exiled among the living. I have built me a soul to fit my dwelling. My cell is so sweet. Free: to drink wine, to smoke, to see ordinary people" (Genet, *Our Lady* 305). The cell still calls to him, but so does life and it is towards life that our narrator feels most called: "I already feel that I no longer belong to the prison. Broken is the exhausting fraternity that bound me to the men of the tomb. Perhaps I shall live" (Genet, *Our Lady* 306).

The prison, however, still exists for his characters and *Our Lady of the Flowers* ends with a letter that Darling writes Divine from prison, which begins conventionally enough but concludes with the signature poetic strategy Genet has employed in the work:

> "Dearest, I'm writing a few lines to give you the news, which isn't good. I've been arrested for stealing ... I'm awfully sorry about what's happened to me. Let's face it, I'm plain unlucky. So I'm counting on you to help me out. I only wish I could have you in my arms so I could hold and squeeze you tight. Remember the things we used to do together. Try to recognize the dotted lines. And kiss it. A thousand big kisses, sweetheart, from
> Your Darling"
>
> The dotting that Darling refers to is the outline of his prick. I once saw a pimp who had a hard-on while writing to his girl place his heavy cock on the paper and trace its contours. I would like that line to portray Darling [Genet, *Our Lady* 307].

The wonderfully mundane letter brings the reader in, close to the couple, then surprises, again, with the ever-presence of the prick and homoerotic desire. The tracing is the transformation of the cock into art, art which never loses the shock value of its un-bourgeois origins. This seems not only an apt portrayal of Darling, but of Genet's work as well.

## *Conclusion*

Later in his life, Jean Genet would continue his fight for the disenfranchised and the degraded and become a political activist. Though he had no particular political leanings, his activity was primarily for causes associated with left-leaning politics. He focused his efforts on prison reform, a movement spearheaded by philosopher Michel Foucault, and the struggles of the Black Panthers and the Palestinians. From each of these came important and influential writings: "Four hours at Shatila" arguably his most important political article described the attack on a Palestinian town and "The Blacks" was one of the several plays that cemented his literary reputation. Among his influential works was the introduction to the prison letters of George Jackson, a black left-wing activist and Black Panther, who was killed in prison by guards a day before his trial. The introduction, written in 1971, contains clear reflections of his concerns in *Our Lady of the Flowers*:

> Out of the multiple slaughter of blacks—from Soledad Prison to Attica—George Jackson, assassinated by the elite sharpshooters—that is gunmen for the elite—rises up, shakes himself off, and is now illustrious, that is luminous, the bearer of a light so intense that it shines on him, and on all Black Americans. Who was George Jackson? An eighteen-year-old black man imprisoned for eleven years for being an accomplice in a theft of seventy dollars [Genet, "Preface to *L'Assassinat de Georges Jackson*" *Declared Enemy* 91].

In the pettiness of the crime committed, the injustice of his death, and the quasi-canonization of George Jackson, he closely resembles the executed young men, "the flowers" of Genet's first novel.

Genet's canonical stature in the world of modern literature was fostered as well by the work of Jean-Paul Sartre, *Saint Genet,* a monumental psychological study of what Sartre thought was a quintessential existential being. Genet for him was the champion amoral pornographer, who wrote from prison a work to which he could masturbate. Genet has had to live down the work's scandalous reputation propagated by Sartre. The eroticism, Genet asserted in an interview, is to serve the poetry: "Today I think that if people are touched sexually by my books, it is because they were badly written, because the poetic emotion should be so forceful that no reader could be moved sexually" (Genet, "Interview with Madeleine Gobeil" *Declared Enemy* 8). Genet did overcome earlier assessments of his work and is now considered in the company of the greatest French writers of his time. Like many artists and writers at the margins in the 1930s and 1940s, his work has become part of the canon of modern literature.

## Works Cited

Bersani, Leo. "The Gay Outlaw." *Diacritics* 24.2–3 (1994): 4–18. JSTOR. 19 Feb. 2014.

Genet, Jean. "An Interview with Jean Genet." An interview by Edward De Grazia, *Cardozo Studies in Law and Literature* 5.2 (1993): 307–24. JSTOR. 19 Feb. 2014.

\_\_\_\_\_. *Our Lady of the Flowers.* Trans. Bernard Frechtman. New York: Grove Press, 1963. Print.

Gaitet, Pascale. *Declared Enemy: Texts and Interviews.* Stanford: Stanford University Press, 2004. Print.

\_\_\_\_\_. "Sleeping with the Enemy: Jean Genet's Erotic Reconfiguration of the Occupation." *SubStance* 27.3 (1998): 73–84. JSTOR. 19 Feb 2014.

Sartre, Jean-Paul. *Saint Genet. Actor and Martyr.* Minneapolis: University of Minnesota Press, 2012. Print.

White, Edmund. *Genet: A Biography.* New York: Alfred A. Knopf, 1993. Print.

# In the Shadows of Prison: Sayyid Qutb's Visions of a Perfect World

PETER C. VALENTI

## Summary

Sayyid Qutb was a mid-twentieth-century schoolteacher, writer, literary critic, and activist who opposed the Egyptian government, advocating a radical new agenda for the country and for the Islamic world as a whole. He was deemed so dangerous that the Egyptian government executed him in 1966. Later extremists, such as Usama bin Laden, have cited his ideology and personal example. This has caused some U.S. media and analysts to dub Qutb "the godfather of terrorism." However, there is an overlooked component to Qutb's intellectual journey—eleven years as a political prisoner. His two most famous works, *In the Shade of the Qur'an* and *Milestones*, were written in prison and were dramatically influenced by Qutb's time there. The prison experience affects all those who are incarcerated, and in this case it dramatically reshaped Qutb; in the confines of his prison cell he formulated an uncompromisingly stark manner in which to view the world.—J.W.R.

## Introduction

"Apparently, a church dance in Greeley, Colo., led to 9/11." Thus opens an article in *The New York Times* written by Alessandra Stanley in 2007. She continues:

> In 1948 Sayyid Qutb, an Egyptian writer who became the father of the radical Islamist movement, was sent to the United States to temper his contempt for the West. What he saw over two years—postwar consumerism, suburban lawns, men and women dancing "breast to breast"—only further inflamed his conviction that the

West was the enemy of Islam and doomed. Mr. Qutb went on to work up a pseudospiritual justification of Islamic terrorism that inspired and emboldened many, including Osama bin Laden and his deputy, Ayman al–Zawahri [sic]. And that modest Colorado mixer ... was Mr. Qutb's "epiphanic moment," as Malise Ruthven, a Middle East expert, puts it in "Jihad: The Men and Ideas Behind Al Qaeda"....

Stanley's article was a review of an 11-part series on PBS, "America at a Crossroads," examining the post–September 11, 2001, world. Both a review article and emblematic of the public discussion regarding the causes of 9/11, Stanley concluded that people like Usama bin Laden and Qutb were fueled by anti–Western hatred, expressing the view that "it's a worthy and worthwhile examination of the clash between Islam and the West, but it's also the kind of sorrowful, all-knowing look backward that makes viewers wonder why all these journalists, experts, scholars and former government officials were not more outspoken about the impending crisis."

There are three interesting points about the arguments in this article, and similar ones in the media since 9/11. First, it utilizes reductionist and teleological clichés about the motivations of so-called Muslim fundamentalists. The implication is Muslim fundamentalists have psychosocial hang-ups with social activities and habits that "we" in the "modern world" find innocuous and trivial. A prime example is how Stanley begins her article, which accepts Ruthven's argument reducing the catalyst for Qutb's supposed anti–Western ideology to a dance. Stanley also pointedly notes that Bin Laden "did not shake hands with women, wear shorts at soccer practice or listen to music."

Yet the supposition that Muslim fundamentalists are motivated by an intense hatred of the West demonstrated by their reaction to Western sociocultural norms elides the long historical relationship of the European Great Powers, and later the U.S., with the Arab and/or Islamic world. The last 200 years of interventions, wars, colonization, and foreign policies have had a lasting impact. These events are well-known and routinely cited in the Arab and/or Islamic World as outstanding grievances (and, subsequently, motivations for hostility or revenge). Whether outsiders agree with interpretations of Arabs or Muslims about the impact of—for example—U.S. policies that supported dictators in the Middle East, attempted to or actually overthrew governments (the 1953 coup in Iran the classic example), and the continued support the United States has given to Israel and its policies, to ignore this historical context and processes leaves a person with no other explanatory factor as to what motivates these fundamentalists, thus making the suggestion explicit in Stanley's narrative that—as per the Bushian argument—"They hate us for our freedoms [in this case, dancing]" seem correct.

Second, Stanley's language exemplifies long-held assumptions that the

West is the engine of history. This trope posits that the so-called Third World and its ideologies, movements, and intellectuals are influenced by, reacting to, or motivated by the West. It is correct that Qutb, and people like him, were highly critical of the West, though their first and most lasting experience of the West was through colonization. Qutb's time in the United States did make him reflect on a variety of topics, nevertheless the argument reduces the long evolution of his thinking to just being a result of his encounter with the West (in this case, a dance). This argument ignores the complex—and more important—domestic influences and motivations for his thinking. Qutb reserved far more ire and focus for the Islamic World. When he did discuss the West's impact on the Islamic World it was mostly as a *symptom* of what he saw as the decline of the Islamic World and not as the *cause*. Moreover, to use the argument that his time in the United States caused his "epiphanic moment" ignores his concerns in his writings predating his trip to the United States.[1]

The third and most relevant point is that if there was one experience that radically and unequivocally shaped Qutb, it wasn't a dance or the trip to the United States, but rather his 11 years as a political prisoner in Egypt. While elements of his ideology were worked out prior to imprisonment, it was the harrowing experiences in prison, including torture and murder of fellow prisoners, which forced him to live in a complex mental world that was both confining and liberating. This better explains much of his later ideology, and to underscore this point, his most famous and influential works, *Milestones* and *In the Shade of the Qur'an* (henceforth *ISQ*), which became inspirational texts for later radical organizations, were both written in prison. Emphasizing his prison experience in shaping his mental universe is key to understanding his radicalization as well as the subtext for most of his late writings. As one author put it:

> There is no doubt that the prison environment and repression inside President [of Egypt, Gamal 'Abd al-] Nasser's prisons were the nurseries that hatched these takfir jihadist ideas seen in Qutb's *Milestones* ... which has become since then a manifesto for jihadist Islamists throughout the world. The first kafir (infidel) in Qutb's mind during his imprisonment, 1954–1964, 1965–1966, was President Nasser [Musallam 202].[2]

## *Biography*

Sayyid Qutb Ibrahim Husayn Shadhili was born in 1906 in the village of Musha, in the south of Egypt near Asyut. Musha was a small farming community; most villagers were Muslim, but there was a sizeable Christian minority. His childhood was typical for rural Egypt in that Qutb was taught to respect and follow various moral and social duties, and he grew up in an atmosphere that emphasized religious practices and cultural norms such as hospitality and generosity.[3]

Qutb was deeply influenced by contemporary nationalist agitations. Egyptians were resentful of British imperial domination of Egypt (Britain occupied it in 1882), and they voiced a sense of cultural pride—which included a central role for Islam—and desire for independence. Qutb's father encouraged him to participate in nationalist activities, including reading nationalist papers to illiterate villagers. Rural Egyptians had a deep mistrust of the state, seeing it as an oppressive and extractive institution, far away in Cairo, manipulated by British colonial authorities. Echoing the concerns of his fellow villagers, Qutb often expressed suspicions or disappointments about soldiers, state ministers, law, and justice. His deep sense of justice was a driving force that motivated him throughout his life.

The post–World War I nationalist upheavals in Egypt made travel to Cairo difficult, but eventually in 1921 his family sent him to the capital. After finishing his secondary studies, in 1929 he entered the *Dar al-'ulum*, Cairo's teacher training college. *Dar al-'ulum* taught a mixed curriculum of "traditional" religious sciences, such as Qur'anic commentary (exegesis) and jurisprudence, and "modern" scientific subjects such as economics, history, and politics. The college was intentionally meant to decrease the influence of the preeminent institution of learning in the Islamic world, al-Azhar, founded in the year 970. While there, Qutb was exposed to many of the great nationalist and intellectual movements of the time. In 1933 he graduated with a degree in Arabic language and literature.

After graduation he taught elementary education around the country for seven years as a Ministry of Education employee. In the provinces he was further exposed to the economic and social ills of Egypt, deepening his concern for social justice. From 1936 onward he worked in Cairo; in 1940 he was promoted to the offices of General Culture and Translation and Statistics. This job entailed inspector responsibilities over education facilities. Furthermore, since his college days Qutb worked for a variety of newspapers and magazines as an editor and contributor. He wrote articles, novels, collections of poetry, and reviews. He moved in the artistic and intellectual circles of Cairo. At this time Qutb embraced literary modernism, also expressing enthusiasm for Western literature.

Qutb's literary activities and publications are too numerous to list,[4] so other than those mentioned throughout this essay, one more will be highlighted here. In late 1947 Qutb along with seven others[5] founded a journal called *al-Fikr al-jadid* (New Thought). The journal's purpose was to bring attention to contemporary social conditions, in particular the plight of the urban and rural poor. The journal exposed the corruption and nepotism of Egyptian officials. After only 12 issues the government closed it down. Despite its brief life we can see this journal as a manifestation of Qutb's life-long concern for social justice and quest for solutions; it was also another fork in the road that put him at odds with the government. *Al-Fikr al-jadid* is also the tentative beginning of what became a more thorough exploration of these issues in his well-received book *Social Justice in Islam*, first published in 1949, and in later Islamist works.

As mentioned earlier, the argument that Qutb's time in the United States caused him to formulate anti–Western ideology is grossly reductionist. Rather the salient point to be made is that Qutb was shaped much more by his experiences in Egypt, especially his time in prison. While the trip to the United States did have some importance in terms of confirming his ideas, Qutb's thinking had changed long before he got on the boat for New York. Around 1939 Qutb began to shift his literary focus to the Qur'an and religious topics. Doing so, whether in the Islamic world or elsewhere, is not inherently a sign of radicalization. The Qur'an, as the font of the Arabic language, literature, and Islamic civilization, is a natural component of study for any Arab intellectual, whether a Muslim or not. His decade of research and publishing on the Qur'an and other religious issues, and gradual shift away from writing on poetry and literature, served as a foundation he could draw upon while later in prison.

But it is valid to ask: what led this esteemed literary critic, known for his prodigious publications on (non-religious) poetry, novels, and short stories as well as his generally secular nationalist political persuasion, to shift focus to religious topics? From 1939 onwards, a number of developments motivated Qutb's shift. A general but important context was the massive political, social, and economic disruptions caused by World War II; Egypt was still occupied by Britain and was a critical strategic location. Egyptians suffered a great deal from wartime hardships, still felt years later. British promises of political change in return for Egyptians' support during the war went unfulfilled. The political system—specifically the monarchy—was held in contempt and seen as little more than corrupt puppets of the imperialists.[6] Qutb, always distressed by social injustice, poverty, political ineptitude and corruption, saw the war exacerbate these conditions greatly. Also, the 1930 and '40s were witness to a revival of intellectual interest in Islamic history in tandem with an evolving dissatisfaction with the unfulfilled promises of liberal and nationalist political parties and institutions (repressed by the British) (Smith).

Furthermore, Qutb, like Egyptians in general, was disturbed by the effects of the British-supported Zionist movement in Palestine, culminating in the dislocation of approximately 750,000 Palestinians in 1948 with the creation of Israel. Prior to 1948 he believed that Zionism (post–1948, Israel) was another example of Western imperialism in the Middle East; later he added that Israel represented a historical enmity of Jews toward Islam. Qutb, like Arabs in general, was dismayed by what he saw as the U.S. abandoning its role as champion of justice, democracy, and anti-imperialism by ignoring Palestinian pleas for self-determination (Calvert, *Origins* 98–101, 120–22, 167–69).

More personal reasons for his shift include the death of his mother in 1940 and a failed engagement in 1943. These events plus his health problems, which continued to plague him throughout his life, caused periods of depression and a reason to "turn to his religion for refuge" (Musallam 12–14, 65–72).[7] Living in this particular historical and personal context, the 1940s were, as one author describes it, a period of "alienation of Sayyid Qutb" (Musallam 73).

## Trip to the United States

Contrary to Stanley's assertion, Qutb was not "sent to the United States to temper his contempt for the West." The reasons were far more complex. The Ministry of Education's official reason was to study new pedagogy and curriculum. Due to his political and social criticism it seems an arrest was imminent, and so friends in the government arranged for him to leave the country. It is possible that those in the government who did not like his views hoped to remove him for a few years (Calvert, *Origins*, 139). In any case, in November 1948 he left, and he returned in August 1950. He lived throughout the United States, much of his time taking classes in academic institutions.

The choice to go the States (instead of the UK) was logical. Qutb had a favorable view of American culture and literature and was curious to see the country. He was impressed by American film and had a deep passion for classical music. His writings express admiration for U.S. technical and scientific achievements.[8] He later wrote in an Egyptian newspaper of the reputation of "America," describing what are very likely his own (initial) views: "America, the New World, is that vast, far-flung world that occupies in the mind's eye more space than it really does on this earth. Imaginations and dreams glimmer on this world with illusion and wonder" (Qutb, "The America" 9). Qutb came to the U.S. curious but also with a strong sense of morality and worth of Egyptian—or Islamic and "Eastern"—identity. He didn't accept the idea that the Third World needed to be remade by Western civilization; indeed, witnessing the impact of Western imperialism in the Middle East, he was already suspicious of the claims of the allegedly superior political systems and values of the West.

His curiosity and open-mindedness led him to meet different types of people in various settings, including Easter and Christmas celebrations in homes, and churches (according to an Arab-American friend of his at the time, often),[9] and it is from his impressions of these that Stanley's article explains his supposed motivations. Qutb, who certainly had traditional views about the nature of religious institutions, was quite shocked that a house of God was used on Sunday for, according to one advertisement, "snacks, magic games, puzzles, contests, fun," and, as he famously witnessed, a provocative dance. His reaction to this, which will be useful to quote here, is indicative both of how he viewed the role of religion and, as is clear in the last line, his acceptance of difference:

> And these ministers would say to you: 'But we are unable to attract this youth by any other means!'
>
> But none of them asks himself: 'What is the value of attracting them to the church, when they rush to it in this way, and spend their time in this manner? Is church attendance a goal in and of itself?' Is it not for the edification of feelings and manners? ... But what can I say? Strange things can happen in this world! For God has created all kinds of people and things [Qutb, "The America" 19–21].

Throughout Qutb's later writings he referred to what he saw as the overt materialism and loss of spirituality in the United States, verifying his suspicion of secularism. Qutb came to believe that people in the United States had lost their respect and awe for nature and God's beneficence to humanity. Additionally, the strong American individualism and prominent sexuality, he felt, diminished the strength and value of family, having detrimental effects on society. Other encounters impressed upon him that the U.S. was not the champion of Third World independence and self-determination that he had hoped.

Finally, one cannot ignore another important aspect of his visit to the States. As a man of dark complexion, Qutb was exposed to the harsh realities of American racism.[10] Experiencing racism in the United States had the effect of further alienating him and doubting the validity of so-called enlightened American (Western) values and societies. His later writings identify the hypocrisy of American (Western) claims regarding equality and human dignity while emphasizing the freedom and justice inherent in Islam.[11] One section in *ISQ* contains a scathing indictment of American racism (Carré 293).

## Return to Egypt

Despite some authors' insinuations, Qutb didn't return to Egypt and enter a new radical phase. Instead, he continued advocating his previously held convictions. Other than material and technological achievements, he hadn't seen anything in U.S. society that necessitated remaking Egypt in the Western image. If anything, the trip strengthened his *preexisting* positions; the fact that he wrote *Social Justice in Islam* prior to the trip is evidence of this point. Rather it was domestic developments that directed his actions after his return to Egypt, and he maintained a reformist position into the 1950s (post-trip). The true radicalization happened in the late 1950s, well after the trip to the United States, so there is no direct causality, as claimed, between the trip and his later views.

Qutb returned to work at the Ministry of Education. As Qutb was evolving intellectually he took note of new organizations emerging in Egypt. The most important for Qutb's life story is the Muslim Brotherhood (henceforth MB). In the late 1930s Qutb became aware of the MB and slowly grew more sympathetic to its views. In 1953, he officially joined. Until that point he had contact with the MB but one can not say he embraced its program. Certainly MB members were enthusiastic about him after the publication of *Social Justice in Islam*. The MB issued reprints of his earlier work. By early 1952 he started writing a column for the MB magazine *al-Muslimun* entitled "Fi zilal al-Qur'an" (In the Shade of the Qur'an) which was a serialized Qur'anic exegesis. Thus were sown the seeds of his later book.

The MB was founded in 1928 by Hasan al-Banna (1906–49), who, like Qutb, was a product of *Dar al-'ulum*. The MB saw itself as a reformist organization serving the spiritual and educational needs of Egyptians. To these ends, it promoted an ethical and devotional lifestyle in addition to offering literacy classes and charity activities. The MB also hoped to strengthen Egyptians' religious and cultural identity in the face of British domination, which it saw as having debilitating effects on society. By the 1940s it had around 500,000 members, and had spread throughout the Arab Middle East. By this time it ran many institutions, including charities, youth organizations, as well as press, film, radio, and publishing houses. Starting in the 1940s the MB began fielding political candidates.[12] Its political activism and antagonism of the government, in tandem with a faction of the MB utilizing more violent means, led to al-Banna's assassination followed by a tense relationship with the monarchy until the latter's overthrow in 1952.

## Intellectual Influences

Qutb was influenced by contemporary Islamist revivalist writers, in particular Abulhasan 'Ali Nadvi (1913–99) and Sayyid Abu al-'Ala Mawdudi (1903–79), both from the Indian subcontinent. These men's works were translated into Arabic through the 1940s–'50s, allowing Qutb to read them.[13] Qutb drew heavily on both authors to expand upon his preexisting ideas,[14] perhaps more so from Mawdudi.

Like Qutb, Mawdudi was greatly concerned by the impact of British imperialism, and all of his practical interaction with "Western civilization" was the colonial experience. He also faced government persecution (under colonial and Pakistani governments) and spent time in jail.[15] Like Qutb, his most influential work was a multi-volume Qur'anic exegesis, *Tafhim al-Qur'an*; like Qutb's *ISQ*, it is modernist and does not rely on traditional clerical scholastic methodology or sources (also like Qutb, partly written in jail).

Qutb was inspired by Mawdudi's argument that it was not enough to reform the personal piety and religious practices of average Muslims. Individuals could only truly be transformed and bettered by a dramatic reformation of society and especially of the government that led it. Additionally, Mawdudi took the Islamic concept of the *hakimiyah* (sovereignty)[16] of God and placed great emphasis on this, arguing that once a person was truly Muslim (either converting to Islam or no longer being just a nominal Muslim), he/she must acknowledge that submission and obedience belong to God alone. As he argued, "A Muslim is *not a Muslim* by *appellation* or *birth*, but by virtue of abiding by holy law" (Maududi, *Fundamentals* 21–22). Notice Qutb's similar language in his late work: "Islam is not a few words pronounced by the tongue, or birth in a country called Islamic, or an inheritance from a Muslim father" (Qutb, *Milestones* 108; also 29).

Lastly, according to Mawdudi, God's commandments, like His oneness, are exclusive and cannot be shared with, altered by, or replaced with another system. Thus a true government and society should only acknowledge, and be based upon, God and His commandments and the example set by Prophet Muhammad. Manmade laws and systems are seen as both faulty and premised on the idea that some humans know better than others (in the case of a liberal democracy, that the majority chooses what is best) as well as contravening what God wants for humanity.[17] Any practice that was not in conformity with this previous argument can be seen as unIslamic, or as he called it, *jahili*.

His use of this Arabic term is both innovative and powerful. In traditional Islamic scholarship, the term *jahili* (an adjective) represents a period in time in history, *al-Jahiliyah*, or "Time of Ignorance." This was the period, specifically in Arabia, prior to the life of Prophet Muhammad (570–632). Muhammad advocated a return to the original monotheism of Abraham and criticized the beliefs and practices of (polytheistic) pre–Islamic Arabia. This meant that the historical *al-Jahiliyah* ended with the lifetime of Prophet Muhammad. 1300 years later Mawdudi was using the term in a different way. For him it transcended time and space and not only described a historical period but also a mode of individual and social existence. Thus Mawdudi's life mission was to remove *jahili* influences and practices in the Islamic world (he was doubtful if this was the proper term)[18] in order to (re)create the proper sociopolitical system that addresses modern needs by utilization of a pure (and purified) and correct interpretation of Islamic sources. This revisionist usage of the term *jahili* was extremely powerful, as well as polarizing, and had immense influence on Qutb.

Political agitation was not new in Egypt, but 1951–52 saw notable protests against the British presence as well as the government. Various groups were involved in confrontations with British and government forces; loss of life was common for the Egyptian protestors. Qutb was an enthusiastic supporter of these activists. The tense situation culminated in the July 23, 1952 "revolution" in which the monarchy was overthrown by a secret cell, the Free Officers, inside the Egyptian military. The Free Officers had met at Qutb's house to liaison with MB members and plan the revolution.[19] Over time one officer rose to lead the new revolutionary government: Gamal 'Abd al-Nasir (commonly called "Nasser"). Qutb, like most Egyptians, was overjoyed by this so-called revolution, and it should be added that he and Nasser had a preexisting warm and respectful relationship. Qutb threw himself into the work of building a new government and society. His credentials as a social critic (and previous connections to the revolutionaries) got him appointed as an advisor to the government, with special focus on education; he was even given a radio program. This work lasted for the next six months.

Eventually Qutb began to question his role in the government. Friction emerged between the MB and the Free Officers in late 1952; the Free Officers began to see the MB as a political threat. Finally, Nasser and the other Free Officers embraced a secular nationalism which had little public role for Islam whereas Qutb and his MB allies disagreed. Despite his initial closeness to the Free Officers, Qutb felt it necessary to signal his dedication to Islamic social reform by resigning from the government and officially joining the MB in February 1953. To reiterate, until 1953 he had been sympathetic to the MB but was not a member; his joining presaged a wider rift between the MB and government and increased the prestige of the MB by having the widely respected figure of Qutb as a member. It should be added that Qutb, and the

MB leadership, felt used by Nasser and his officer revolutionaries. Qutb was elevated to very prominent positions in the MB, and the MB joined in protests against the new government.

## Prison Cell as Islamic World

The impact of Qutb's 11 years in jail on his intellectual trajectory is undeniable, and it is the contention of this essay that it was the crucible in which he came to his most radical conclusions (and revisions of his own work). While he was already of an Islamist orientation prior to entering prison, there is no way of saying whether he would have come to the same conclusions had he not gone to prison. Also, prior to his incarceration, the Muslim Brotherhood did not embody nor promote any of these (Qutbian) ideas[20]—and the organization officially repudiated Qutb's most radical core arguments by the end of the 1960s—so it cannot be said that he was unduly influenced by them.[21] Actually Qutb still maintained a moderate Islamist position even in his first few years in jail. His ideas at this point could be best described as social reformism. It is only over the accumulating years in jail that Qutb moved to a radical position.

Just as MB members began meeting with dissident factions inside the government resulting from power struggles, the MB was declared an illegal political party. However, the ax came down on the MB in late 1954. While President Nasser was giving a speech on October 26, an assassin tried to shoot him, missing completely (debate remains whether this assassination was staged or a conspiracy within a conspiracy).[22] Under the pretext of this conspiracy, Nasser was able to target all political rivals—as many as 20,000 people were arrested. The most prominent target was the MB, as the assassin caught was a MB member. Qutb, along with thousands of other Muslim Brothers, was imprisoned. Qutb was convicted of "anti-government" activity and sentenced to 15 years hard labor. During his court appearances, observers noted signs of torture on him. He famously lifted up his shirt during the trial, revealing his wounds, and stated "the principles of the revolution have been applied on us in prison" (al–Khalidi 347–49).[23]

For all Muslim Brothers in general and Qutb specifically, time spent in prison was initially an experience of bewilderment, disillusionment, and despair. They were shocked at how quickly relations with the new revolutionary government had deteriorated, putting the MB at the receiving end of its hostility, and they were not even sure if their own organization had the ideological vision and ability to go forward under these new circumstances (Zollner 412–15). A number of Brethren eventually began slowly and cautiously addressing perceived faults in strategy or ideas; Qutb became the most prolific in doing so.

Egyptian prisons were notorious (and unfortunately remain so) for their conditions and methods. Dank, unsanitary conditions and poor nutrition were coupled with frequent torture. Unsurprisingly for a 50-year-old who entered prison with health conditions, Qutb's situation immediately grew worse. His arthritis, angina pectoris, and lung problems were exacerbated, he developed rheumatism, and probably contracted tuberculosis (al-Khalidi 347–49, 361–65). Frail and often sick, Qutb spent most of his time in the prison hospital; he wrote a good deal of his work while in a hospital bed.[24] To understand Qutb's prison writing, we must foreground torture and health problems as constant elements that affected his views. Evidence of this slips through his prose, such as during his discussion of obstacles the first Muslims (during Prophet Muhammad's lifetime) faced in the *al-Jahiliyah*.[25]

Despite the terrible afflictions he suffered, the sources are unanimous in painting Qutb as an exemplary prison comrade who shared food, diffused conflicts, assisted sick prisoners, and even managed to take care of a stray cat. All throughout, he saw his religious devotion and practice as the bedrock upon which he could maintain his steadfastness and moral character in the face of the horrors around him.[26] In the confines of his prison cell he constructed an Islamic society.

Even though Qutb began to revise his earlier work in prison, his truly radical work started in 1957. This is important to further substantiate the point that Qutb's so-called anti–Western ideology and "epiphanic moment" came not while in the United States but rather in an Egyptian prison. The event in question occurred when some MB prisoners refused to fulfill labor duties at the prison quarry; guards then shot the prisoners in their cells, killing 21 and wounding scores more. At the time Qutb was in the prison hospital, but saw the bloody bodies as they were brought in after the massacre (al-Khalidi 355–57). Both the secondary sources and the tone of Qutb's own writing verify that this was the moment of absolute rupture. Until this point he saw himself as an Islamist reformer hoping to effect change in society. However, the catalogue of his terrible experiences in jail and 1957 massacre convinced him that no real social change could happen under an illegitimate political system; sweeping and revolutionary changes were needed. What was at stake was the end of immorality, oppression, and injustice. He now saw the situation in Egypt, and indeed in the world, in stark black-and-white terms.

In the intensely rigid and harrowing life of prison, he constructed an ideal—some might say imaginary—world. Calvert alludes to Qutb's propensity to live a "dream life" which rounded out the "the limited range of experiences and influences" of prison life. He later adds that he "felt like a foreigner in the world" (Calvert, *Origins* 24, 200; Moussalli 35). He no longer had time for the frivolous writings of his past; with a new zeal he felt it necessary to find the solutions for not only Egyptians but all of humanity. His work took on a new urgency, underscored by the possibility that he could easily die in prison from health problems or at the hands of oppressive jailors.

He was able to finish his multivolume *ISQ* because his publisher sued the government for losses suffered from lack of contract fulfillment, and a court order allowed Qutb to write.[27] Other works followed, including revising *Social Justice in Islam*,[28] and all had to go through a censorship committee, which explains that while his vision was often stark he usually lacks specific details. Like any skilled writer operating under censorship, he found writing strategies to evade and obfuscate. On the other hand, this necessitated a wider latitude of interpretation by his readers as to how to implement his vision, often leading to more radical manifestations of his ideology.

During the years of his incarceration Qutb's fame grew. More international pressure was placed on Nasser to release him. When Qutb suffered a heart attack in 1964, Iraqi President 'Abd al–Salam 'Arif intervened.[29] Always practical, Nasser did not want Qutb's death in prison on his hands, and he was attempting to moderate his relationship with political dissidents. Qutb was released in May 1964, but was weak and sickly. At home he was greeted by well-wishers, and Islamist visitors treated him with great deference. He was offered a position in the Iraqi government but he felt he should remain in Egypt. He began meeting with the Nizam 1965 (see below) but he was cautious. Their feelings—not surprisingly—were that they needed to be prepared once the government renewed its persecution of them; they did discuss ideas for militant action, including assassinating Nasser, but none of these reached planning stages (Calvert, *Origins* 240–44).

For the next year he was involved with the Nizam 1965 as well as with MB leaders. By summer 1965 the government discovered the secret Nizam 1965. Qutb and his brother, Muhammad, were arrested; his sister and two nephews were also arrested (one of the latter dying in prison). Other MB members were arrested and tortured. Muhammad Qutb was reportedly tortured to within an inch of his life. In April 1966 Qutb and 42 other Islamists were tried on counts of subversion, terrorism, and sedition. Excerpts of *Milestones* were used in the trial against him; prosecutors, just as later militants, read between the lines in the passages calling for the replacement of *jahili* systems. Qutb's defense was that these passages discuss an evolutionary process over a period of time (Qutb, *Milestones* 28–29, 31, 120, 136).

Initially six defendants were sentenced to death, but Nasser commuted the penalty for three, leaving Qutb and two close companions, 'Abd al–Fattah Isma'il and Yusuf al–Hawwash, to face death by hanging. On August 29, 1966, the executions were carried out. Qutb reportedly shook hands with the guards prior to his hanging; this may seem strange, but until the end he lived a man of his principles.

## The 30 Volumes of In the Shade of the Qur'an

Even though Qutb's *Milestones* has gotten more attention in the non–Islamic world—seen as his definitive ideological treatise—the most important of his works is *ISQ*. This work is his most monumental and influential legacy. *ISQ* is a 30-volume Qur'anic exegesis that is Qutb's statement on how to read the Qur'an as well as what Muslims must do based on that reading. *Milestones* is really a crystallization of ideas Qutb made in *ISQ*.[30] Finally, comparing the slim *Milestones* to the huge *ISQ*, we can see how Qutb himself certainly felt that *ISQ* was his greatest achievement. The majority of his prison years were spent writing and revising its many volumes.

Not only radical Islamists appreciate *ISQ*—a good number of moderate Muslims do as well. Qutb is viewed as an intellectual who sacrificed his life challenging the oppressive political and religious elite of his day. More importantly, the considerable popularity of *ISQ* as a Qur'anic exegesis is precisely because of the methodology used by Qutb. Qutb tried to make the Qur'an as accessible as possible. Qutb, utilizing his extensive skills in literary criticism and his ability to condense complicated ideas into simple, powerful statements, writes in a style that can be appreciated by elites and the less educated. Qutb makes reference to recent scientific developments as confirmation and explanation of Qur'anic phenomena. Finally, Qutb eschews the established traditional norms of Qur'anic exegetical literature: he avoids using highly technical, obscure vocabulary and its overly-referential style (reliance on the pre-existing religious scholarship)—he makes limited references to other Islamic scholars.[31] These features led clerics (many being government-appointed) to dismiss Qutb's work.

Thus *ISQ* is a conscious effort to bypass the methodology of the Islamic scholarly tradition to understand the Qur'an.[32] Like Martin Luther, he claimed that average believers can interpret the holy book themselves; Qutb is a popularizer and, as with Luther, subjecting scripture to popular interpretation opens a "Pandora's box" that can lead to all kinds of new readings of the holy book. This was a revolutionary act with incredible political and social ramifications. Therefore, despite Qutb's emphasis on the absoluteness of God and His commandments, his masterwork of *ISQ*, in both its writing style and methodology, is a modernist innovation.

Qutb first began writing *ISQ* in the early 1950s as a column in an MB periodical which then grew into a book project; he finished the latter volumes in jail. He finished all the volumes by 1959, but then immediately started revising the collection, starting with the first volume.[33] It is impossible to review in great detail the 30 volumes of *ISQ*, so some overall themes will be examined. A good quote to begin with is from volume 1; when commenting on 2:213 (that is, *surah* 2, verse 213), Qutb writes:

> It is worth pausing here to consider the statement that the Book[34] is *"setting forth the Truth."* This is an affirmation that the Book ... has come with the definitive and absolute truth. It is the ultimate, pre-eminent and sole arbiter and judge of all human thought and behavior. Without this authority society would be at a loss, life would descend into chaos, confusion and strife, and mankind would know no peace or happiness. This is vital in determining the source of human values, thought and understanding, and for defining the laws that govern human relations. The source is God, and God alone.

He later adds: "The fact is that it was necessary for a definite and firm standard to exist as a reference point for all mankind. It was likewise necessary that this standard should come from a source above the human mind and independent from it." He inevitably concludes:

> Society will progress and improve as long as it adheres to the teachings of God's Book.... Right and wrong in terms of religious faith are not to be decided by human individuals or through a ballot box ... the norms, traditions, systems, and laws people may adopt and accept as a way of life for human society at any particular time in history have no merit or consistency if they are at variance or in contradiction with God's Book [Qutb, *ISQ* Vol. 1 247–49].[35]

It is not enough to have some/certain Islamic practices implemented—it must be a complete and comprehensive system. The idea of a separation of mosque and state, or different spheres for people's religious and social lives, is antithetical to his understanding: "we cannot simply take one legal provision of one principle of Islam and try to implement it in a non–Muslim social setup" (Qutb, *ISQ* Vol. 4 95–96). If no human mind is perfect, it follows that any system (political, social, intellectual) designed by human reason is bound to have flaws. The best use of reason in his opinion was in dedication to understanding the fullness of the Qur'anic message. One of his major assumptions in this regard seems to be the ultimate possibility of clarity of revelation whereas he ignores the role of (subjective) human agency in interpreting and implementing it.[36]

Regarding Islamic scholarship or political and social developments of the past, his view is that Islamic history, indeed the current state of the Islamic world, had lost its essential Islamic character.

> In Muslim society, for example, serious deviations have occurred at certain stages of its history, and at present there is a worsening decline.... For genuine Islamic life to be resumed and a distinctive Muslim society to be rebuilt, those parts of Muslim history have to be cast aside ... [Qutb, *ISQ*, Vol. 1, 249; *Milestones* 13].

Qutb felt there were few elements in the Islamic world to draw upon for a (re)newed society. What was needed was a plan of action to put this renewal into effect. For his "plan" as to how to do this, we turn to his other prison work.

## *The Book* Milestones

Despite all the attention this book has received, whether from the radicals who embrace it or from journalists, writers, and "security analysts" in the U.S. who point to it, Qutb actually viewed it as minor compared to his other works. In size alone it is a handbook (though portability may have enhanced its success); comparison to the impressive *Social Justice in Islam* or the compendious collection of *ISQ* makes it appear minuscule. As was revealed by memoirs of the participants and the 1966 court trial that condemned Qutb to death, *Milestones* was first written as a study guide for select members of the MB (many of whom previously prisoners).[37] This small group, later dubbed "Nizam 1965" (or Organization 1965), was to be a new, invigorated, and activist "vanguard" of Muslims that would work towards creating an Islamic society; essentially Qutb was rejecting the mainstream MB, both in terms of methods and ideology, and instead creating a more select group of believers. While it cannot be inferred that these goals were predicated on militant methods (or Nizam 1965 was even capable of doing so), the organization clearly had the (long-term) goal of eventually replacing the government of Nasser. Thus, it is possible to see the potential for militancy. Obviously, so did the court that tried Qutb.[38]

Published in January 1964, *Milestones* is organized as a series of essays that frame belief and action as intertwined necessities for true Muslims. As the name implies, it is a handbook for working along the path of revolution to an ultimate and true Islamic order. Surprisingly, it got through the censors, being reprinted five times before the government banned it in mid–1964. In order to pass through the censors, Qutb again utilized a strategy of broad statements and obfuscation. Anyone searching for a detailed program of revolution or the desired Islamic state will be disappointed.

> The people who do not understand the character and nature of Islam demand that it provide theories and a completed constitution for its system.... These people want Islam ... [to] be reduced to the level of ordinary human theories and laws ... [Instead] First, the hearts and consciences of a people must be committed to a belief system that forbids submission to anyone other than God and that rejects the derivation of laws from any other source ... when such a group of people is ready and also gains practical influence in the society, various laws will be legislated according to their practical needs [Qutb, *Milestones* 28–29; also 35].

As evident, "Qutb's mature Islamism thus makes the revolutionary process central to its concerns.... [It] does not extend beyond the stage of struggle to envision precisely what a 'proper' Islamic state should look like" (Calvert, *Origins* 211).

Perhaps the two most important themes in this book are the central role played by *jahiliyah* and revolution.[39] Qutb nods to Mawdudi's use of the concept of *jahiliyah* and stretches it further—so far, we might say that he makes a radical break with Mawdudi. Mawdudi saw what could be called a "mixed" society, making allowance for what he calls "partial Muslims" in distinction to "full Muslims" who are those who "completely merge into Islam their full personality and entire existence.... Everything is subservient to Islam" (Maududi, *Fundamentals* 69; see 67–71). For Mawdudi this state of being a "partial Muslim" also can include levels of unbelief:

> Now if a person sets aside the system propounded by God and decides to work according to some other system, he, in reality, follows the path of *Kufr* [unbelief].... And if he obeys the directions of God in some matters and, in some others, gives preference over these to selfish desires or customs or man-made laws, then he is involved in *Kufr* to the extent he has rebelled against the laws of God. Someone is half *Kafir*, someone fourth and someone one-tenth or one-twentieth. In short, *Kufr* is there in proportion to the extent of rebellion against the law of God [Maududi, *Fundamentals* 49–50].

While Mawdudi admits that most Muslims stray from a complete obedience to God's laws and proper Islamic practice (Maududi, *Fundamentals* 64, 67), as can be seen above he still allows for them to be seen as Muslims, at least nominally.[40]

Earlier in his life, Qutb recognized a formulation not unlike Mawdudi. However, as he formulated in his 2nd edition of *ISQ* and *Milestones*, Qutb makes no such allowance. A person is either a Muslim or not; a person either fulfills Qutb's definition of Muslim or doesn't. Extending this logic, either a society is Islamic or not. If not, it is *jahili*. It is impossible, he writes, to have "a situation which is half–Islam and half-*jahiliyyah*" (Qutb, *Milestones* 112; also 114). Since Qutb came to feel that there are no true Islamic societies on earth, and there haven't been since the earliest days of Islam,[41] the whole world, both of non–Muslims *as well as the Islamic world*, is in a state of *jahiliyah*: "all the societies existing in the world are *jahili*" (Qutb, *Milestones* 66; also 7, 79, 117).[42] This needs to be emphasized: while Qutb as well as those who later expand upon his ideas were opposed to Western systems of governance and society,[43] he reserved his greatest hostility for the governments of the Islamic world. While he opposed the expansion of European or U.S. global hegemony, his primary target was the status quo in Egypt as well as other Arab, Middle Eastern, and Islamic countries.[44]

Qutb's stark vision of the world smacks of Manichaeism. There is no middle ground here. Given Qutb's context as a prisoner in terrible circumstances under an oppressive state, it would seem natural that Qutb could not fathom any form of accommodation. He says as much: "It is not for Islam to compromise with the concepts of *jahiliyyah* current in the world or to coexist in the same land together with a *jahili* system." Elsewhere he proclaims no compromise and "nor can we be loyal to it" (Qutb, *Milestones* 111; also 16, 39). This is a radical personal position to take. However, despite his extreme judgement of the unIslamic nature of people and society, he does not overtly utilize *takfir*. There may certainly be some convolutions involved in his avoidance of *takfir*, due to the doctrinally serious consequences of this practice, yet it is entirely possible for someone to interpret the thrust of his argument—read between the lines—as leading to this conclusion.[45] Here is a telling passage: "people are not Muslims, even if they proclaim to be, so long as they live the life of *jahiliyyah*. If someone loves to deceive himself or to deceive others ... it cannot change anything of actual reality. This is not Islam, and the deceived are not Muslims. Today a prime task of the Call to Islam is bringing these ignorant people back to Islam and make [*sic*] them into Muslims all over again" (Qutb, *Milestones* 118). Qutb takes us to the edge of the *takfir* precipice but doesn't plunge over; he speaks generally of societies and behavior, but does not specifically identify individuals or set out a rubric for *takfir*. In later iterations of his ideology as adopted and integrated with other radical ideas—as, for example, seen among al–Qaeda affiliated groups in Iraq—the ideologues are not hesitant to identify specific individuals and groups (for example, Shi'is), and list rigorous criteria for declaring somebody an unbeliever (if they do not do x, y, and z).

This connects to the other theme of the book, one which has had powerful resonance ever since. If it is to be determined that a given society is not Islamic—easy to do for Qutb and his later followers who saw themselves engulfed in unIslamic societies—then it is the duty of (true) Muslims to work for a revolutionary change of that society. While overtly hostile to nationalism, he posits that all man-made systems that organize society and government along principles other than religious belief are bound to be oppressive. Faith should be the only criterion:

> All men are equal regardless of their color, race or nation.... Man is able to change his beliefs, thinking, and attitude toward life, but he is incapable of changing his color and race, nor can he decide in what place or nation he is to be born. Thus it is clear that a society is civilized only to the extent that human associations are based on a community of free moral choice, and a society is backward in so far as the basis of association is something other than free choice. In Islamic terminology, it is a *jahili* society [Qutb, *Milestones* 81].[46]

Those who are within this society and decide not to choose Islam (that is, remain Christian, for example) have respected participatory roles, but are subordinate. Qutb is emphatic about forced conversion being forbidden (Qutb, *Milestones* 46, 59–60). However readers feel about this overall formulation, we should note that Qutb equates full membership as voluntary association (choice of religion) over hereditary factors about which we have no choice.

In creating this new Islamic society, Muslims may not be ultimately successful in this revolution (and use of the term *jihad* is appropriate here)—and Qutb and many assume martyrdom will be their end—but they are fulfilling God's expectations to make the effort. His interpretation of the life of Prophet Muhammad is key in this regard.[47] Qutb underscored Muhammad's difficult struggle to create a new God-ordained society in Medina (in the years 622–32) after he abandoned the unIslamic society of his birth—the city of Mecca—in which true believers were ridiculed and oppressed. The Prophet and his first Muslim followers implemented God's commandments as revealed; they incrementally removed those practices which were unIslamic. They faced immense obstacles and constant threats to their lives by the attacks made by Meccans; with telling language Qutb refers to these as "the Prophet ... bearing tortures for 13 years" (Qutb, *Milestones* 21). Ultimately, the Prophet and the first Muslims were successful; with absolute surety, Qutb felt this would again be the case in the present age.

## *The Martyr's Legacy*

Shortly after Qutb's execution in 1966 an article circulated entitled "Why Did They Execute Me?" in which Qutb speaks from the grave. Written in jail prior to his 1966 trial (though government censors removed references to torture), he outlines his explanation of his circumstances and makes his last riposte to the Egyptian government. He actually saw the article as a confession and final statement, assuming the end was near; since the government had already extracted confessions from his associates, at this point he had nothing to hide. He argues that it was state violence toward the MB that forced the organization to try to prepare itself militarily for defensive purposes; Nizam 1965 was the ultimate example of this. As a final nod to his overall thesis found in *ISQ* and *Milestones*, he again argued that Islam is a comprehensive way of life, and being a true believing Muslim necessitates all that this entails (as he saw it).

Today Qutb is widely considered a martyr, partially due to the successful campaign by the MB and his family to promote this image. This title of martyr is commonly used by sympathizers of his work, and even more so by radicals who claim his intellectual lineage. Even though the MB published the aforementioned book *Preachers Not Judges* as a rejection of some of Qutb's ideas, it still held him up as an exemplary Muslim Brother. For a non–Qutbist Muslim to acknowledge his martyrdom is also an explicit condemnation of the Nasser government as repressive, so politics overlap with considerations of Qutb's legacy.

After being released from jail, Muhammad Qutb went into exile in Saudi Arabia, as did many other MB members. There he taught Islamic studies and continued to edit and publish his brother's writings, sometimes attempting to moderate more radical interpretations. He was an important link in continuing his brother's legacy and teaching it to new generations. Some of these students later combined preexisting Saudi schools of religious thought—so-called "Wahhabism"—with Qutbism as well as adding more radical trends (the so-called *takfiri*), which has produced a number of political dissidents in Saudi Arabia and Islamist radicals elsewhere.

Empathetic authors (not the same as sympathetic) often make a salient point: later Islamists have taken Qutb's ideas or terms and interpreted them in ways that Qutb would not have agreed with. One example of this sentiment is "Had the Nasser regime not executed Qutb in August [1966], the possibility was fair that Qutb would have clarified many of the controversial terms he had posited in his prison writings. Instead, with Qutb gone, his writings were left wide open for radical interpretations" (Musallam 202). Regardless of the veracity of this claim, it is the case that Islamist radicals have cited Qutb. Al-Zawahiri was reportedly spurred to action when he learned of Qutb's execution, eventually leading the group Islamic Jihad. Its two most important thinkers, 'Umar 'Abd al–Rahman and 'Abd al–Salam Faraj, expanded upon the stark dichotomy in Qutb—they rejected his more gradualist-revivalist and educational plans and wanted immediate violent revolution. Islamic Jihad later merged into Bin Laden's al–Qaeda. Al-Zawahiri, long-considered the "brains" behind al–Qaeda, and now its leader after Bin Laden's assassination, has written admiringly of Qutb.[48]

The interpretations that these radicals offer of Qutb are certainly among the *possible* interpretations of his work. As noted above, Qutb opened a Pandora's box when he popularized Qur'anic exegesis for the non-specialist/non-cleric.[49] Qutb set up such a stark dichotomy of the world—Islam vs. *jahiliyah*—that it enabled people to eliminate nuance, complications, and compromise from their ideology. Finally, Qutb's argument that the governments of the (so-called) Islamic world were illegitimate—not to mention those of the rest of the world—and that they needed to be replaced with legitimate Islamic governments, is also suggestive of either an immediate or eventual revolution to remove those governments.

Despite the inspirational role of Qutb's work to violent radicals like Bin Laden, there are some problems with the argument that this is a natural or exact link. Qutb himself never advocated anything like terrorism.[50] He doesn't dwell at any length on violence, though he did admit in "Why Did They Execute Me?" that his group tried to stockpile weapons. However, while Qutb is certainly suggestive of revolution aimed at governments, nowhere in Qutb's works is there an advocacy of attacks against civilians, whether non-Muslim or Muslim (these kinds of attacks are hallmarks of groups like al-Qaeda). As a matter of fact, the mental and exegetical gymnastics that groups like al-Qaeda undergo in order to justify killing children, women, and elderly are a pointed disavowal of very specific injunctions of the Qur'an and *hadith*.[51] Finally, there are important ideological differences between al-Qaeda and Qutb, despite the former's use of the latter. Qutb describes a world that is not Islamic, including the lands in which Muslims live. *ISQ* and *Milestones* see Islam in a state of arrest; for this reason he wanted to rebuild a new Islamic society. However, even the most ardent radicals like Bin Laden didn't embrace this formula. They operate on the assumption that if a government is attacked or overthrown (such as Saudi Arabia), and if enough Muslims are drawn (or dragged) into this fight, they will reunite and repower the Islamic world. This assumption, then, sees much (most?) of the Islamic world as the vanguard from which to reconstitute the proper Islamic order. Qutb saw nothing Islamic in the societies from which to draw upon.

## Notes

1. For a well-researched and far better understanding of Qutb's time in the U.S. and how he felt the experience reinforced preexisting beliefs, see Calvert, "'The World Is an Undutiful Boy!'"
2. See later in this chapter for an explanation of the Arabic terms in the quote.
3. See Qutb's autobiography of his childhood (published in 1946), translated as *A Child from the Village*.
4. For a list in English of Qutb's major works, see Calvert, *Origins* 348–49.

5. Including his brother Muhammad, Naguib Mahfouz, and Muslim Brotherhood member Muhammad al-Ghazali.

6. The evolution of Qutb's thinking and writing seem to follow the "phases of development in the works of colonized writers" as outlined by Fanon in his revolutionary text, *The Wretched of the Earth*, 158–59.

7. Qutb was in the hospital multiple times during his trip to the United States in 1949–50 (See Calvert, *Origins*).

8. Even in his late, more radical years (see Qutb, *Milestones* 7).

9. Interview with Saeb Dajani, found in Brogan.

10. One instance happened in Greeley, Colorado, when Qutb and another Egyptian were barred from entering a cinema. Qutb mentioned other incidents to his friend Dajani. See Brogan.

11. For example, in his later editions of *Social Justice in Islam* Qutb pointed to the "organized extermination" of American Indians and discrimination of African Americans (see the translation in Shepard, *Sayyid Qutb and Islamic Activism* 59).

12. For the classic study on the MB, see Mitchell.

13. Qutb actually wrote the introduction to the 2nd edition of the Arabic translation of Nadvi's book (which translates as *What the World Has Lost by the Decline of the Muslims*). The chronology outlined above means that Qutb read Mawdudi and Nadvi after he had already written *Social Justice in Islam*, so their influence was on works after that book (as well as on Qutb's revisions of *Social Justice*). Actually, Qutb met Nadvi in September 1950 on Hajj in Mecca and gave him a copy of his *Social Justice in Islam* (see al-Nadwi 101–6).

14. Nevertheless, as I have tried to show throughout this essay, Qutb was most influenced by and reacting to local developments. As Abu-Rabi' notes, the influence of Mawdudi and other thinkers was important but should not be overemphasized (Abu-Rabi' 139).

15. For a good study of Mawdudi (Nasr).

16. *Hakimiyah* of God is not a Qur'anic term, though it is derived from *hukm* (rule, judgment) which is found in the Qur'an. Mawdudi's exact term in Urdu was *hukumat-i ilahiya* (which means "divine government"). See chapter 5 in Nasr for an outline of Mawdudi's arguments—and this evolution—on this important aspect of his ideology. As a matter of fact, it has been noted that Qutb probably got the term *hakimiyah* from the Arabic translator of Mawdudi's work (see Akhavi 378, 396) (note 7). Also, see Khatab, "'Hakimiyyah' and 'Jahiliyyah.'"

17. A pithy statement in this regard is "The popular slogan ... 'Rule of man over man is exploitation; submission to Allah the Creator is the only way to emancipation'—best captures the essence of Mawdudi's argument" (Nasr 88).

18. As Nasr argues, "Like other contemporary Islamic revivalists, Mawdudi did not view Islamic history as the history of Islam but as the history of un-Islam or *jahiliyah*. Islamic history, as the product of human choice, was corruptible and corrupted. For him, Islamic history held no value and manifested no religious truths, except during its early phase. The history of Muslim societies was not so much a testimony of divine will as an account of the fall of Islam.... The Islamic state [he wished to create] therefore had to stand outside the cumulative tradition of history of Muslim societies" (Nasr 60). As can be seen, Mawdudi, like Qutb, rejected nearly the entirety of the Islamic tradition, embodied in its history, scholarship, and institutions; this point, in and of itself, and not necessarily the nature of the government these men advocated, is what actually makes the term "radical" so applicable.

19. It is incontrovertible that there was a meeting at Qutb's house days before the July 1952 coup but debate still exists among scholars as to the extent and nature of the cooperation. Furthermore, both Qutb (and MB) were enthusiastic about the plans of the Free Officers, and among the latter were admirers of Qutb and the MB, but it is also clear that both groups saw each other as tools for their particular goals (see Calvert, *Origins* 180–83).

20. That is, the more radical ideas he worked out in his revised editions of his works written in prison.

21. The most important statement in this regard by the MB was by their General Guide in his posthumous (and collectively-written) book which only alluded to Qutb but certainly rejected his (and Mawdudi's) most radical interpretations. It seems to me that the entire chapter dedicated to *hakimiyah* was, in and of itself, a direct response to Qutb, as was the very suggestive language contained therein. Among the book's many salient points is the argument that the suffering of MB members in jail pushed them to extremes. Its title translates as *Preachers not Judges*. Due to censorship, the book was published nearly a decade after its composition. I was able to read the second edition. See al-Hudaybi. There have been claims that the state intervened in the production of this book. For one version of this claim, see Khatab 149–51.

22. While most observers accept that the would-be assassin was a member of the MB, questions remain as to whether it was a "set up" (given his pitifully poor performance) and who knew about the plot in the MB; indications are that the leadership of the MB, and Qutb, did not.

23. A British Foreign Office report noted the torture evident on the prisoners (Calvert, *Origins* 193).

24. Due to her reputation as a liberal reformer, a very popular translated book used in the U.S. to understand the Egyptian prison experience is Saadawi. An actual MB prison memoir available in English is al-Ghazali. For further and more detailed reading on the critical role of the prison experience on Qutb (Abu-Rabi'; Moussalli; Tripp; Calvert, *Origins* 193–98; al-Khalidi 345–73).

25. For example, he writes: "The Muslim encountered nothing burdensome except the torture and oppression of those who rejected Islam. But he had already decided in the depth of his heart that he would face the future with equanimity. Therefore no pressure from the jahili society could have any effect on his firm resolve. Today too we are surrounded by *jahiliyyah*" (Qutb, *Milestones* 15; qtd. in 129–31, 133–37).

26. Those works written by followers of his ideology emphasize his afflictions to underscore his martyrdom, but nevertheless this fact alone does not detract from the reality of his prison experience.

27. A number of scholars have suggested that the Egyptian government also allowed this to happen because Qutb's (growing) celebrity as an imprisoned intellectual hurt it in the wider Third World political arena, and so now they could claim the conditions of his incarceration were mild enough to allow him productive work. While plausible, there is no access to government records that could substantiate this claim.

28. This essay focuses on *ISQ* and *Milestones*, but his revisions of *Social Justice* are equally interesting and demonstrate my argument (Shepard, "The Development" 196–236).

29. While 'Arif was a nationalist military man like Nasser, he utilized religion as a political tool in a way that Nasser avoided. Furthermore, during the turbulent late 1950s in Iraq, 'Arif himself had been a prisoner and had read *ISQ*—we might see this as a spiritual bond of imprisonment.

30. He says as much, as four chapters in *Milestones* are from *ISQ* (Qutb, *Milestones* 9–10).

31. Part of this methodology was probably practical—in jail he did not have access to the kinds of libraries that normal exegetes do.

32. It should be reiterated that Qutb was not a cleric nor did he have a clerical training, thus partially explaining his unconventional exegetical methodology. This fact underscores, again, the novelty in both Qutb's approach to interpreting the Qur'an as well as the reception and consideration he has received as a religious authority by those sympathetic to his views. Calvert gives a good review of Qutb's approach (See Calvert, *Origins* 173–75).

33. His execution curtailed these plans. Thus the volumes covering *surah*s 33–114 were written in prison up to the year 1959, *surah*s 16–32 are as published prior to his incarceration in 1954, and *surah*s 1–15 have a 1st edition and a 2nd edition, the latter being revised in his post-1959 phase in prison. It is when comparing the 1st and 2nd edition volumes, as well as

the pre–1957 prison massacre and post-massacre writing, that we can see the clear evolution of his radicalization.

34. A generic term that means the message, or Word, of God that has been revealed throughout history culminating in the Qur'an.

35. Also see Khatab, "'Hakimiyyah'" 159–60, 164–65.

36. We should add that he avoids addressing the intellectual context of any hermeneutical exercise, as briefly addressed in Nayed, 359–62.

37. The most important reading material given to the members of Nizam 1965 was by Qutb and Mawdudi (See Zollner, 418).

38. Zollner, 418–19; this concept of a vanguard to lead a revolution was not new. For Qutb's context, see Calvert, *Origins*, 16–18. The court—as well as later followers—could "read between the lines" and interpret that Qutb, in his indirect fashion, announces a "declaration of war" against (assumedly) the Egyptian government in *Milestones*, 20–21.

39. It should be noted that there was an evolution of his interpretation of *jahiliyah*, and this is nicely traced in Khatab, *Political Thought*. Also, Shepard, "Doctrine" 532–33.

40. *Takfir* is declaring a person as disbelieving in God (he/she is a *kafir*). His discussion is ironic given his branding of some Muslims "half *Kafir*" or "fourth … one-tenth … one-twentieth," but at least he still allowed for that person to be accepted as a "partial Muslim" and not full *kafir*.

41. Though one author points out that Qutb's language is suggestive that earlier Islamic states were at "lower levels" of Islam; the point when the Islamic world became non–Islamic, that is, *jahili*, started during the European imperialistic period onwards (Shepard, "Doctrine" 529–30).

42. He is explicit on page 67: "all the existing so-called 'Muslim societies' are also *jahili* societies."

43. It should be added that Shepard sees this argument of Qutb also in a defensive light: "Only an Islamic society can properly be said to be 'civilized.' Thus, Qutb inverts the usual Western judgment on the Islamic world" (Shepard, "Doctrine" 527).

44. As a matter of fact, Qutb would strenuously deny the validity of my usage of such terms as "Islamic world" and "Islamic country"—which I use for sake of ease of discussion—since he would point out that just because there are individual Muslim believers in a country doesn't make it necessarily "Islamic"—and, of course, in this highly narrow view, he is correct.

45. As Zollner comments, therefore it is again necessary to complicate common critiques of Qutb because Qutb himself did not explicitly outline *takfir*. It was later interpreters of Qutb who emphasized the idea of *takfir*—or, put another way, they brought Qutb's argument to its most extreme possible conclusion (see Zollner, 423–25; Shepard, "Doctrine" 529).

46. Also 40–41, 46, 88, 103, 107–10.

47. It should be noted that looking to the example of the Prophet Muhammad, and interpreting said example to support one's particular religious and/or political agenda, is an old practice.

48. Al-Zawahiri was prolific in his praise of Qutb in his book *Fursan taht rayat al-nabi*.

49. Another important example: the fact that Bin Laden felt able to make *fatwa*s (legal interpretations), even though this is only a prerogative of trained clergy, is a result of the open Pandora's box.

50. Though an ill-defined term, as it is popularly understood this means use of nontraditional violent or military tactics that may include civilian targets for purposes of spectacle and symbolism.

51. It should also be added that the assumption of a direct transmission of Qutb's ideas down a "direct genealogical line" to Bin Laden ignores both the specific and very different historical contexts (and motives) of both men's lives as well as the role of the agency and individualized interpretation of Qutb's works by later militants like Bin Laden. For a critique of scholarship that makes those assumptions, see Zollner.

## Works Cited

Abu-Rabi', Ibrahim M. *Intellectual Origins of Islamic Resurgence in the Modern Arab World*. Albany: State University of New York Press, 1996. Print.

Akhavi, Sharough. "The Dialectic in Contemporary Egyptian Social Thought: The Scripturalist and Modernist Discourses of Sayyid Qutb and Hasan Hanafi." *International Journal of Middle East Studies* 29.3 (1997): 377–401. Print.

Brogan, Daniel. "Al Qaeda's Greeley Roots." *5280 Magazine: Denver's Mile-High Magazine* (June–July 2003): n.pag. Print.

Calvert, John. *Sayyid Qutb and the Origins of Radical Islamism*. New York: Columbia University Press, 2010. Print.

———. "'The World Is an Undutiful Boy!': Sayyid Qutb's American Experience." *Islam and Christian-Muslim Relations* 11.1 (Mar. 2000): 87–103. Print.

Carré, Olivier. *Mysticism and Politics: A Critical Reading of* Fi Zilal al–Qur'an *by Sayyid Qutb*. Trans. Carol Artigues. Rev. W. Shepard. Leiden: E.J. Brill, 2003. Print.

Fanon, Frantz. *The Wretched of the Earth*. Trans. Richard Philcox. New York: Grove Press, 2004. Print.

al-Ghazali, Zainab. *Return of the Pharoah: Memoirs in Nasir's Prison*. Trans. Mokrane Guezzou. Keicester: The Islamic Foundation, 1994. Print.

al-Hudaybi, Hasan. *Du'at la qudat: Abhath fi al-'aqidah al-islamiyah wa-minhaj al-da'wah ila Allah*, 2nd ed. Beirut: Dar al-salam, 1978. Print.

Al-Khalidi, 'Abd al-Fattah. *Sayyid Qutb: Min al-milad ila al-istishhad*. Damascus: Dar al-qalam, 1991. Print.

Khatab, Sayed. "'Hakimiyyah' and 'Jahiliyyah' in the Thought of Sayyid Qutb." *Middle Eastern Studies* 38.3 (2002): 145–70. Print.

———. *The Political Thought of Sayyid Qutb: The Theory of* Jahiliyyah. New York: Routledge, 2006. Print.

Maududi, Sayyid Abul A'la. *Fundamentals of Islam*. Lahore: Islamic Publications, 1992. Print.

Mitchell, Richard P. *The Society of the Muslim Brothers*. New York: Oxford University Press, 1993. Print.

Moussalli, Ahmad. *Radical Islamic Fundamentalism: The Ideological and Political Discourse of Sayyid Qutb*. Beirut: American University of Beirut, 1992. Print.

Musallam, Adnan A. *From Secularism to Jihad: Sayyid Qutb and the Foundations of Radical Islamism*. Westport: Praeger, 2005. Print.

Al-Nadwi, Abu al-Hasan. *Shaksiyat wa-kutub*. Damascus: Dar al-qalam, 1990. Print.

Nasr, Seyyed Vali Reza. *Mawdudi & the Making of Islamic Revivalism*. New York: Oxford University Press, 1996. Print.

Nayed, Aref Ali. "The Radical Qur'anic Hermeneutics of Sayyid Qutb." *Islamic Studies* 31.3 (1992): 355–63. Print.

Qutb, Muhammad. *Sayyid Qutb, al-shahid al-a'zal*. Cairo: Al-Mukhtār Al-Islāmi, 1974. Print.

Qutb, Sayyid. "'The America I Have Seen': In the Scale of Human Values." *America in an Arab Mirror: Images of America in Arabic Travel Literature: An Anthology 1895–1995*. Ed. Kamal Abdel-Malek. New York: St. Martin's Press, 2000. 9–27. Print.

———. *A Child from the Village*. Ed. and Trans. John Calvert. William Shepard. Syracuse: Syracuse University Press, 2004. Print.

———. *In the Shade of the Qur'an: Fi Zilal al–Qur'an*. Vol. 1. Ed. and Trans. M.A. Salahi. A.A. Shamis. London: MWH, 1979–. Print.

———. *In the Shade of the Qur'an*. Vol. 4. Ed. and Trans. Adil Salahi. Ashur Shamis. Leicester: The Islamic Foundation, n.d. Print.

Saadawi, Nawal El. *Memoirs from the Women's Prison*. Trans. Marilyn Booth. Berkeley: University of California Press, 1994. Print.

Shepard, William. "The Development of the Thought of Sayyid Qutb as Reflected in Earlier and Later Editions of 'Social Justice in Islam.'" *Die Welt des Islams* 32.2 (1992): 196–236. Print.

\_\_\_\_\_. *Sayyid Qutb and Islamic Activism: A Translation and Critical Analysis of* Social Justice in Islam. Leiden: E.J. Brill, 1996. Print.

\_\_\_\_\_. "Sayyid Qutb's Doctrine of 'Jahiliyya.'" *International Journal of Middle East Studies* 35.4 (2003): 521–45. Print.

Smith, Charles. "The 'Crisis of Orientation': The Shift of Egyptian Intellectuals to Islamic Subjects in the 1930's." *International Journal of Middle East Studies* 4.4 (1973): 382–410. Print.

Stanley, Alessandra. "'America at a Crossroads': The World since 9/11 in Detail and Sorrow." *The New York Times* 14 Apr. 2007. Web. 19 Mar. 2014.

Tripp, Charles. "Sayyid Qutb: The Political Vision." *Pioneers of Islamic Revival*. Ed. Ali Rahnema. London: Zed Books, 1994. N.p. Print.

Zollner, Barbara. "Prison Talk: The Muslim Brotherhood's Internal Struggle During Gamal Abdel Nasser's Persecution, 1954 to 1971." *International Journal of Middle East Studies* 39.3 (2007): 411–33. Print.

# Martin Luther King, Jr., "Letter from a Birmingham Jail" and Nonviolent Social Transformation

JOYCE APSEL

## Summary

"Letter from a Birmingham Jail" (1963) by Martin Luther King, Jr., has become a classic description and defense of civil disobedience, and a hallmark of the U.S. Civil Rights Movement. Rooted in resistance to racism, and embracing the dignity of the individual, King's words anticipate the modern human rights revolution with their emphasis on the mutuality of human beings, and the interdependence of their rights. This essay looks at the letter's historical context—King's imprisonment for protesting without a permit, his leadership of the Southern Christian Leadership Conference, and the movement's need for a manifesto—and its religious and philosophical influences, from African American church sermons to Gandhi's nonviolent philosophy and activism. "Letter from a Birmingham Jail" has become a rallying cry against oppression, and for justice worldwide.—J.W.R.

## Introduction

> "Injustice anywhere is a threat to justice everywhere. We are caught in an inescapable network of mutuality, tied in a single garment of destiny."
> —Martin Luther King, Jr., "Letter from a Birmingham Jail"

This essay focuses on Martin Luther King's "Letter from a Birmingham Jail" (dated April 16, 1963), and how its content and context represent a significant milestone in the history of the U.S. Civil Rights Movement, and in nonviolent social movements globally; it is a universal manifesto for freedom and equality. The letter was first published in book form in *Why We Can't Wait* (1964), a collection of King's writings about Birmingham, Alabama, and is widely available online.

Martin Luther King, Jr. (1929–1968), often along with his lieutenant Ralph D. Abernathy, Sr. (1926–1990), and thousands of other activists, was thrown in jail repeatedly for protesting U.S. segregation laws and practices over the course of the Civil Rights Movement during the 1950s and '60s. On Good Friday 1963, King and Abernathy were among some fifty people arrested in Birmingham for "parading without a permit," leading a protest in violation of a court-issued injunction banning the march. Such acts of civil disobedience against what King described as unjust laws were hallmarks of the Civil Rights Movement to end racial segregation.

During his eight days of imprisonment in the Birmingham jail in 1963 (he would serve time again there in 1968), King read an open letter, published in a five-day-old copy of the *Birmingham News*, critical of "a series of demonstrations by some of our negro citizens, directed and led in part by outsiders." The letter was written and signed by eight white local clergymen urging an end to demonstrations that they believed could lead to further hatred and violence; instead, they supported what they referred to as restraint, and use of the courts and negotiations with the Birmingham civil authorities. King's written response—explaining why Negroes could *not* wait, and that "I am in Birmingham because injustice is here"—began in scribbles on the edges of the newspaper. Over the rest of what he described as his "confinement" in prison, he continued to write down his ideas; many were based on earlier sermons and speeches. Sections of the letter were smuggled out by his lawyers, further edited, and typed in the following days. Initially, there was limited publicity of the letter, or reaction to it; however, it was later picked up by several national papers and periodicals. The letter was eventually reprinted and circulated widely, providing a moral and intellectual basis for the nonviolent movement and its campaigns, and helped to gain financial and popular support as well. Just as "We Shall Overcome" became its protest song, the letter by Martin Luther King, Jr., penned in the Birmingham jail, became the written rally cry for the Civil Rights Movement, and the most widely read manifesto of its goals. King's stirring language and content has made "Letter from a Birmingham Jail" a classic in the literature of social protest worldwide. "If Birmingham could be cracked, the direction of the entire nonviolent movement in the South could turn. It was our faith that 'as Birmingham goes, so goes the South'" (King, "How It Began" 4).

## Historical Background

Birmingham, Alabama, was founded in 1871, six years after the Civil War ended, and it was referred to as "The Magic City" early on because of its rapid economic growth as a Southern industrial center for iron, steel, and manufacturing. At the same time, Birmingham adopted the practices and policies of segregation that characterized the antebellum South, becoming a center of Jim Crow support where the white population strongly supported racial segregation. "Whites Only" and "Colored" signs dotted the city's public and private facilities, and segregation was strongly enforced. The city acquired a reputation as a segregationist stronghold and a bastion of the Ku Klux Klan. Birmingham was nicknamed "Bombingham"; one neighborhood was known locally as "Dynamite Hill," reflecting the extent of violence against African American persons and their property: by one estimate, over fifty homes were bombed in the city between 1947 and 1965.

Birmingham was one of a number of places that resisted the changes mandated by a series of court cases dismantling the legitimacy of racial segregation in schools, public transportation and facilities, voting, and other areas. The May 17, 1954, U.S. Supreme Court judgment *Brown v. Board of Education* of Topeka, Kansas, was a watershed event, overturning the earlier "separate but equal" rulings, and declaring segregated educational facilities unconstitutional. However, it turned out that the ruling to end segregation in schools "with all deliberate speed" proved very slow in action, and the implementation of integration in schools, public facilities, and other places met a series of legal and other obstacles; the law was often ignored and fought against by segregationists and their supporters. In Birmingham in the early 1960s, discrimination against African Americans—who made up 40 percent of the population—continued with segregation in public and private institutions and spheres, employment access limited to low-paying jobs without benefits, and obstruction of voter registration. The Ku Klux Klan had close ties with city officials, including the commissioner of public safety, Eugene "Bull" Connor. In general, targeted racial violence against African Americans and their property was carried out with impunity. Periodic physical violence took place, including killing and maiming. For example, there was the kidnapping of Edward Aaron, an African American out walking with his girlfriend, who was forced to crawl and then castrated; his bleeding wound was doused with turpentine and set on fire. Assistant pastor Charles Billups, an ally of the activist Reverend Shuttlesworth, was beaten with chains, and the letters KKK were branded on his stomach (McWhorter 155). Martin Luther King, Jr., in his essay "Bull Connor's Birmingham," describes an environment where "the silent password is fear": "You would be living in the largest city of a police state, presided over by a governor—George Wallace—whose inauguration vow had been a pledge of 'segregation now, segregation tomorrow, segregation forever!' You would be living, in fact, in the most segregated city in America."

Even though the National Association for the Advancement of Colored People (NAACP) was outlawed in Alabama by the state legislature in order to prevent demonstrations, local black leaders and groups continued to petition and take initiatives against white supremacy. Reverend Fred Shuttlesworth (1922–2011) was among the most prominent activists in Birmingham's fight for civil rights. He organized a petition, signed by over seventy black clergy, calling for the hiring of African American police officers. The city commissioners were presented with the petition but refused to act on it, claiming it would anger the white community. Like King and other civil rights activists, Shuttlesworth was the object of physical attacks and repeated threats, and both his home and church were bombed. In 1956, Shuttlesworth and other ministers joined to form a new organization called the Alabama Christian Movement for Human Rights (ACMHR) as a vehicle to organize for civil rights. The ACMHR was supported primarily by lower-middle-class African Americans (in contrast to more well-to-do African American community members, who were often reluctant to directly challenge the status quo). ACMHR pushed for equal opportunity for the economic and social advancement of African Americans, and led a series of actions—from sitting in whites-only sections of buses (modeled on the earlier Montgomery public bus boycott), to Shuttlesworth trying in 1957 to register four students (including two of his own) in a white school.

In May 1961, Birmingham became one of the destinations of the Freedom Riders campaign, initiated by the Congress of Racial Equality (CORE), in which black and white members traveled together on buses to integrate public bus stations. The burning of one bus outside Anniston, Alabama, as well as knife attacks on Freedom Riders when their bus arrived at Birmingham's Trailways bus station on Mother's Day, 1961, reflected the local authorities' tolerance of violence against desegregationist supporters. In October 1961 a judge ruled that the city's parks, playgrounds, and swimming pools had to be desegregated; Connor and the two other city commissioners responded by closing down the facilities. From a series of reports by Harrison Salisbury of the *New York Times* describing the racism in Birmingham and calling it an American Johannesburg, to images of police brutality under chief Bull Connor, bad publicity began to have a negative economic impact on the city. Hence, a group of more moderate businesspeople—who supported segregation—worked to change the city's government as a means of getting Bull Connor out of office. The two leading contenders in the next mayoral election were Connor and Albert Boutwell, a lawyer and segregationist who had the support of the business community, and who disapproved of the public and violent methods used by Connor.

Meanwhile, Fred Shuttlesworth and others argued that the Southern Christian Leadership Conference should bring its campaign to Birmingham. In September 1962, the SCLC held its convention there, and Martin Luther King, Jr., and his supporters were at a crossroads. King's earlier campaign to desegregate facilities in Albany, Georgia, had proved unsuccessful, and there was increasing criticism of his leadership. Attention was more and more focused on the action of students and younger activists following sit-ins at Greensboro, North Carolina, and on the Freedom Riders and the publicity surrounding them. The SCLC was a relatively small organization, competing with the NAACP, CORE, and the Student Nonviolent Coordinating Committee (SNCC) for support from the African American and white communities in its fight against racism, and to achieve civil rights and equality.

After some hesitation, the SCLC leaders realized they needed a winning strategy in order to remain viable; they took up Shuttlesworth's appeal, and their "do-or-die" Birmingham campaign to end segregation began to take shape. Lessons learned from the earlier demonstrations in Albany resulted in attempts to better coordinate with local organizers and churches, provide nonviolent training workshops, and put more emphasis on getting effective publicity out about what was taking place. However, success was far from certain; King and the SCLC were initially met with suspicion from some local black clergy, and opposition from much of the black middle class and the small elite sector of Birmingham black society, who viewed the organization as too confrontational, as well as being outsiders. There was also ongoing criticism from SNCC and younger activists; for example, King had refused to participate in the Freedom Rides, and the SCLC was seen as too moderate and outdated to bring about effective change in civil rights now.

In April 1963, there was a series of new sit-ins and protests, including a small group of picketers in downtown Birmingham carrying signs saying "Equal Opportunity and Human Dignity" and "Birmingham Merchants Unfair," led by blind jazz singer Al Hibbler and others. As the demonstrations faltered, the SCLC under King's leadership finally resolved not to wait any longer: now was the time to take action. They decided to openly, publicly violate the court injunction against protest marches, and to nonviolently accept the consequences of their actions. King, along with Abernathy and Shuttlesworth, saw this public protest—a protest staged expressly to result in their arrest and imprisonment—as part of the spectacle they needed to create in order to publicize their cause. (King often wrote and spoke about the "creative tension" brought about by nonviolent actions as necessary to prod change.)

On Good Friday, King, with Abernathy and Shuttlesworth by his side, led a nonviolent march in downtown Birmingham for racial justice and integration; the event was covered by the national media. As King writes in "New Day in Birmingham," an essay about the example of civil disobedience, "We decided that Good Friday, because of its symbolic significance, would be the day that Ralph Abernathy and I would present our bodies as personal witness in their crusade" (70). With other nonviolent protestors, they were filmed being arrested and thrown into police vehicles. According to historian Diane McWhorter, King's "subsequent confinement at the Birmingham Jail yielded the 'Letter' that consecrated his reputation." She points out that there is a legend that it was SCLC member Reverend Wyatt Walker who, after the editing was completed, said, "This is going to be one of the historic documents of this movement. Call it 'Letter from a Birmingham Jail'" (McWhorter 335).

## *Writing "Letter from a Birmingham Jail"*

The influence of Martin Luther King, Jr., and the reputation his public letter has generated, seems inevitable. But during his lifetime, King was a controversial figure throughout the United States, among African Americans as well as whites. As pointed out earlier, the 1963 Birmingham campaign came at a time when King's leadership and the SCLC strategy were being challenged by other organizations and leaders, including the NAACP, CORE, and SNCC. "In hindsight King's status as civil rights leader is seen as 'natural' but many civil rights activists did not; in fact most protestors at the time belonged to other organizations" (Miller 11). King would also be criticized by Malcolm X and other Black Power advocates for not being radical enough, and for his moderation and acquiescence to white authorities. On the other hand, King was viewed as "poisonous"—a dangerous menace to public safety and order—not only by segregationists but from white moderate political leadership and advocates of the gradual dismantling of segregation. What, then, distinguished Martin Luther King, Jr., as a leader and public figure, and contributed to the significance of "Letter from a Birmingham Jail" for the Civil Rights Movement?

King became a media magnet and "superstar," and this was to a large degree because of his language—his skill in persuading moderate whites on the sidelines to accept racial equality. King's strength as a leader in part stemmed from his "ability to translate the message of the folk pulpit into ... an idiom most suited to persuade white listeners" (Miller 11). And in "Letter from a Birmingham Jail"—just as in the "I Have a Dream" speech delivered six months later at the March on Washington—the content included themes of freedom and deliverance that resonated across different racial and socioeconomic communities. If the messenger and the message had resonance, a series of events over the next years, from his receiving the Nobel Peace Prize to his assassination in 1968, added as well to his reputation, and that of "Letter from a Birmingham Jail."

Once out of jail, King and others realized that they needed another spark to keep the pressure on. In response to the urging of one of SCLC's visionaries, Reverend James Bevel (Rieder 108), and other nonviolent activists—and with initially considerable misgivings—King and the SCLC endorsed the Children's Crusade. During the last ten days of April, Bevel, along with Andrew Young, Dorothy Cotton, and others, conducted training sessions on nonviolence, and encouraged young people to join and march together in a movement for peaceful protest. On May 2, 1963, the Children's Crusade publicly began; and on the following day, when children and students, including the K-12 brigade, marched in protest in Birmingham, Bull Connor ordered them to stop; when they continued to march and sing, Connor ordered them to be forcibly stopped. The images from Birmingham—police, firemen, and supporting onlookers deploying police dogs and hoses against children and other young people protesting nonviolently—flashed around the world. Reactions against the violence, and in support of ending racial segregation, came from politicians and leaders, including those who had previously urged gradualism. President John F. Kennedy's speech on race to the county on June 11, 1963, emphasized the need to end segregation. Ironically, a day later, in the Protestant periodical *The Christian Century*, "Letter from a Birmingham Jail" was published; in August it appeared in *The Atlantic* magazine with the headline "The Negro Is Your Brother," and that same month King delivered the "I Have a Dream" speech.

Both racial violence and nonviolent protest continued to mark the landscape of segregation and civil rights. In May, King, Shuttleworth, and Abernathy announced a settlement with Birmingham authorities agreeing to desegregation demands in exchange for an end to protests. But tensions and violence continued. On September 15, 1963, the Sixteenth Street Baptist Church in Birmingham was bombed, killing four African American girls in the basement who were there to attend Sunday School. Martin Luther King, Jr., was among those who spoke of their martyrdom and redemptive suffering, while delivering the eulogy at their funeral.

King grew up listening to the preaching of his father, Martin Luther King, Sr., and absorbed the themes and images from thousands of sermons he heard delivered from African American pulpits, as well as in progressive Protestant churches during his theological study at Boston University, and later on visits to churches throughout the United States. King borrowed from these different traditions and individual theologians, integrating the Bible, particularly Old and New Testament stories and images, into his speeches and writings. This ability to synthesize religious themes, universal ethics, and everyday stories of the devastating, destructive effects of racial violence on individuals and families, together with themes of nonviolence and justice, became the hallmark of King's message—through the open letter, sermons, speeches, and writings.

The popular image of Martin Luther King, Jr., spontaneously writing a letter of protest from his jail cell needs further contextualization. For some time, King and his small group of advisers, including Reverend Wyatt Walker, who was in charge of publicity for the SCLC, realized they needed some type of statement or letter to promote their cause in various newspapers throughout the U.S. and internationally, in order to gain support. Earlier on, a writer from the *New York Times* had suggested that King write a letter to the paper about the movement; ironically, the *Times* declined to print "Letter from a Birmingham Jail," and it was eventually published in the *New York Post*. Also, King and others were keenly aware of the tradition of political prisoners such as Gandhi and their letters from jail, as well as the apostolic tradition, particularly that of Paul, getting out Christ's message through a series of epistles. King had published a series of speeches in the volume *Stride to Freedom*, but it had not generated the widespread readership the organization hoped for.

Also, while King and others expected to serve time in jail, conditions and treatment varied; in Birmingham, King was put in solitary confinement for twenty-four hours. He describes the darkness and his sense of frustration and worry in the essay "New Day in Birmingham." As he writes in an "author's note" on the first page of the published letter, after finally being allowed to speak to his lawyers, he received an old copy of the *Birmingham News* from "a friendly Negro trustee." In it, King read the public letter signed by eight white clergy critical of the protests, and he decided to respond to their criticism and their call for gradualism. The content of King's letter evolved over the following days; he used the clergy's brief statement as a taking-off point for discussing why civil disobedience was necessary, examining segregation and its harms, and criticizing moderates, such as the white clergy who failed to face the urgency of the situation. In fact, the letter emphasizes how much their cooperation contributed to perpetuating the institutions and oppressions of segregation.

King began writing a response in his cell on April 16, 1963, putting down his thoughts in the form of notes on the edges of the newspaper. The letter is an example of the influence of oral traditions. It is a synthesis, incorporating ideas and phrases from earlier sermons—both those he had listened to in childhood, and his own sermons and speeches delivered at various meetings and civil rights events. King turned the letter into a defense not only of his actions but of civil rights protest in general, a rationale for the significance of civil disobedience. He pointed to the timidity of his accusers and other well-intentioned clergy and white moderates who refused to take a radical stand against injustice, and hence became accomplices to it. He uses the example of just and unjust laws to explain that anyone who breaks an unjust law "must do it openly, lovingly." If an individual breaks a law that his conscience tells him is not just, and "willingly accepts the penalty by staying in jail to arouse the conscience of the community over its injustice, then this person" is "expressing the very highest respect for law."

There was a strong oral tradition in the battle for civil rights, which became a cornerstone of the movement in the 1950s and later. This was in part linked to the important role played historically by African American churches, ministers, and communities in preaching the gospel of freedom. From hymns of freedom and resistance, to the pulpit as the center of community organizing, to the church basement as a place to train in civil disobedience, the movement was both inspired and instructed by its religious roots. The language of the letter reflects King's experience as a preacher first and foremost, as well as his training in theology and philosophy. The language and tone of the letter shifts from polite response to fellow clergy, to prophetic anger, disdain, and outrage. King describes the everyday experiences of the Negro, sometimes using the term "nigger" in discussing the demeaning mistreatment and pernicious harms of segregation and racism. Being put—or often shoved or thrown—into jail becomes part of the badge of honor of resistance.

## *Nonviolence and Human Rights*

The expanded, edited version of what has come down as the text of "Letter from a Birmingham Jail" includes description of key aspects of a range of nonviolent tactics, reflecting a mixture of King's theological/philosophical background and his experience preaching and in civil rights organizing and practices. King emphasizes the concepts of love, mutuality, and interdependence of human beings, their communities, and their rights. Rooted in the dignity of the individual and belief in the possibility of human improvement and moral courage, King's words anticipate the modern human rights revolution as it will emerge in the post–Cold War era after decades of posturing over which rights trumped others. King's message conveys the importance of mutuality: human beings and their rights—civil, cultural, economic, political, and social—are interdependent. Political philosopher Gene Sharp describes a series of tactics used in the history of nonviolent social movements. These include speaking out, marching, petition, boycott, and sit-in. Filling the jails with political dissenters is another tool, along with publicizing one's goals, including writings—from pamphlets to books to letters. Hence, King's letter of protest during his imprisonment is deeply rooted within the history and methods of nonviolent dissent. And from Socrates to Christ, and Thoreau to Gandhi, King was aware of being part of this heritage, and found inspiration in their deeds and words.

## Content of the Letter

"Letter from a Birmingham Jail" was addressed to a series of different audiences in Birmingham—clergymen and laypeople, whites and blacks—as well as being a nationwide appeal for support of the activities and goals of the movement for racial equality, and to end segregation. In many respects, it was a wake-up call describing the corrosive effects of U.S. racism, not only on blacks but on society as a whole. King explained why actions of civil disobedience against a series of unjust laws were being carried out now, and defended such actions as well.

The letter begins with the particular and local—addressed to "My Dear Fellow Clergymen," it immediately points out that King, too, is a member of the clergy, a man of God, and one who is "confined here in the Birmingham city jail." He has read the clergymen's criticisms that "our present activities" are "unwise and untimely," and decided to take the time to respond. In an "author's note," King names the eight fellow clergymen. (While King wrote in his conclusion that he hoped to meet them, he in fact never did so. Historian S. Jonathan Bass, in *Blessed Are the Peacemakers*, traces the impact of the letter on each clergyman's life and faith. These men were forever affected by the notoriety attached to their signature on what at the time they saw as a reasonable call for moderation and order [see also Chappell's account].)

The irony that recurs throughout the letter appears in the opening paragraph's statement that King is "confined" in prison; of course, the fact that he is sending out a message suggests that even if he and others are imprisoned, they *cannot* be confined, and that they can and will get their message out. Also, by describing the clergymen as "men of genuine good will," he sets up a category of "well-intentioned" individuals on the sidelines, including church leaders. He will shift voice in later paragraphs, critiquing the assumptions of those who are urging Negroes to practice restraint and "wait" while racial violence and injustice continue.

The letter then proceeds with a double-explanation of why King is in Birmingham. First he writes politely, like a gentleman in a debate, about his role as president of the SCLC and being invited to Birmingham by one of its affiliates, the Alabama Christian Movement for Human Rights, to be "engaged in a nonviolent direct action program if such were deemed necessary," along with several staff members. "So, I am here because I have basic organizational ties here" (King, "Letter" 77). He then shifts to a moral, universal explanation for his presence in the city, with the voice of an indignant prophet: "Beyond this, I am in Birmingham because injustice is here." Just as the Apostle Paul left his village to respond to the Macedonian call for aid, and spread the gospel of Jesus Christ throughout the Greco-Roman world, King links his mission as responding to the larger call "to carry the gospel of freedom beyond my particular hometown." He rebuts the accusation of being an "outside agitator" and takes issue with the "narrow, provincial" concept of communities. In emphasizing how all communities and states are interrelated, the letter introduces a philosophy rooted in universal ethics and themes that will become popularized through speeches such as the one at the March on Washington: "I cannot sit idly by in Atlanta and not be concerned about happens in Birmingham. Injustice anywhere is a threat to justice everywhere. We are caught in an inescapable network of mutuality, tied in a single garment of destiny. Whatever affects one directly affects all indirectly" (King, "Letter" 77).

King takes issue with the clergymen's statement deploring the recent demonstrations in Birmingham, criticizing their failure to express concern for the underlying causes that made such protests necessary. He ironically points out to the clergymen that they would certainly want to go beyond a superficial social analysis, and look deeper into why the Negro community was left with no alternative but to mount a struggle against racism, given the white power structure in Birmingham. The letter then gives a short primer of the four basic steps of a nonviolent campaign: (1) collecting data to determine if there are current injustices; (2) negotiation; (3) self-purification; and (4) direct action. After following all these steps in Birmingham, King declares: "There can be no gainsaying of the fact that racial injustice engulfs this community." In fact, this city "is probably the most thoroughly segregated city in the United States." The letter then describes the pervasiveness of racism, from the "ugly record of police brutality" to unjust treatment in the courts, to "more unsolved bombings of Negro homes and churches than in any city in this nation" (King, "Letter" 78).

## *Why We Can't Wait: Direct Nonviolent Action Against Segregation and Racism*

In fact, King explains, over the years there were a series of good-faith negotiations attempted by Negro leaders—first with the political leadership, and later with those in the economic community—but they all failed. For example, after meeting with local merchants who promised to remove "humiliating racial signs" from their stores, leaders of the ACMHR, including Reverend Shuttlesworth, consented to call a moratorium on demonstrations. However, the signs remained; once again, a promise had been broken. King writes that under such circumstances, and aware of the difficulties, "there was no alternative but to prepare for direct action in which ... we would present our very bodies as a means of laying our case before the conscience of the local and national community" (King, "Letter" 78). Beginning the process of self-purification, including setting up workshops on nonviolence, "[we] repeatedly asked ourselves the questions: 'Are you able to accept blows without retaliating?' and 'Are you able to endure the ordeals of jail?'" (King, "Letter" 79).

Throughout the letter, King discusses the method and purpose of nonviolent direct action and how it creates a crisis, a creative tension that so dramatizes an issue that a community can no longer ignore it. He writes that while some may be shocked by the word "tension," he embraces not violent but nonviolent, constructive tension; such tension is needed for growth. King turns to the example of Socrates, who felt how necessary it was "to create a tension in the mind so that individuals could rise from the bondage of myths and half truth"; similarly, we too must see how necessary nonviolent gadflies are in order to create the tension in society that will help people move out of prejudice and racism "to the majestic heights of understanding and brotherhood" (King, "Letter" 79).

King addresses accusations of irresponsibility directed at the recent demonstrations, which had been called "untimely," and describes how the Negro leadership had negotiated and waited, over and over again, to take nonviolent direct action. For example, Reverend Shuttlesworth and others had put off plans to boycott stores in March 1963, around the Easter shopping season, so as not to interfere with the run-off mayoral election between Bull Connor and Albert Boutwell. However, once the election was over, they were determined to move ahead with nonviolent direct action. Why not give the new administration time to act? some had asked. Because, answers King, Mr. Boutwell is also a segregationist, and, like Connor, "dedicated to maintaining the status quo." As King points out: "We will be sadly mistaken if we feel that the election of Mr. Boutwell will bring the millennium to Birmingham" (King, "Letter" 80). King then extends the lessons and disappointments of Birmingham to a larger overview of historical change. He points out: "My friends, I must say to you that we have not made a single gain in civil rights without determined legal and nonviolent pressure. History is the long and tragic story of the fact that privileged groups seldom give up their privileges voluntarily.... We know through painful experience that freedom is never voluntarily given by the oppressor; it must be demanded by the oppressed" (King, "Letter" 80).

The issue of "waiting," and its link to the gradualist approach advocated by many white moderates—including the Birmingham clergy who signed the Call to Unity letter in the *Birmingham News*—is repeatedly refuted in King's text. He writes that, for the Negro, this message has "a piercing familiarity" and in fact almost always means "never." King picks up on a current controversy over malformations in newborns due to the distribution of the drug thalidomide to pregnant women, writing that "wait" has served as a "tranquilizing thalidomide, relieving the emotional stress for a moment, only to give birth to an ill-formed infant of frustration." He goes on to quote: "justice too long delayed is justice denied."

King points out that Negroes have waited over 340 years for their constitutional and God-given rights. He points to the decolonization process in Asia and Africa where nations are moving toward political independence quickly, and contrasts this with the United States where the pace is creeping along "toward gaining a cup of coffee at a lunch counter" (King, "Letter" 81). King then describes a series of examples from daily life to demonstrate why those who have never felt "the sting of the darts of segregation" may counsel waiting, but those who live daily under this yoke can no longer do so. The examples of the corrosive effects of racism range from lynching to police brutality and even to "kill your black brothers and sisters with impunity." He points out that most of the 20 million Negro brothers are "smothering in an airtight cage of poverty in the midst of an affluent society." King weaves from the international to the local in describing the effects of racism. He describes his children asking why they cannot go to the public amusement park, quoting his five-year-old son: "Daddy, why do white people treat colored people so mean?" The day-in, day-out humiliations are captured in descriptions of the "nagging signs reading 'white' and 'colored'; when your first name becomes 'nigger,' your middle name becomes 'boy' (however old you are) and your last name becomes 'John,' and ... your wife [is] never given the respected title 'Mrs.'" He describes the fear and "sense of nobodiness" that characterizes the Negro's existence in a racist society, and explains that there is a point at which human beings are no longer willing to endure such torment, adding sarcastically, "I hope, sirs, you can understand our legitimate and unavoidable impatience" (King, "Letter" 82 ).

## Just and Unjust Laws

A centerpiece of the letter is King's explanation and contextualization of the meaning and application of just and unjust laws, and the use of nonviolent social protest to counter unjust ones. King picks up on the seeming contradiction that, on the one hand, civil rights advocates "diligently urge people to obey" the 1954 Supreme Court desegregation decision, and yet they support breaking other laws. In looking to a greater moral authority, he cites a series of ethical models, including St. Augustine, who wrote that "an unjust law is no law at all"; St. Thomas Aquinas; the Jewish philosopher Martin Buber; and the Protestant theologian Paul Tillich. King describes segregation laws as ones that are "morally wrong." He goes on to explain that even laws which on their face appear just, may in their application be unjust. He cites the example of his present arrest: he has been charged with violating the Birmingham ordinance of parading without a permit. Such a legal rule is, he writes, "unjust when it is used to maintain segregation and to deny citizens the First Amendment privilege of peaceful assembly and peaceful protest" (King, "Letter" 83).

Anticipating criticism, King disavows that he is supporting anarchy in the form of "rabid segregationists" who defy the law; instead he maintains that breaking an unjust law must be carried out "openly, lovingly, and with a willingness to accept the penalty" (King, "Letter" 85). And, in fact, someone who is willing to act from his conscience accepts the penalty of imprisonment, and who hopes to arouse the community's conscience about the law's injustice, "is in reality expressing the highest respect for law" (King, "Letter" 84).

King traces civil disobedience throughout history, citing examples in the Bible, and from Roman times to the Boston Tea Party. He provides an ecumenical message stating that what Hitler did in Germany was "legal," and what the freedom fighters did in Hungary was "illegal." But, he writes, if he had lived in Nazi Germany he would have "aided and comforted" Jews, just as, in a Communist-supported country where Christianity was suppressed, he would disobey those laws.

A recurring theme, and one addressed to a broad, white audience, was King's criticism of people who refused to take a stand—white moderates, in particular. He describes them as people who are "more devoted to 'order' than to justice"; "paternalistically," they "set the timetable of another man's freedom" (King, "Letter" 84). The tone of the letter shifts to indignation and anger at those who for example, signed the public letter urging restraint, and at a letter King received "from a white brother in Texas" who points out that all Christians know that eventually colored people will receive equal rights, but "it is possible that you are in too great a religious hurry" (King, "Letter" 86).

In what has become a famous phrase rousing the conscience of the reader, King writes, "We will have to repent in this generation not merely for the hateful words and actions of the bad people but for the appalling silence of the good people" (King, "Letter" 86). Later, he also specifically writes of the white churches and their leadership as a major disappointment. He points out that there are now and then exceptions, such as Reverend Stallings (who was a signatory to the public letter in the Birmingham newspaper, but who also welcomed Negroes to Sunday worship) and the small, Catholic Springhill College that integrated several years previously. But these are exceptions, and over several pages King describes the "laxity" and silence of the church to speak out, for example, against the words and practices of Governors Barnett or Wallace, or to support "bruised and weary Negro men and women when they decided to rise from the dark dungeons of complacency to the bright hills of creative protest" (King, "Letter" 91). Describing himself as the son, grandson, and great-grandson of preachers, King cries out, "Yes, I see the church as the body of Christ. How we have blemished and scarred that body through social neglect and through fear of being nonconformists."

## *The Negro Community, "Somebodiness," Discontent and Extremism*

King briefly describes two contrasting forces within the Negro community. First, he writes, the impact of years of oppression has drained a sense of "somebodiness" and self-respect from some, creating complacency. The other force is hatred, which comes dangerously close to advocating violence, as does Elijah Muhammad's Muslim movement (King, "Letter" 87). King sees himself as standing between these forces of complacent "do-nothingism" and the despair and hatred of the black nationalist. He writes that he is "grateful to God that, through the influence of the Negro church, the way of nonviolence became an integral part of our struggle." King links the struggle for freedom in the United States with decolonization efforts around the world:

> Oppressed people cannot remain oppressed forever. The yearning for freedom eventually manifests itself, and that is what has happened to the American Negro.... Consciously or unconsciously, he has been caught up by the *Zeitgeist*, and with his black brother of Africa and his brown ad yellow brothers of Asia, South America and the Caribbean, the United Sates Negro is moving with a sense of great urgency toward the promised land of racial justice [King, "Letter," 87–88].

King goes on to discuss how discontent can be creatively channeled through nonviolent action to effect change. He discusses being called an "extremist"—a description, he has come to realize, that he and others should embrace. He goes on to describe Jesus as an extremist for love, and Amos as one for justice: "Let justice roll down like waters and righteousness like an ever-flowing stream." King continues with a series of religious and national figures such as John Bunyan, Abraham Lincoln, and Thomas Jefferson—examples of men of conscience—and then asks the reader: "So the question is not whether we will be extremists, but what kind of extremists we will be? Will we be extremists for hate or for love? Will we be extremists for the preservation of injustice or for the extension of justice?" (King, "Letter" 88).

## *Conclusion: Nonviolence in the Face of Violence; Hope for Deliverance and Justice*

In his final pages, King weaves a series of images and voices. On the one hand, his is a prophetic voice condemning those who urge restraint and praise the authorities for keeping order, who fail to look more deeply at, for example, how the Birmingham police use violence and mistreat Negroes. But King also commends those who serve as models—such as James Meredith, who faced angry mobs to desegregate his university; a seventy-two-year-old woman in Montgomery who boycotted segregated buses and said, "My feets is tired, but my soul is at rest"; and people of all ages "sitting in at lunch counters and willingly going to jail for conscience's sake" (King, "Letter" 94). Here is the prophetic voice of hope and deliverance, from a hopeful visionary:

> One day the South will know that when these disinherited children of God sat down at lunch counters, they were in reality standing up for what is best in the American dream and for the most sacred values in our Judaeo-Christian heritage, thereby bringing our nation back to those great wells of democracy which were dug deep by the founding fathers in their formulation of the Constitution and the Declaration of Independence [King, "Letter" 94].

King observes that this letter is much longer than he expected it to be. He goes back to his opening theme of confinement, pointing out that, since he is alone in a narrow jail cell, what else is there to do but "write long letters, think long thoughts and pray long prayers?" (King, "Letter" 95) And then, with an ironist's touch, he begs forgiveness if he has said anything unreasonable or overstated the truth. King ends by stating that he hopes "racial prejudice and misunderstanding will be lifted from our fear-drenched communities, and in some not too distant tomorrow the radiant stars of love and brotherhood will shine over our great nation with all their scintillating beauty." He concludes with, "Yours for the cause of Peace and Brotherhood, Martin Luther King, Jr."

Of course, King may have been "confined," but his public letter got his message out. King's "Letter from a Birmingham Jail" was written and published more than half a century ago, and its universal message of deliverance and nonviolent struggle against injustice continues to inspire individuals and communities around the world.

## Works Cited

Bass, S. Jonathan. *Blessed Are the Peacemakers: Martin Luther King, Jr., Eight White Religious Leaders, and the "Letter from Birmingham Jail."* Baton Rouge: Louisiana State University Press, 2001. Print.

Branch, Taylor. *Parting the Waters: America in the King Years, 1954–1963.* New York: Simon & Schuster, 1988. Print.

Chappell, David L. *Waking from the Dream: The Struggle for Civil Rights in the Shadow of Martin Luther King, Jr.* New York: Random House, 2014. Print.

King, Martin Luther. *The Autobiography of M. L. King, Jr.* Edited by Clayborne Carson. New York: Warner Books, 1998. Print.

\_\_\_\_\_. "How It Began," in SCLC newsletter, July 1963, vol. 1, no. 1.

\_\_\_\_\_. *I Have a Dream: Writings & Speeches That Changed the World.* Edited by James M. Washington. San Francisco: Harper, 1986. Print.

\_\_\_\_\_. "The Negro Revolution—Why 1963?," "Bull Connor's Birmingham," "New Day in Birmingham," "Letter from Birmingham Jail," in *Why We Can't Wait.* New York: Mentor, 1964. Print.

McWhorter, Diane. *Carry Me Home: Birmingham, Alabama, The Climactic Battle of the Civil Rights Revolution.* New York: Simon & Schuster, 2001. Print.

Miller, Keith. *Voice of Deliverance: The Language of Martin Luther King, Jr. and Its Sources.* New York: Free Press, 1992. Print.

Rieder, Jonathan. *Gospel of Freedom: Martin Luther King, Jr.'s Letter from Birmingham Jail and the Struggle that Changed a Nation.* New York: Bloomsbury Press, 2013. Print.

# About the Contributors

Joyce **Apsel**, Ph.D., J.D., teaches in the Global Studies and Liberal Studies programs at New York University and was a recipient of the NYU Distinguished Teaching Award (2009). Her research focuses on issues of comparative genocide, human rights and peace studies. She is also president of the Institute for Study of Genocide and former president of the International Association of Genocide Scholars.

Peter **Diamond** is a member of the Liberal Studies faculty at New York University and is coordinator of its core program. He has taught courses on American political thought, liberal theory, nationalism and globalization, cultural membership, democratization, and the ethics of war and peace. He received a Ph.D. in the history of political thought from Johns Hopkins University.

Sean **Eve** teaches at New York University in the Liberal Studies program. After graduating from Cornell University and doing his graduate work at the Institute of Film and Television at NYU, he spent a decade as a playwright and screenwriter. His productions in London and New York include *American Heart*, *By Land*, *Paint*, and *Cecile Had Won a Million Dollars*.

Brendan **Hogan** is a master teacher in New York University's Liberal Studies program. Trained in philosophy, he has published a variety of articles on the pragmatism, philosophy of social science, and political philosophy.

Stephanie **Kiceluk** teaches humanities in the Liberal Studies program at New York University. She earned a Ph.D. at Columbia University and has trained with the New York Freudian Society. Her work on the narrative construction of the self, the study of trauma, and psychoanalysis and the nature of stories has won numerous awards including ACLS and NEH grants.

Farzad **Mahootian** teaches in the Global Liberal Studies program at New York University. He has an interdisciplinary background, with a Ph.D. in philosophy (Fordham) and an MS in chemistry (Georgetown). His research focus is the relevance of myth and metaphor to the history of philosophy and the sciences.

Afrodesia E. **McCannon** teaches global humanities in Liberal Studies at New York University. She received a Ph.D. from the University of California–Berkeley in comparative literature. Her research interests are in medieval memoir, particularly *The Life of Saint Louis* by Jean de Joinville.

Joseph J. **Portanova** received a Ph.D. in Byzantine and Hellenistic history from Columbia University. He has taught in the Liberal Studies program (formerly General Studies Program) at New York University since 1984. He is the author of several introductory texts for students in liberal studies.

Martin F. **Reichert** received a Ph.D. in comparative literature from New York University. He has taught in the Liberal Studies program for more than two decades. He also taught in Würzburg, Germany, and Florence, Italy. Recent courses explored religious violence, cultural foundations, sensory studies, and global identity.

J. Ward **Regan** has a Ph.D. in U.S. labor and cultural history (SUNY Stony Brook). He has been teaching in NYU's Liberal Studies and Global Liberal Studies programs for more than 20 years.

Tilottama **Tharoor** is a master teacher in the Liberal Studies program at New York University. She received a Ph.D. in English from New York University in 1998. Areas of interest and research include nineteenth and twentieth century literature, post-colonial studies and feminist theory and literature.

Peter C. **Valenti** is a master teacher in New York University's Liberal Studies program. His academic background is in history and Middle Eastern and Islamic studies. He has specialized in the social and political history of Saudi Arabia and the Persian Gulf, as well as pursuing research in state-formation in Iraq, Islamist movements, and Arabic literature.

Phil **Washburn** is a master teacher in the Liberal Studies program at New York University. He is the author of *Philosophical Dilemmas: A Pro and Con Introduction to the Major Questions and Philosophers*, 4th ed. (Oxford, 2014), *The Vocabulary of Critical Thinking* (Oxford, 2010), and the editor of *The Many Faces of Wisdom: Great Philosophers' Visions of Philosophy* (Prentice-Hall, 2003).

Heidi **White** teaches philosophy and intellectual history in the Global Liberal Studies program at New York University and she serves as the chair of the Politics, Rights, and Development concentration. She has a doctorate in philosophy from the New School for Social Research She has been an N.E.H. fellow and has twice received the Deutscher Akademischer Austauschdienst for study in Germany.

Rolf **Wolfswinkel** is a professor of modern history in the Liberal Studies program at New York University. He studied modern history and literature in Amsterdam, the Netherlands. He is interested in topics related to the Second World War and the Holocaust.

# Index

Aaron, Edward 232
'Abd al-Nassir, Gamal *see* Nasser, Gamal
'Abd al-Rahman, Umar 223
Abernathy, Ralph D. 231, 234–35
abolitionism 98, 99
*Achilles in Vietnam* (Shay) 70
Acquaviva, Cardinal 65
action from principle: King on 240, 241–43; Thoreau's concept of 93, 94, 103, 104, 106
Adams, John: on Paine 79, 91–92*n*1
Adams, Sam 72, 85
Africa, decolonization in 242
African Americans: discrimination against 210, 225*n*11, 230–46; extremism and 244–45; as lacking sense of "somebodiness" 244; middle class 233; slavery and 93, 98, 100, 101, 103
African National Congress 94
*The Age of Reason* (Paine) 8, 78–92; banning of 84; contemporary relevance of 91; cosmology in 88–89; first draft of 81; historical context of 83; organized religion critiqued in 79, 83–90; scientific principles espoused in 84, 85, 87, 90
*Agrarian Justice* (Paine) 82, 91
Ahmadnagar prison 153–54, 157–59, 160, 165
Alabama Christian Movement for Human Rights (ACMHR) 233, 240, 241
Albany, Ga. 234
Alcott, Bronson 98, 99, 100
Alexander the Great 164
Algiers: Cervantes' imprisonment in 63, 69, 70, 73
Alligny-en-Morvan, France 193
*America at a Crossroads* (PBS series) 205
"The America" (Qutb) 209, 210
*The American Crisis* (Paine) 79, 80
American Indians 99, 100, 225*n*11
American Revolution 78–79, 80, 86, 90–91
Amman, Max 177
Amritsar, India 156
analytic philosophy 124–25, 126, 131–35
anarchism 99, 101
anti-Semitism 170, 174, 178

Apartheid 140
*Apology* (Plato) 17, 18, 19–24
*Apology* (Xenophon) 20
'Arif, 'Abd al-Salam 216, 226*n*29
Aristotle 28, 38, 134
Armistice: negotiation of 171–72; seen as betrayal of Germany 167, 170–71, 172, 173
Arrian 164
*Arthashastra* (Kautilya) 145
Arthur, King 50, 57, 59–60
Ascham, Roger 48
Asia: decolonization in 242
Asiatic Registration Act (Black Act; 1907) 139, 148
atheism 85
*Atlantic* 236
Attenborough, Richard 142
Augustine, Saint 42, 43, 44, 243
*An Autobiography* (Gandhi) 138, 151–52*n*5
*An Autobiography* (Nehru) 154, 161
*Autos-de-fe* 68–69
Aventine Secession 181
*Awntyrs off Arthure* 55
Ayer, A. J.: *Language, Truth and Logic* 135
Azad, Maulana Abdul Kalam 159
al-Azhar 207

*The Bagnios of Algiers* (Cervantes) 67, 72–73
Bakhtin, Mikhail 76
*The Ballad of Reading Gaol* (Wilde) 119
al-Banna, Hasan 211
Barnett, Ross 244
Barthes, Roland 76
Bass, S. Jonathan: *Blessed Are the Peacemakers* 239
Bate, Catherine 52
Bavaria 175
Baxter, Nathaniel 48
Bencivenga, Jim 6
Bequart, Andre 170
Berlin: 1936 Olympics in 179; planned march on 174–76
Bevel, James 236
Bible: Paine's critique of 83, 84, 86–88, 89–90

249

## Index

Bierkeller Putsch 167–68, 175
Billups, Charles 232
bin Laden, Usama 204, 205, 223, 224, 227n49
Birmingham, Ala. 231; Civil Rights Movement in 233–35; racial violence and segregation in 232, 233, 236, 241
*Birmingham News* 231, 242
Black Act (Asiatic Registration Act; 1907) 139, 148
Black Muslims 244
Black Panthers 202
Black Power 235
*The Blacks* (Genet) 202
*Blessed Are the Peacemakers* (Bass) 239
Boer War (1899–1902) 143
Boethius, Anicius 8; *Consolation of Philosophy* 34–45; imprisonment of 34, 35, 37; on Plato 36
Boston Tea Party 243
Boston University 237
Boutwell, Albert 234, 242
Brixton Prison 124, 130
Brook Farm 96
Brown, John 93, 101–2, 105
*Brown v. Board of Education* 232
Buber, Martin 243
Buckingham, Humphrey Stafford, Duke of 49–50, 51
Buddha 17
Bukharin, Mikhail 187, 188
"Bull Connor's Birmingham" (King) 232–33
*Bürgerbräukeller* 175
Burke, Edmund: *Reflections on the French Revolution* 80

Calvert, John 215–16; *Sayyid Qutb and the Origins of Radical Islamism* 220
Cambridge University 126, 127, 128, 153, 155
Canavaggio, Jean: *Cervantes* 63
capitalism: Gramsci on 183, 189, 190–91
carceral system 6–7, 10
Carnap, Rudolf 134
Carson, Edward 109, 110
Cassiodorus 35
Catholic Church 84, 86, 193
Caxton, William 46–47, 55
*Cervantes* (Canavaggio) 63
Cervantes, Miguel de 8, 62–77; Algerian captivity of 62, 63, 69, 70, 73; *The Bagnios of Algiers* 67, 72–73; *The Commerce of Algiers* 67, 72; *Eight Interludes* 67; excommunication of 69; images of captivity in writings of 70, 72; possible Jewish ancestry of 64, 65; Spanish imprisonment of 62, 63, 69–70; *The Voyage to Parnassus* 76; see also *Don Quixote*
Cervantes, Rodrigo de 65
Chaves, Cristobal de 69
Children's Crusade (U.S.) 236
*The Christian Century* 236
Christian metaphysics 37, 40
Christianity: Paine's critique of 83, 84; racism and 244
civil disobedience: Gandhi and 93, 143; King and 230, 231, 235, 237–39, 243; Nehru and 93, 155–56; Thoreau and 93, 94; see also nonviolent resistance
Civil Disobedience Movement 150
Civil Rights Movement 9, 230–46
Clarence, George, Duke of 51, 53
Clark, Ronald 127
Cobbett, William 83
Cocteau, Jean 194
Cold War 13–14, 166
colonialism 83; British 83, 143–44, 153, 154, 161, 163–64, 165, 207, 208, 212; decolonization and 242, 245; resistance to 8; see also Gandhi, Mohandas K.; Nehru, Jawaharlal; Qutb, Sayyid
*The Commerce of Algiers* (Cervantes) 67, 72
*Common Sense* (Paine) 79, 80, 85, 86
communism/Communists 170, 174
Communist Party of Italy (PCI) 183, 191
Congress of Oppressed Nationalities 157
Congress of Racial Equality (CORE) 233, 234, 235
Congress Party 154, 155, 156, 157, 159, 161
Connor, Eugene "Bull" 232, 233–34, 236, 241–42
conscientious objectors 124, 127, 129, 130–31
*Consolation of Philosophy* (Boethius) 34–45
Constitution, U.S. 93, 100
Cornelius Plot 54
*Corydon* (Gide) 194
Cotton, Dorothy 236
Counter Reformation 73
courage: nonviolent resistance and 145, 149; of Russell 126, 128, 129, 130, 135
Criminal Law Amendment Act (1885) 109
Cromwell, Oliver 158

Dante 107, 108, 121n5
*Dar al-'ulum* 207
Dawes plan 179
*De Profundis* (Wilde) 8, 107–22; Douglas as depicted in 111–14; image of Christ in 112, 117–18; imprisonment in 115–16; influence of Greek thought in 116–17, 118; Ross and 111, 116, 118–20; Wilde as depicted in 114–15

Declaration of Independence 80, 100
decolonization 242, 245
Defense of the Realm Act (1914) 128
Dehra Dun jail 160
Deism 83–84, 85
Delacampagne, Christian 133
democracy 102, 103
Devji, Faisal 145
*dharma-yuddha* 145–46
*The Dial* 97
*Dialogues Concerning Natural Religion* (Hume) 34
Diaz de Toledo, Fernan: *Instrucion* 64
Dickens, Charles: *A Tale of Two Cities* 7
direct action *see* action from principle
*Discovery of India* (Nehru) 9, 153–66
do-gooders: Thoreau on 103–4
*Don Quixote* (Cervantes) 62–77; as act of self-assertion 71; autobiographical references in 72; as book about books 68, 71, 75–76; Captive's Tale section of 72, 73; madness in 66, 67, 68; self-reference in 68
Douglas, John Sholto *see* Queensberry
Douglas, Lord Alfred 108, 119, 120, 121n9; as depicted in *De Profundis* 111–14
Douglas, Sibyl Montgomery *see* Queensberry, Marchioness of
Drexler, Anton 173–74
Dulcinea (char.) 65–66

Eastern Roman Empire 37
Ebert, Kurt 171
Eckhart, Dietrich 174
*Economic and Philosophic Manuscripts of 1844* (Marx) 187
"economism" 187
Edward IV, King of England 48, 51, 53
Edward of Lancaster, Prince of Wales 53–54
Egypt 204; British imperialism in 207, 208, 212; prison conditions in 215, 226n24; social and political unrest in 208, 213–14
*Eight Interludes* (Cervantes) 67
Eliot, T. S. 48
Elizabeth I, Queen of England 48
Ellman, Richard 108
Emerson, Ralph Waldo 94, 95–96, 99; *Essays, Second Series* 97; *Nature* 96; reform associations criticized by 96–97
*Enchiridion* (Epictetus) 44–45n3
Enlightenment 85, 86, 87
Epictetus 41; *Enchiridion* 44–45n3
*Epistle VII* (Plato) 17, 26–27
Erskine, Thomas 84
Erzberger, Matthias 171–72
Espionage Act (1917) 136n4
*Essays, Second Series* (Emerson) 97
*Euclid's Elements of Geometry* 87

evil, problem of 38–39, 42–44
extremism, African American 244–45

Fabian Socialism 155
faith, reason vs. 39
Faraj, 'Abd al-Salam 223
fascists, Fascists 9, 181–82
Feder, Gottfried 170, 173
Fest, Joachim 178
Field, P. J. C.: *The Life and Times of Sir Thomas Malory* 47, 48, 50, 51–52
*al-Fikr al-jadid* (New Thought) 207–8
Fitch, John 89
Ford, Henry 190–91
"Fordism" 190–91
forms, theory of 28–29
fortune, fickleness of 39–41
Foucault, Michel 6, 10, 55, 202
"Four hours at Shatila" (Genet) 202
France: German occupation of 194
Francis of Assisi, Saint 117, 119
Franklin, Benjamin 79
Free Officers 213–14, 225n19
free speech 129
free will 34, 43–44
Freedom Riders campaign 233, 234
Frege, Gottlob 133, 134, 135
French Revolution 78–79, 80–82, 86, 89, 90–91, 189
Friedlander, Paul 20
*Fronterlebnis* (front experience) 170
*Fundamentals of Islam* (Mawdudi) 212, 220

Gagnier, Regenia 114, 115
Galileo 86
*Gandhi* (film) 142
Gandhi, Indira 154
Gandhi, Maganlal 147
Gandhi, Mohandas K.: assassination of 150; *An Autobiography* 138, 140, 151–52n5; civil disobedience and 93; early life of 141–42; imprisonment of 138–39, 140–41, 144, 150–51n2, 154, 237; in India 143–46, 150, 150–51n2; Indian independence movement and 150; Nehru and 155–56, 163, 164; *Satyagraha in South Africa* 9, 138–52; in South Africa 138, 139–40, 142–43, 146–50, 151n3, 152n7; Thoreau's influence on 94, 105; *see also* satyagraha
Garces, Maria 70, 72
Garrison, William Lloyd 97, 99–100
Genet, Camille Gabrielle 192
Genet, Jean 8, 62, 192–203; *The Blacks* 202; "Four hours at Shatila" 202; imprisonments of 193, 194; *The Maids* 193; in military 193–94; prison reform efforts of 202; *see also Our Lady of the Flowers*

German Socialist Party (SPD) 171, 174
German Workers Party (DAP) 173
Germany: Hitler's rise in 167–79; Weimar Republic in 174, 175, 179
Gide, André: *Corydon* 194
Girard, René 140
*The Glimpses of World History* (Nehru) 154, 161
Global North 190
Global South 190
God: as beyond human understanding 39, 44; Deist view of 83–84, 85; as first cause 88; problem of evil and 38–39, 42–44
Gokhale, B. G. 157–58
Goldman, Emma 94
Gopal, S. 158, 160
*Gorgias* (Plato) 21
Göring, Hermann 172, 174, 176
gospel of freedom 238, 240
Gougeon, Len 98
Gramsci, Antonio: on capitalism 183, 189, 190–91; conjunctural vs. organic distinction of 188–89, 191; early life of 180–81; "economism" critiqued by 187; hegemony concept of 185, 189–90, 191; humanism of 190; imprisonment of 184–85; Marxism critiqued by 183–84, 185–90; *The Prison Notebooks* 9, 180–91; scientific positivism critiqued by 187
Gramsci, Gennaro 183
Gramsci, Francesco 180
"Great Books," definition of 5
Great Britain 11; colonialism of 83, 143–44, 153, 154, 161, 163–64, 165, 207, 208, 212; prison system in 110, 124, 130–31
Great Depression 194
Greek thought: *De Profundis* and 116–17, 118; *see also* Socrates; Socratic discourse
Greensboro, N.C. 234
Guenivere 56–58
Guha, Ramachandra 165
Gutmann, Hugo 170

*hadith* 224
*hakimiyah* 212, 225n16, 226n21
Haldane, Richard 110–11
Hanisch, Reinhold 169
happiness 41, 42, 43, 44
Harpers Ferry raid 93, 101, 105
Harrow 155
al-Hawwash, Yusuf 217
Hegel, G. W. F. 96
hegemony: Gramsci's concept of 185, 189–90, 191
Heiden, Konrad 178
Henry VI, King of England 51, 53–54
"Herald of Freedom" (Thoreau) 97

*Herald of Freedom* 97
Hess, Rudolf 174, 176, 177
Hibbler, Al 234
Hindenburg, Paul von 171
Hindus/Hinduism: Muslims and 150, 163; Nehru on 164–65
Hiroshima, nuclear bombing of 149
historians, as explorers 62–63
Historical Materialism *see* Marxism
*History of India* (Mill) 163
Hitler, Adolf 9, 167–79, 243; anti-Semitism of 170, 174, 178; appointed chancellor of Germany 179; army service of 168, 169–70, 172–73; in Bierkeller Putsch 167–68, 175; DAP joined by 173–74; early life of 168–69; early parole granted to 178; in failed March on Berlin 174–76; imprisonment of 167, 176–77; as Nazi Party leader 174–76; racism of 167; *see also Mein Kampf*
Hitler, Alois 168
Hitler, Klara 168
Hoar, Samuel 98
Holland, Vyvyan 120
Holy Grail 49, 56, 57
homosexuality 121n9; of Genet 194; laws against 109–10, 114, 120; in *Our Lady of the Flowers* 194, 195–97; of Wilde 108, 109–10, 114, 119
"How It Began" (King) 231
human rights, interdependence of 239, 240
humanism 158, 160, 190
Hume, David 91; *Dialogues Concerning Natural Religion* 34
Hundred Years War 50
Hungary 243–44
hypocrisy 67

"I Have a Dream" speech (King) 236, 240
"*Ich hatt' einen Kameraden*" (Uhland) 171
*The Importance of Being Earnest* (Wilde) 108–9, 113
*In the Shade of the Qur'an* (Qutb) 9, 204, 216, 217–19, 220, 223, 224
India: British salt monopoly in 157; British stifling of industrial growth in 162, 164, 166; capacity for assimilation of 162; Gandhi in 143–46, 150, 150–51n2; history of 161–62; independence movement in 150, 155–57, 163; non-alignment policy of 166; partition of 150, 159, 161, 162; poverty in 156, 163, 165, 166; prison conditions in 140, 158–59; as secular, pluralist state 162, 166; Western view of 163–64; *see also* Nehru, Jawaharlal
Indian National Congress *see* Congress Party
Inquisition 68

institutionalized violence *see* violence, institutionalized
*Instrucción* (Díaz de Toledo) 64
intellectuals, Gramsci on 188–89, 191
*Introduction to Mathematical Philosophy* (Russell) 9, 123–37
Iraq 221
Islamic Jihad 223
Islamic World: Qutb's criticism of 219, 220–21, 224; Qutb's influence in 204, 223–24; West and 205–6
Islamists 9; Qutb cited by 223–24
Isma'il, 'Abd al–Fatah 217
Israel 205, 209
Italy: Fascists in 9, 181–82; labor movement in 182–84; racism in 182; social and political unrest in 182; unification of 189

Jackson, George 202
Jacobins 81, 82
*jahili* 212–13, 216, 220–21
*al-jahiliyah* 212–13, 215, 220–21, 224, 225n18, 227n39
Jefferson, Thomas 82, 88
Jesuits 73–74
Jesus Christ 17, 87, 88, 90; in *De Profundis* 112, 117–18
Jews 170, 209, 243
jihad 146, 222
Jim Crow 232
Jinnah, Muhammad Ali 161
Joan of Arc 50
Job (biblical char.) 37–38, 42, 44
*Journal* (Thoreau) 94

Kachhalia, Ahmad Muhammad 147
Kahr, Gustav von 175, 176
Kallenbach, Hermann 149
Kant, Immanuel 91, 96
Kautilya, *Arthashastra* 145
Keitel, Wilhelm 172
Kennedy, John F. 236
Keynes, John Maynard 155
King, Martin Luther, Jr. 9, 10, 230–46; assassination of 236; "Bull Connor's Birmingham" 232–33; on direct action 240, 241–43; Gandhi's influence on 138, 237; "How It Began" 231; "I Have a Dream" speech 236, 240; imprisonment of 231, 235–36, 237–38; "New Day in Birmingham" 235, 237; and nonviolent resistance 105, 138, 231, 234–35, 238–46; *Stride to Freedom* 237; Thoreau's influence on 94, 105; *Why We Can't Wait* 231; *see also* "Letter from a Birmingham Jail"
King, Martin Luther, Sr. 237
*King Henry V* (Shakespeare) 46

Kittredge, G. L. 47
knowledge: self- 24, 26; Socrates' concept of 18, 22, 23–24, 26–27
Kopf, David 157, 160
Ku Klux Klan 232
Kubizek, August: *The Young Hitler I Knew* 168

Lancaster, House of 50, 52
Lancelot 50, 55, 56–59
*Lancelot* 55
Landsberg-am-Lech prison 167, 176–78
Lane, Charles 98, 100
language: analytic philosophy and 125, 133–34, 135; self-construction and 74–75; written vs. spoken 26–27
*Language, Truth and Logic* (Ayer) 135
Lawrence, T. E. 194
laws: just vs. unjust 9–10, 94, 238, 243–44
League of Nations 179
*Lebensraum im Osten* 178
legal systems: institutionalized violence and 10, 11–12, 14–15, 20–21
Lenin, V. I. 12
Lepanto, Battle of 69, 72
"Letter from a Birmingham Jail" (King) 9, 230–46; on civil disobedience 238, 239, 243; as Civil Rights Movement manifesto 230, 231, 235–36; gradualist approach rejected in 242, 245; on just and unjust laws 238, 243–44; as primer on nonviolent protest 240; publication of 236; on silence of good people 240; writing of 235–38
Lewis, C. S. 47, 48, 58
*Liberator* 97, 100
*The Life and Times of Sir Thomas Malory* (Field) 47, 48, 50, 51–52
Lincoln, Abraham 102
logical positivists 134–35
Lossow, Otto Hermann von 175, 176
Louis XVI, King of France 81, 88
Louisiana Purchase 82
loyalty: in *Le Morte Darthur* 56, 58
Loyola, Ignacius de 73–74; *Spiritual Exercises* 74
Lucknow jail 157
Ludendorff, Erich von 171, 175, 176
*Lusitania*: sinking of 127
Lustig, T. J. 47, 50, 57
Luther, Martin 217
Luxembourg Prison 78, 81–82
Lytton, Constance 94

McCrory, Donald 66
McGaha, Michael 64
*The Maids* (Genet) 193

Malcolm X 235
Malory, Elizabeth Walsh 48
Malory, Nicholas 48
Malory, Robert (crusader) 49
Malory, Robert (Thomas's son) 48
Malory, Thomas 9, 46–61; brigandage of 49–50; death of 48; imprisonment of 50, 51, 52–54; rape charge against 49, 52; *see also Le Morte Darthur*
Manichaeism 221
March on Rome 174, 175
March on Washington 236, 240
Margaret of Anjou, Queen of England 53, 54
martyrdom 222
Marx, Karl: *Economic and Philosophic Manuscripts of 1844* 187; "The Poverty of Philosophy" 186
Marxism 160, 177; Gramsci's critique of 183–84, 185–90
Massingham, H. J. 136n3
material world: attachment to 38; Myth of the Cave and 25; soul's separation from 25, 31
Mawdudi, Sayyid Abu al-'Ala 212–13, 225n13, 225n18; *Fundamentals of Islam* 212, 220; *Tafhim al-Qur'an* 212
*Mein Kampf* (Hitler) 167–79; anti-Semitism in 178; Armistice seen as betrayal in 167, 170–71, 172, 173; *Lebensraum* concept in 178; original concept of 177
*Meno* (Plato) 17, 18, 21
Meredith, James 245
Merlin 55–56
*Merlin* 55
Mettray prison 193–94
Mexican War 98, 100, 103
Middle East, U.S. policies in 205
*Milestones* (Qutb) 9, 204, 212, 216, 217, 219–22, 223, 224
Military Service Bill (1916) 129
Mill, John: *History of India* 163
Miller, Keith: *Voice of Deliverance* 235
miracles: Paine's debunking of 89
Mohenjo Daro 161
Monroe, James 82
Moore, G. E. 126, 133
Moorehead, Caroline 124
moral injury 70–71
moral motivation 41–42
moral sense 101
*Mort Artu* 55
*Morte Arthur* 55
*Le Morte Darthur* (Malory) 9, 46–61; authorship questions about 46–47; composition of 54–55; imprisonment in 52–53; loyalty as theme of 56, 58; revisionist versions of 48; wholeness in 54–57, 59, 60

Moses 17
Mughal empire 162, 164
Muhammad, Elijah 244
Muhammad, Prophet 17, 88, 212, 213, 222
Munich 173
Murad, Hajji 73
Muslim Brotherhood (MB) 211, 213–15, 216, 218, 219, 223, 225n19, 226n21
Muslim League 161
Muslims: fundamentalist see Islamists; Hindus and 150, 163; separate state demanded by 159, 161, 162; *see also* Islamic world
Mussolini, Benito 169, 170, 174, 175, 176, 181
myth: Bible and 84, 90; in Socratic discourse 27–29
Myth of the Cave 25

Nadvi, Abulhasan 'Ali 212, 225n13
Nagasaki, nuclear bombing of 149
Naini Jail 157
Nasr, Seyyed Vali Reza 225n18
Nasser, Gamal 213–14, 216, 217, 219, 226n29
National Association for the Advancement of Colored People (NAACP) 233, 234, 235
National Convention, French 81, 82, 88
Natural Law 84, 88, 91
Natural Rights 91
*Nature* (Emerson) 96
*Navajivan* 140
Nazi (National Socialist) Party 170, 174, 179
Nehru, Jawaharlal 153–66; *An Autobiography* 154, 161; civil disobedience and 93, 155–56; *Discovery of India* 9, 153–66; early life of 154–56; Gandhi and 155–56, 163, 164; *The Glimpses of World History* 154, 161; as humanist 158, 160; imprisonment of 153–54, 156–60; as India's first prime minister 153, 154, 165–66; partition opposed by 161, 162; secular, pluralist India envisioned by 162, 166; socialism of 155, 157, 166; Soviet Union and 157–58
Nehru, Kamala 155, 158, 161
Nehru, Motilal 154, 155, 157, 158
Nelson, James 111, 116
neoliberalism 191
"New Day in Birmingham" (King) 235, 237
New England Non-Resistance Society 99
*New York Post* 237
New York Stock Exchange, crash of 179
*New York Times* 204–6, 233, 237
Nicea, Council of 87–88, 90
9/11 terrorist attacks 204, 205
Nizam 1965 216, 219
No Conscription Fellowship (NCF) 124, 125, 127, 129

Non-Cooperation Movement 144
nonviolent resistance: courage and 145, 149;
  Gandhi and 105, 138, 145–46; Nehru and
  155–56; Thoreau on 93, 94, 100, 105; U.S.
  Civil Rights Movement and 105, 138, 231,
  234–35, 236, 238–46; *see also* civil disobedience

Oakeshott, Walter 47
Olympics of 1936 (Berlin) 179
organized crime 12–13, 14
organized religion: connection between
  state and 84, 85–86, 90; knowledge of
  God's will claimed by 86; Paine's critique
  of 79, 83–90
*Oscar Wilde: A Critical Study* (Ransome)
  120
Ostrogoths 34, 36
*Our Lady of the Flowers* (Genet) 8, 192–
  203; capital punishment in 200–201; homosexuality in 194, 195–97; prison as depicted in 192, 197–200, 201

pacifism 99, 124
Paine, Thomas 8, 11, 78–92; *Agrarian Justice*
  82, 91; *The American Crisis* 79; American
  Revolution and 78–79, 80, 91; atheism
  charge against 85; childhood and early career of 79–80; *Common Sense* 79, 80, 85,
  86; death of 83; death sentence of 78, 88;
  French Revolution and 78–79, 80–81, 89,
  91; imprisonment of 78, 81–82, 89; John
  Adams on 79, 91–92*n*1; *The Rights of
  Man* 80–81, 82, 85, 91; *see also The Age of
  Reason*
Pakistan 150, 159, 161, 162
Palestine/Palestinians 202, 208–9
Patel, Sardar Vallabhai 159
Paul, Saint 237, 240
Peano, Giuseppe 131
*Pennsylvania Magazine* 80
Pentonville Prison 110
*Phaedo* (Plato) 17, 24–32
*Phaedrus* (Plato) 17, 26
Phillips, Wendell 97–98
philosophy: as learning to live well 19, 32,
  33; as practicing dying 25, 31, 33
*The Picture of Dorian Gray* (Wilde) 108
Pilorge, Maurice 198, 200
Plato 17; *Apology* 17, 18, 19–24; Boethius on
  36; *Epistle VII* 17, 26–27; *Gorgias* 21;
  *Meno* 17, 18, 21; *Phaedo* 17, 24–32; *Phaedrus* 17, 26; *Protagoras* 21; *Republic* 41–42,
  159
"A Plea for Captain John Brown" (Thoreau)
  101–2
poison gas 127

political machines 14
political power *see* ruling power structure
political prisoners 8–10, 46, 237
politics: Thoreau's contempt for 101, 102–3,
  105–6
"The Poverty of Philosophy" (Marx) 186
Priestly, Joseph 89
*Principia Mathematica* (Whitehead and Russell) 124, 131
prison/imprisonment: as depicted in *De
  Profundis* 115–16; as depicted in *Our Lady
  of the Flowers* 192, 197–200, 201; in Egypt
  215, 226*n*24; in Great Britain 110, 124,
  130–31; history of 6–8; in India 140, 158;
  as necessary part of political struggle 93;
  political prisoners 8–10, 46, 237; in South
  Africa 139–40
*The Prison Notebooks* (Gramsci) 9, 180–91
prisoners of war 8
*The Problems of Philosophy* (Russell) 126, 135
prophecy: Paine's debunking of 89
*Protagoras* (Plato) 21
Proust, Marcel 194
Puritans 12

al-Qaeda 221, 223
Quakers 85
Queensberry, Marquess of 108–9, 110, 112,
  115
Queensberry, Marchioness of 108
*Queste del Saint Graal* 55
Quit India Movement 150, 157
Quixote (char.) 71; "madness" of 66, 68; as
  reader 75–76; self-construction of 74–75
Qur'an 208, 224; Qutb's exegesis of 217–19
Qutb, Muhammad 216, 223
Qutb, Sayyid 204–29; "The America" 209,
  210; in call for revolutionary change 221–
  22; early life and career of 206–9; execution of 217; imprisonment of 206, 208,
  214–17, 221; *In the Shade of the Qur'an* 9,
  204, 206, 216, 217–19, 220, 223, 224; influence of 204, 223–24; Islamic World
  criticized by 219, 220–21, 224;
  Manichaeist worldview of 221; *Milestones*
  9, 204, 206, 212, 216, 217, 219–22, 223,
  224; Muslim Brotherhood and 211, 213–
  15, 216, 218, 219, 223, 225*n*19, 226*n*21; *Social Justice in Islam* 208, 211, 216, 219,
  225*n*13; U.S. trip of 204–5, 206, 209–10,
  211; "Why Did They Execute Me?" 222–
  23, 224

racism 167, 182; corrosive effects of 239,
  242–43; in U.S. 210, 230–46
Ransome, Arthur *Oscar Wilde: A Critical
  Study* 120

rape: Malory charged with 49, 52
Rathenau, Walther 172
Rathore, L. S. 157
Reading Prison 110, 111
reason, faith vs. 39
*Reflections on the French Revolution* (Burke) 80
"Reform and Reformers" (Thoreau) 97, 98
reform associations 96–98
Reform Bill (1832) 124
Régnier, Eugenié, and Charles 193
Reign of Terror 78, 79, 81, 82
*Relacions* 68–69
religion: Nehru on 164–65; satyagraha and 145–46; *see also* organized religion
*Republic* (Plato) 41–42, 159
resistance: public vs. private 100, 101, 104
"Resistance to Civil Government" (Thoreau) 9–10, 93–106
Ribbentrop, Joachim von 172
Richard III, King of England 54
Riddy, Felicity 50
*The Rights of Man* (Paine) 80–81, 82, 85, 91
Ripley, George 96
Rivers, Anthony Wydeville, Earl of 55
Robespierre, Maximilien 78, 81, 82, 89
Rogers, Nathaniel P. 97
Röhm, Ernst 173, 174
Ross, Robert 111, 116, 118–20
Rousseau, Jean-Jacques 44
rule of law 102
ruling power structure 7–8, 9; and Gramsci's concept of hegemony 185, 189–90, 191; institutionalized violence as tool of 10–15; *see also* state
Rupprecht, Crown Prince of Bavaria 175
Russell, Bertrand 155; analytic philosophy and 124–25, 126; antinuclear activism of 123, 125; antiwar activism of 9, 123–24, 125–31, 135, 136n2; devotion to truth of 125, 128, 135; government attempts at intimidation of 127–28; imprisonment of 124, 128, 129, 130–31; intellectual courage of 126, 128, 129, 135; *Introduction to Mathematical Philosophy* 9, 123–37; Nobel Prize for Literature awarded to 125; *Principia Mathematica* 124, 131; *The Problems of Philosophy* 126, 135; public contempt for 127, 128; trials of 123–24, 127–28
Russell, Lord John 124
Russian Revolution 128–29, 157, 183, 184, 185

*Saint Genet* (Sartre) 194, 203
Salisbury, Harrison 233
Santayana, George 126
Sardinia 182, 180

Sartre, Jean-Paul: *Saint Genet* 194, 203
satyagraha 138, 155–56; courage and 145, 149; coversion of adversary as goal of 145, 149, 150; as experiment 148; meaning of term 144–45; role of religion in 145–46
*Satyagraha in South Africa* (Gandhi) 9, 138–52
*Sayyid Qutb and the Origins of Radical Islamism* (Calver) 220
Schicklgruber, Anna Maria 168
Schwartz, Benjamin 160
science: Paine's advocacy of 84, 85, 87, 90
scientific positivism 187
Sedition Act (1918) 136n4
segregation 231, 232, 233–35, 241, 243
Seisser, Hans von 175, 176
self-knowledge 24, 26
self-purification 138, 150, 240, 241
self-reform 95, 104, 105, 106
September 11, 2001, terrorist attacks 204, 205
Seville, Royal Prison in 69, 70
Shakespeare, William 50–51, 53, 67; *King Henry V* 46
Sharp, Gene 239
Shaw, George Bernard 155
Shay, Jonathan: *Achilles in Vietnam* 70
Shuger, Dale 68
Shuttlesworth, Fred 232, 233, 234–35, 241–42
silence: of good people 244
16th Bavarian Infantry Regiment 168, 169
Sixteenth Street Baptist Church, Birmingham 236
slavery 93, 98, 100, 101, 103
"Slavery in Massachusetts" (Thoreau) 101
Smith, Joan 49, 52
Smuts, Jan 147–48
*Social Justice in Islam* (Qutb) 208, 211, 216, 219, 225n13
social sciences, ninteenth-century flourishing of 187
socialism/socialists 155, 157, 166, 170
society 11, 13–14
Socrates 8, 10, 17–19, 241; last day of 24–27; philosophical mission of 17, 24, 25–26, 105; trial of 8, 19–24
Socratic discourse 18, 22, 34, 40; myth vs. logic in 27–29
sodomy 109
Somerset, Edmund Beaufort, Duke of 51, 54
Sophists 18, 19, 20, 22
soul: immortality of 17, 18, 24–25, 27, 30–31, 32
South Africa 94; Gandhi in 138, 139–40, 142–43, 146–50, 150–51n2, 152n7; prison conditions in 139–40

Southern Christian Leadership Conference (SCLC) 230, 234–36, 237, 240
Soviet Union 157–58, 186, 187–88
Spain: Cervantes' imprisonment in 62, 63, 69–70; institutionalized hypocrisy in 67
Spanish Civil War 157
*Spiritual Exercises* (Loyola) 74
Springhill College 244
Sraffa, Piero 184
Stallings, Rev. 244
Stanley, Alessandra 204–6, 209, 210
state: connection between organized religion and 84, 85–86, 90; creation of 12–13; power of 7
Statute of Rapes (1382) 52
Staub, Ervin 11
stock market crash of 1929 179
Stoicism 34, 37, 40
Strauss, Leo 65
*Stride to Freedom* (King) 237
Student Nonviolent Coordinating Committee (SNCC) 234, 235
Sturm Abteilung (SA) 171, 173
Summers, Joanna 55
Supreme Court, U.S.: *Brown v. Board of Education* decision 232
*Swadeshi* 155
Swan, Maureen 152*n*8
*Swaraj* 155
Sydney, Philip 48

*Tafhim al-Qur'an* (Mawdudi) 212
*takfir* 221, 223, 227*n*40, 227*n*45
*A Tale of Two Cities* (Dickens) 7
Taliban 12
Texas 98
Thapar, Romila 163
Theodoric, Ostrogoth King 34, 36–37
Thomas Aquinas, Saint 73, 243
Thoreau, Henry David: action from principle advocated by 93, 94, 103, 104, 106; Emerson and 94, 95; "Herald of Freedom" 97; jailing of 93–94, 98–99, 104, 105; *Journal* 94; Mexican War opposed by 98, 103; non-resistance opposed by 99–100; passive and private resistance seen as insufficient by 100, 101; "A Plea for Captain John Brown" 101–2; politics disdained by 101, 102–3, 105–6; "Reform and Reformers" 97, 98; reform associations criticised by 97–98; in refusal to pay poll tax 93–94, 95, 98, 104; "Resistance to Civil Government" 9–10, 93–106; self-reform and 95, 104, 105, 106; "Slavery in Massachusetts" 101; slavery opposed by 93, 94, 98, 100, 103; on violent vs. nonviolent resistance 93, 94, 100, 105; *Walden* 95, 101, 103–4;

at Walden Pond 95, 99, 105; *A Week on the Concord and Merrimack Rivers* 99; "Wendell Phillips Before Concord Lyceum" 97–98
Tillich, Paul 243
Tilly, Charles 11, 12–13
*Times* (London) 176
Tocqueville, Alexis de 102, 103
Tolstoy, Leo 145
Tolstoy Farm 148–49
*Tractatus Logico-Philosophicus* (Wittgenstein) 134–35, 136*n*5
Transcendentalism 96
Transvaal British Indian Association 147
*Tribunal* 124
Tristan 55
Tristram 52, 55
Trotsky, Leon 186
Tucker, P. E. 55, 56
Turin, Italy 182–83

Uhland, Ludwig: "*Ich hatt' einen Kameraden*" 171
United States: Middle East policies of 205; opposition to World War I in 136*n*4; Qutb's trip to 204–5, 206, 209–10, 211; racism in 210, 230–46; Texas admitted to 98
Upanishads 164–65

Vega, Lope de 67
Vietnam War 125
Village, Clement 198
Vinaver, Eugene 47
violence: nonviolent resistance vs. 143, 146, 149
violence, institutionalized 10–15; aura of legitimacy surrounding 13–14; legal systems and 10, 11–12, 14–15, 20–21; morality of 12
virtue: Socrates' concept of 18
*Voice of Deliverance* (Miller) 235
Voight, Lisa 70
*The Voyage to Parnassus* (Cervantes) 76

Wagon-Lits 2419D 172
Wahhabism 223
*Walden* (Thoreau) 95, 101, 103–4
Walden Pond 95, 99, 105
Walker, Wyatt 237
Wallace, George 233, 244
Walnut Street Jail, Philadelphia 6
Wandsworth Prison 110
War of the Roses 9, 46, 50–54
Warwick, Richard Neville, Earl of 51, 53, 54
Washington, George 83
Webster, Daniel 100

*A Week on the Concord and Merrimack Rivers* (Thoreau) 99
Weimar Republic 174, 175, 179
"Wendell Phillips Before Concord Lyceum" (Thoreau) 97–98
West: Islamic World and 205–6
Whitehead, Alfred North 127, 129; *Principia Mathematica* 124, 131
wholeness: in *Le Morte Darthur* 54–57
"Why Did They Execute Me?" (Qutb) 222–23, 224
*Why We Can't Wait* (King) 231
Wilde, Constance 110, 120n2
Wilde, Oscar 8–9, 107–22; American tour of 107–8; *The Ballad of Reading Gaol* 119; Classical education of 116–17; deteriorating health of 110–11; Douglas and 108, 111–14, 119; homosexuality of 108, 109–10, 114, 119; *The Importance of Being Earnest* 108–9, 113; imprisonment of 107, 110–11; *The Picture of Dorian Gray* 108; Queensbury sued by 109, 115; Queensbury's harassment of 108–9; trials of 109–10, 121n9; *see also De Profundis*
Wilhem II, Kaiser 171
Wills, Justice 110
Wistrich, Robert 174

Wittgenstein, Ludwig 127, 133; *Tractatus Logico-Philosophicus* 134–35, 136n5
Wolpert, Stanley 155, 158
Woodville, Elizabeth 53
World War I 183; Hitler in 168, 169–70; onset of 126; Russell's opposition to 9, 123–24, 125–31, 135, 136n2; unpopularity of 124; U.S. oppostion to 136n4
World War II 149, 161, 194, 208

Xenophon: *Apology* 20

York, Richard, Duke of 51
York, House of 50, 53, 54
Young, Andrew 236
*The Young Hitler I Knew* (Kubizek) 168
*Young India* 140
Young plan 179
Ypres, First Battle of 169
Ypres, Second Battle of 127

al-Zawahiri, Ayman 223
Zeno, Eastern Roman Emperor 37
*Zentrum* (Catholic) Party 171–72
Zionism 208–9
Zulu Rebellion (1906) 143

www.ingramcontent.com/pod-product-compliance
Ingram Content Group UK Ltd.
Pitfield, Milton Keynes, MK11 3LW, UK
UKHW041934140426
5217IPUK00014B/466